The Foundations of Knowing

Financial assistance for this book was provided by the Andrew W. Mellon Foundation.

The Foundations of Knowing

Roderick M. Chisholm

University of Minnesota Press □ Minneapolis

Copyright © 1982 by the University of Minnesota.
All rights reserved.
Published by the University of Minnesota Press,
2037 University Avenue Southeast, Minneapolis, MN 55414
Printed in the United States of America.

Library of Congress Cataloging in Publication Data

Chisholm, Roderick M.
    The foundations of knowing.

    Includes bibliographical references and index.
    1. Knowledge, Theory of—Addresses, essays,
lectures. I. Title.
BD161.C467 1981   121   81-19707
ISBN 0-8166-1103-3   AACR2
ISBN 0-8166-1104-1 (pbk.)

The University of Minnesota
is an equal-opportunity
educator and employer.

Contents

BD
161
.C467
1982

Introduction

This book is an attempt to deal positively and concretely with the fundamental questions of the theory of knowledge.

Of the four essays that appear in Part I, the first—"A Version of Foundationalism"—is a revised version of a paper that appeared in Volume Five of the *Midwest Studies in Philosophy* (1980). I attempt there to develop a philosophical theory and express the hope that proponents of alternative programs will be encouraged to do the same. I conclude that no serious alternative in epistemology to foundationalism has yet been formulated.

The other three essays in Part I were written expressly for this book. "Confirmation and Concurrence" is an account of the epistemic significance of confirmation and certain analogous relations. "Knowledge as Justified True Belief" is a defense of the traditional definition of knowledge. And "Knowing that One Knows" applies the results of the previous essays to a traditional epistemological question.

The essays in Part I presuppose a general conception of thought and reference that is summarized in the first essay and defended in detail in my book, *The First Person: An Essay on Reference and Intentionality*. The essays in Parts II and III, which were written before 1978, are readily adaptable to the present point of view.

Part II is an application of foundationalist principles to various areas within the theory of knowledge. Most of these papers have been revised for the present volume. "The Problem of the Criterion" first appeared as The Aquinas Lecture and was published by Marquette University in 1973. "The Foundation of Empirical Statements" is concerned in part with the relation of epistemology to other intellectual disciplines; it was presented to the International Colloquium on Methodology of Sciences held in Warsaw in 1961 and was published in *The Foundation of Statements and Decisions* (Warsaw: Polish Scientific Publishers, 1964), edited by Kazimierz Ajdukiewicz. "*Verstehen*: The Epistemological Problem" is a defense of the use of "intuitive understanding" in application to the problem of other minds. It was presented to the International Colloquium on Knowledge and Understanding held in Biel in 1978 and first appeared in *Dialectica* (Vol. 33, 1979). "What is a Transcendental Argument?" expresses certain misgivings about one way of doing philosophy. It first appeared in *Neue Hefte fur Philosophie* (Heft 14, 1978). "The Paradox of Analysis," written with Richard Potter, offers a nonlinguistic solution to a fundamental problem about the nature of philosophy. It first appeared in *Metaphilosophy* (vol. 12, 1981).

The third and final part of the book, "Theory of Knowledge in America," is a critical history of twentieth-century American epistemology. It first appeared in *Philosophy*, a volume in the series *The Princeton Studies: Humanistic Scholarship in America* (Englewood Cliffs, NJ: Prentice-Hall, Inc., 1964). It is here presented in its original form.

I wish to express my thanks to the editors and publishers of these publications for allowing me to reprint them here.

Part I

Chapter 1
A Version of Foundationalism

Introduction

The present essay is an attempt to deal with the basic problems of the theory of knowledge. The general view that is here defended is appropriately called "foundationalism."

What are the presuppositions of the theory of knowledge? I shall list six such suppositions. In formulating them, I shall use the first person, but I am quite confident that I am speaking for others as well.

1) There are certain things I know and certain things I do not know. I can give examples of each. Like Moore, I know that I have two hands and that the earth has existed for hundreds of years. But I do not know whether it will rain here a year from today and I do not know how many people now live in East Jaffrey. This first presupposition can be put more generally: I am justified in believing certain things and I am not justified in believing certain other things.

2) The distinction between the things I am justified in believing and the things I am not justified in believing need not coincide with the distinction between those of my beliefs that are true and those of my beliefs that are false. In other words, it is quite possible that some of the things I am *not* justified in believing are true. Possibly my senses are deceiving me, but even if they are, I am not justified in believing they are not. And obviously, many of the things I am not

---

I am indebted to critics of earlier formulations. These critics include William P. Alston, Bruce Aune, Fred Dretske, Herbert Heidelberger, Robert Shope, Ernest Sosa, and Timm Triplet.

justified in believing are true. I cannot *now* say, of course, which of my justified beliefs are false. Perhaps there was a time when people were justified in believing the false proposition that all swans are white. This means that they were not justified in believing the true proposition that some swans are not white.

We may say, of the relation between epistemic justification and truth, what John Maynard Keynes said about the relation between probability and truth: "there is no direct relation between the truth of a proposition and its probability. Probability begins and ends with probability. That a scientific investigation pursued on account of its probability will generally lead to truth, rather than falsehood, is at best only probable."[1]

3) Yet there *is* a positive relation between the epistemically justified and the true. For one thing, I am justified in believing a given proposition, if and only if, I am justified in believing that that proposition is *true*. There is still another point about the relation between epistemic justification and truth, but this point is somewhat more difficult to formulate. For the present, we may put it by saying that, if I want to believe what is true and not to believe what is false, then the most reasonable thing for me to do is to believe what is justified and not to believe what is not justified.

4) Epistemic justification, unlike truth, is capable of degrees. Of the things that we are justified in believing, some are more justified than others. We may say, more generally, that certain attitudes are *more reasonable* on certain occasions than are other attitudes on those occasions. (As we shall see, the concepts of the theory of evidence may be explicated in terms of the undefined epistemic locution, "_____ is more reasonable for S at t than_____.")

5) Some of the things I know, or am justified in believing, are justified by certain *other* things that I know, or am justified in believing. For example, I know—and am therefore justified in believing— that there were people in a certain building earlier today. What justifies me in believing this may include the fact that certain people have told me so and that I am justified in believing what they said. And presumably my justification also includes certain general information I have about such buildings and the communities in which they exist.

6) Some of the things I am justified in believing are such that by reflection, I can *know* that I am justified in believing them; and I can find out just *what*, if anything, justifies me in believing them. Thus Russell once observed: "The degree of credibility attaching to a

proposition is itself sometimes a datum. I think we should also hold
that the degree of credibility to be attached to a *datum* is sometimes
a datum."[2] This will hold of so-called empirical or a posteriori beliefs
as well as of beliefs that are a priori. Hence we have another respect
in which the present concept of the justified differs from the concept
of the true. For in the case of what is empirical or a posteriori, delib-
eration or reflection is *not* sufficient to enable us to find out whether
it is true. It is important to distinguish this final point from the first.
According to the first, there are some things I am justified in believing
and some things I am not justified in believing. And according to the
present point, some of the things I am justified in believing are such
that I can find out by reflection that they *are* things I am justified in
believing; and similarly for some of the things I am not justified in
believing.[3]

It may be noted that these presuppositions of the theory of evidence are analogous, in fundamental respects, to the presuppositions
of ethics.

Let us now consider certain basic facts about thought and reference.

On the Primary Object of Intentional Attitudes

It is only within the last decade that philosophers have come to
appreciate the difficulties involved in what might be called the "he,
himself" locution—the locution "There exists an x such that x believes *himself* to be wise," as contrasted with "There exists an x such
that x believes x to be wise." The difficulties arise because the first
locution implies the second and not conversely, thus leaving us with
the question, "What does the first tell us that the second does not?"

The second locution could be true and the first false in the following situation. I look in the mirror, or look at my hand, and believe
with respect to the person that I see that he is wise; I am then an x
such that x believes x to be wise. But it may yet be at the same time
that I do not believe *myself* to be wise, for I may have a very poor
opinion of myself and not realize that *I* am the person I am looking at.

Does the first sentence ("There exists an x such that x believes
himself to be wise") express some proposition that is not expressed
by the second? It is not possible to give a plausible account of what
this proposition would be.

To understand the difference between the two locutions, we have
to rethink the nature of believing and of other so-called propositional

attitudes. Instead of thinking of these atttitudes as involving, in the first instance, a relation between a person and a *proposition*, we think of them as involving a relation between a person and a *property* — a property that the person attributes to himself. If I believe myself to be wise, then I directly attribute the property of wisdom to myself. If I believe *you* to be wise, then there is a certain *other* property that is such that, in directly attributing *that* property to myself, I *indirectly* attribute to you the property of being wise. Suppose, for example, that you are the only person I am talking with. And suppose I (directly) attribute to myself the following property — that of talking with exactly one person and with a person who is wise. Then I indirectly attribute to you the property of being wise. The property I attribute to myself singles you out as the thing to which I bear a certain relation; by directly attributing the one property to me, I indirectly attribute the other property to you.

Thus we begin with the undefined locution, "x directly attributes to y the property of being F." And we assume that direct attribution is necessarily such that, for every x and y, if x directly attributes a certain property to y, then x is identical with y. Given this undefined locution, we may now define the locution "x *indirectly attributes* to y the property of being F" as follows: There is a relation R such that x stands in R to y and only to y; and x directly attributes to x the property of standing in R to just one thing and to a thing that is F."

So-called *de dicto* believing — the acceptance of propositions — may be viewed as one type of indirect attribution. If I accept a certain proposition, then I indirectly attribute to it the property of being true. (In so doing, I may single it out as the sole thing I am conceiving in a certain way. The proposition, say, that all men are mortal may be the sole thing pertaining to mortality that I am now conceiving.) But we shall assume that, whenever I do attribute a property to myself, then I *also* accept a certain proposition. Thus if I attribute wisdom to myself, I will also accept the proposition that someone is wise.

I assume, however, that there are no "first-person propositions" — e.g., that although the first-person sentence "I am wise" expresses my direct attribution of wisdom to myself, it does not express a proposition. My reasons for holding this are set forth in detail in *The First Person: A Study in Reference and Intentionality*.

The version of epistemology that follows, then, presupposes this general theory of believing. But everything that I shall say is readily adaptable to the view according to which the basic form of believing is propositional. Indeed, if that view were true, the following could be considerably simplified.

Some Epistemic Concepts

Traditionally, knowledge may be identified with justified true belief. If, as we are now assuming, the basic sense of believing is direct attribution, then a kind of knowledge exists that may be associated with justified true direct attribution. We now consider this knowledge.

The simplest way of setting forth the vocabulary of the theory of evidence, or epistemology, is to take as undefined the locution, "_____ is more reasonable than _____ for s at t" (or, alternatively, "_____ is epistemically preferable to _____ for S at t"). Epistemic reasonability could be understood in terms of the general requirement to try to have the largest possible set of logically independent beliefs that is such that the true beliefs outnumber the false beliefs. The principles of epistemic preferability are the principles one should follow if one is to fulfill this requirement. (It should be noted that the requirement is so formulated that the requirement to have true beliefs receives greater emphasis than the requirement not to have false beliefs.)

The epistemic locution we have taken as undefined is obviously applicable to propositional acceptance, or de dicto belief, where we can say that accepting one proposition is more or less reasonable than accepting another. But its application can readily be extended to direct attribution.

To characterize the relevant epistemic concepts in their application to such attribution, we shall introduce the concept of *withholding* the attribution of a property. Consider a person and a property such that (a) the person does *not* directly attribute that property to herself and (b) she does not directly attribute the *negation* of that property to herself: such a person may be said to *withhold* the direct attribution of that property.

Among the general principles of epistemic preferability is that such preferability is transitive and asymmetric. If one attribution, or withholding, is more reasonable for a given subject at a given time than a second, and if the second is more reasonable than a third, then the first is more reasonable than the third. And if one is more reasonable than another, then the other is not more reasonable than the one.

We may also affirm the following principle: If, for a certain subject

at a certain time, withholding the direct attribution of a given property is *not* more reasonable than the direct attribution of that property, then the direct attribution of that property *is* more reasonable
than the direct attribution of the negation of that property. This
principle has its analogue in the following de dicto epistemic principle:
if withholding a proposition is *not* more reasonable than accepting it,
then accepting it is more reasonable than accepting its negation. "If
agnosticism is not more reasonable than theism, then theism is more
reasonable than atheism."[4]

Given these principles and others, we may formulate definitions of
a variety of fundamental epistemic concepts. We could say, for example, that the direct attribution of a given property is is epistemically *unacceptable* for a given subject at a given time, provided only
that withholding that property is more reasonable for that subject at
that time than directly attributing it. In saying that the attitude is
"unacceptable," I do not mean that the believer *finds* it unacceptable.
I mean something more objective—something that could also be put
by saying that the attitude ought not to be taken, or that it is an attitude that it would be unreasonable to take. We could say that an attribution is *counterbalanced* if and only if the direct attribution of
that property is no more nor less reasonable than is the direct attribution of the negation of that property.

We may also distinguish several different epistemic levels that the
direct attribution of a property may occupy for a given subject at a
given time. Thus we have:

> Having some presumption it its favor;
> Acceptability;
> Being beyond reasonable doubt;
> Being evident;
> Being certain.

Each of these concepts may be said to provide a sense for the expression "epistemically justified"—certainty constituting the highest degree of epistemic justification, and having some presumption in its
favor the lowest.

A direct attribution of a property could be said to *have some presumption in its favor*, provided only that the direct attribution of
that property is more reasonable than the direct attribution of its negation. A direct attribution of a property is *acceptable* if it is not
unacceptable. A direct attribution of a property could be said to be
beyond reasonable doubt provided only that the direct attribution of

that property is more reasonable than withholding that property.

Ascending to still higher epistemic levels, we may now consider *the evident.* We may say that the direct attribution of a property is *evident* for a given person provided the attribution is beyond reasonable doubt for that person and is one of those attributions on which it is reasonable for her to base her decisions. (A person may be said to "base her decisions" on a given attribution provided she uses that attribution as a premise from which she calculates those probabilities on which she acts.)

Finally there is the concept of objective certainty. The direct attribution of a property may be said to be objectively *certain* for a person provided these conditions hold: the direct attribution of that property is beyond reasonable doubt for that person; and it is at least as reasonable for him as is the direct attribution of any other property. If the attribution of the property of being F is thus certain for a subject, then he may be said to be certain that *he* is F.

These epistemic expressions may be read in another way. For example, if we may say, of the property of being F, that the direct attribution of that property is beyond reasonable doubt for a certain subject x, then we may also say: "It is beyond reasonable doubt for x that *he* is F." And analogously for the other epistemic concepts just defined.

We must take care not to be misled by syntax at this point. The propositional locution, "It is beyond reasonable doubt for x that *he* is F," may tempt one to suppose that there is a certain proposition corresponding to the expression "he is F" and that this proposition is one that is beyond reasonable doubt for the subject x. But "It is beyond reasonable doubt for x that he is F" does not imply that there is a proposition corresponding to the expression "he is F." In this respect, "it is beyond reasonable doubt" may be compared with the locution, "He believes himself to be F." The latter tells us only that he has directly attributed the property of being F to himself; and the former tells us only that, for him, directly attributing that property is more reasonable than withholding it.

The epistemic concepts that thus apply to direct attributions have their analogues that may be applied to propositions.

The Self-Presenting

Certain properties—all of them implied by what psychological or "Cartesian"—may be said to *present themselves* to the subject who has them. One example is feeling sad; another is thinking about a golden mountain; another is believing oneself to be wise; and still another may be suggested by the awkward locution, "is appeared redly to."[5]

The mark of a self-presenting property is this: every property it entails is necessarily such that, if a person has it and also considers whether he has it, then *ipso facto* he will attribute it to himself.[6] Thus we do not *define* such properties by reference to certainty, but we will formulate a material epistemic principle relating such properties to certainty.

We may distinguish the self-presenting from "the self-presented." A property that is self-presenting may not be considered by the person who has it and therefore it will not be *self-presented* to that person.[7] But if the person who has it considers his having it, then he will accept the fact that he has it and the property may be said, therefore, to be self-presented.

Whatever is self-presenting is *implied by* what is psychological. That is to say, for every self-presenting property, there is a psychological property which is necessarily such that, if one has the psychological property then one has the self-presenting property. And whatever is self-presenting *involves* what is psychological. That is to say, every self-presenting property is necessarily such that, if one conceives that property, then one conceives some psychological property.[8]

I would say that *thinking*, as Descartes conceived it, is self-presenting. Consider the activities he refers to in the following passage:

By the word thought I understand all that of which we are conscious as operating in us. And that is why not alone understanding, willing, imagining, but also feeling are here the same as thought. . . . If I mean to talk only of my sensation, or my consciously seeming to see or to walk, . . . my assertion now refers only to my mind, which alone is concerned with my feeling or thinking that I see and I walk.[9]

The properties that Descartes here refers to are all such that, if a person has them and if he considers the question whether he has them, then he will attribute them to himself.

Many properties which are *not* psychological are also self-presenting by our definition. An example is the property of being either a stone or considering something. But this property involves and is implied by the psychological property of considering something.

We should note, what may not be clear in the passage from Descartes, that there are *ways of being appeared to* —ways of *sensing*—

that are such that being appeared to in those ways is self-presenting Thus there is what we might call "a way of being appeared to" that is such that, if you are appeared to in that way, and if you consider your being appeared to in that way, then you will attribute to yourself the property of being appeared to in that way. We shall return below to such ways of being appeared to.

Every self-presenting property, then, is a property that is such that, if while having it, you *consider* your having it, then you will *believe* yourself to have it. Let us now note that considering and believing are themselves self-presenting. If you are sad and consider your being sad, then you will attribute sadness to yourself. If you consider your being sad and then consider your considering being sad, then you will believe yourself to consider your being sad. And if you believe yourself to be sad and consider your believing yourself to be sad, then you will believe yourself to believe yourself to be sad.

There is no regress here. We are not saying that if you consider your being sad, then you will believe that you are considering your being sad. And we are not saying that if you believe yourself to be sad, then you will believe yourself to believe yourself to be sad. For we can consider and believe without considering our considering and believing.

Our definition of the self-presenting may be interpreted as telling us that the presence of a self-preseting property is "indubitable." This interpretation is correct if "doubt" is taken to imply conscious withholding of belief. For we have assumed that, if you have a self-presenting property and if you consider your having it, then you will believe yourself to have it; and if you believe yourself to have it, then you cannot at the same time doubt whether you have it. But this type of indubitability should be distinguished from the epistemic concept of *certainty*.

Self-Presentation and Certainty

I have not *defined* self-presenting properties by reference to evidence and certainty. But the presence of such properties is also evident to the subject who has them. And, if we think of certainty as constituting the highest degree of epistemic justification, then we may say that a person's self-presenting properties *are* objects of certainty for that person.

Indeed we may affirm the following "material epistemic principle" pertaining to such evidence and certainty:

P1 ↑

> If the property of being F is self-presenting, then, for every x, if x has the property of being F and if x considers his having that property, then it is certain for x that he is then F.

Every self-presenting property provides us with an instance of P1. Thus we could say:

> For every x, if x has the property of being sad, and if x considers the question whether he is sad, then it is certain for x that he is sad.

And if considering is also self-presenting, and if you consider your considering whether you are sad, then it will be certain for you that you are considering whether you are sad.

Our principle illustrates what some have called the *supervenient* character of epistemic justification; for it tells us how positive epistemic status "is supervenient on a set of non-epistemic facts."[10] Other material epistemic principles that I shall formulate also illustrate such supervenience. (We could say that a normative property G "supervenes on" a nonnormative property H, provided only: H is necessarily such that whatever has it has G, but not necessarily such that whoever attributes it attributes G. A "normative" property—for present purposes—could be said to be any property definable in terms of preferability.) Thus the instance of P1 cited above tells us that being certain that one is sad supervenes on the property of being both sad and such that one considers one's being sad.

Principle P1 pertains to what we might call "nonpropositional evidence and certainty." But we may affirm as a corollary the following principle about propositional evidence and certainty: For every x, if it is evident for x that he has the property of being F, then the *proposition* that something is F is one that is evident for x; and if it is certain for x that he has the property of being F, then the proposition that something is F is one that is evident for S.

The evidence that is thus yielded by those of our properties that are self-presenting could be said to constitute that which is *directly evident*—or, more exactly, that which is *directly evident a posteriori*. When we have such properties, then our direct attributions of them are directly evident. So, too, for the attribution of those properties that are *entailed* by the self-presenting. Anything entailed (both implied and involved) by such attributions is also directly evident.

Hence certain negative properties—say, once again, the property of not believing that ghosts exist—may be such that it is directly evident to one that one has them. These properties will not be self-presenting by our definition but they may be entailed by what is self-presenting—say the property of thinking and not believing ghosts exist. (The latter property may be self-presenting even to those who do not have the concept of a ghost. This consequence is essential to the theory of evidence.) But in saying that such properties are self-presenting, we are not saying that they are self-presented.

The Epistemically Unsuspect

The term "foundation," in its application to knowledge, suggests that our knowledge is comparable to a building or to a pyramid. But a different metaphor has been proposed by Otto Neurath. He said that our knowledge is to be compared to a ship or a raft and that the epistemologist is to be compared to a sailor "who, unable to return to dock, must reconstruct his vessel on the open sea, and is therefore forced to make use of the best constituents that are at hand."[11] We have here two quite different ways of looking at knowledge. Must we choose between "the pyramid and the raft"?[12]

The figure of the pyramid suggests that we can use material that is solid, firm, and absolutely reliable. That of the raft suggests we must settle for what is at best makeshift and haphazard. But perhaps *both* figures are accurate. I suggest that we do not have here two different conceptions of knowledge. What we have—metaphors aside—are two different aspects of our knowledge, each of them of fundamental importance. There are two moments of epistemic justification, one of them foundational and the other not.

In considering what it is that we are justified in believing, we should take into account, not only that which is objectively certain and thus foundational for our subject at any given time, but also certain things which may then be said to have *some presumption in their favor* for him. I have said that the direct attribution of a property has some presumption in its favor for a given subject at a given time provided that the direct attribution of that property is then more reasonable for him than is the direct attribution of its negation. Let us now consider such attributions and see how they function in our general epistemic principles.

To locate that which has some presumption in its favor, I shall propose an additional material epistemic principle—and one that is extremely latitudinarian. This is the principle that *anything* we find ourselves believing may be said to have *some* presumption in its favor —*provided* it is not explicitly contradicted by the set of other things that we believe. The principle may be thought of as an instance of a more general truth—that it is reasonable to put our trust in our own cognitive faculties unless we have some positive ground for questioning them.

The principle is this:

> P2 For every x, if (i) x directly attributes to himself the property of being F, and if (ii) x being F is not explicity contradicted by the set of properties that x directly attributes to x, then his being F has some presumption in its favor for x.

The principle is readily extended to propositional belief. Thus we may say that, for every x, if x accepts a proposition or state of affairs that is not explicitly contradicted by any conjunction of propositions each such that it is accepted by x, then that proposition has some presumption in its favor for x. (One proposition "explicitly contradicts" another provided only that it *entails* the negation of the other; the relation between properties is analogous.)

In affirming P2, we follow Carneades who assigned a positive epistemic status to "the uncontradicted."[13] The apparent overpermissiveness of this principle can be corrected by reference to a certain subset of these "uncontradicted" attributions; this subset constitutes our next category.

From among the attributions that thus have some presumption in their favor for our subject, we may now single out those that are "epistemically in the clear." An attribution of a property P may be said to be *epistemically unsuspect*, or *epistemically in the clear*, for any subject, provided only that it is *not disconfirmed* by the set of "uncontradicted" properties we have just singled out. More exactly, a property P is epistemically in the clear for a given subject provided it is not disconfirmed by the set of those properties other than P that have some presumption in their favor for him. And analogously for propositions or states of affairs. (The requisite concept of confirmation is discussed in the following essay.)

According to our latitudinarian epistemic principle P2, anything we believe has some presumption in its favor provided it is not explicity contradicted by anything else we believe. Given the concept of the epistemically unsuspect, we may formulate an additional principle, which will compensate for this permissiveness of P2. We will equate the epistemically unsuspect with that which is epistemically *acceptable*. (We have said that the direct attribution of a property is "acceptable" provided that withholding that property is not more reasonable than attributing that property. And, analogously, a proposition is acceptable provided that withholding it is not more reasonable than accepting it.)

Our third principle, then, is this:

P3   For every x, and every property H, the direct attribution of H is acceptable for S if and only if it is not disconfirmed by the set of all those properties having some presumption in their favor for S.

Analogously, a proposition is epistemically in the clear for x if and only if it is acceptable for x. The principle thus tells us that anything that is epistemically in the clear is epistemically acceptable. But it also tells us that nothing is epistemically acceptable unless it is epistemically in the clear.

Our new principle thus enables us to single out, from the set of beliefs having some presumption in their favor, a subset of beliefs that are also epistemically acceptable.

We are now in a position to formulate our principles of perceptual evidence. These will all make reference to that which is epistemically acceptable, or in the clear.

Appearing and Being Appeared To

We now apply the concept of indirect attribution to throw light on a number of philosophical problems involving the nature of perception. For we may say that perception is, essentially, the indirect attribution of a property to a thing, the thing being considered *as* the thing that is appearing in a certain way.

We being, then, with appearing.

The requisite sense of "appear" is both causal and psychological. Traditionally one had spoken of "sensations" instead of "ways of appearing." One had said that the object of perception, acting on the perceiver's sense-organs, caused him to "have certain sensations." But I would prefer to say that the object of perception causes him to *sense* in a certain way. The subject, who was said to experience a red sensation, does not stand in a sentient relation to an *object* that is a red sensation; rather, is is sentient *in a certain way*—a way that we could describe as "redly." (Compare "she experiences sadness" and "she feels sad": the former suggests, misleadingly, that sadness is one of two things that are related by experiencing; the latter suggests, more accurately, that being sad is a *way* of experiencing.) for philosophical purposes it is convenient to use "is appeared to" in place of "senses."

Let us note the distinction between (a) "There exists a y such that y appears to x in a certain way" and (b) "x is appeared to (senses) in a certain way." The first implies something about an external stimulus object; it tells us, in part, that y, acting as a stimulus object, causes the subject to be in a certain sentient state. But the second implies nothing about an external object and tells us only about the state of the subject. In cases of fantasy, dreaming, and hallucination, the second may be true whereas the first is false. For then one will be sensing —one will be appeared to—in a certain way even though no external stimulus object is causing one to sense in that way.

The expression "being appeared redly to," as we shall interpret it, must *not* be interpreted as having the same sense as any of the following expressions: "being appeared to by something that is red": "being appeared to in the way one is normally appeared to by things that are red": or "being appeared to in the way in which one believes that red things normally appear." The expression "being appeared redly to" has what I have called its *noncomparative* sense in this use.[14]

"Being appeared redly to," in this noncomparative use, refers to a property that is self-presenting in the sense that we have defined. That is to say, being appeared redly to is necessarily such that, if a person is appeared redly to and if he considers his being appeared redly to, then he will attribute to himself the property of being appeared redly to. This use of "being appeared redly to" is "noncomparative," since the sense of the expression "red", in this use, has not *logically* connected with the sense that the word "red" has when physical things are said to be red.

Can we, then, characterize "y appears redly to x" in terms of being appeared redly to and certain causal concepts? Here we must presuppose the concept of *functional dependence*: if y appears in a certain way to x, then the way x is appeared to will be functionally dependent on the nature of y. That is to say, y will be so related to x that, merely by varying y continuously with respect to certain of its properties, one can vary continuously the way in which x is appeared to. More specifically, if y is appearing visually to x, then y has properties that are such that, by varying them, one can vary the way in which x is visually appeared to. And analogously for the other sense-modalities.

The functional dependence that relates the appearing object and the way of being appeared to is also *structural*, since it essentially involves different *parts* of the object that appears. If, for the moment, we permit ourselves the sense-datum language ("He senses a red appearance") instead of the language of being appeared to ("He is appeared to redly"), we can easily describe this structural relation. The appearance is divisible into parts that correspond to different parts of the thing that presents the appearance. The table-top, for example, may present a uniform visual appearance; yet by varying the color, say, of the left half of the table-top we can vary the color of the left half of the visual appearance. (If we restrict ourselves to the language of being appeared to, we cannot thus speak of the "parts" of a way of being appeared to. But we can distinguish various *aspects* of the way of being appeared to and we can put our point by reference to them.)

The way that an external thing appears will be thus structurally dependent, not only on the thing that is appearing, but also on the relevant sense-organ. Perhaps we can distinguish the role of the sense-organ from that of the object of appearance by saying this: the nature of the appearance is *directly* dependent on the state of the sense organ; and it is *indirectly* dependent on the state of that physical thing on which the state of the sense-organi is directly dependent.

The *medium* in which an object appears will also affect the way in which the subject is appeared to. Indeed, continuous variations in the former may produce continuous variations in the latter. But the medium will not have the kind of structural relation that we have been considering to the way of being appeared to. For it will not normally be the case that different aspects of the way of being appeared to will correspond to different proper parts of the medium. Hence we need not say that it is always the medium of perception that appears to the subject. It is the *object* of perception that appears.

We may now formulate a simple appearance principle. What we have a right to affirm, I suggest, is a generalization on the following: "*Being appeared redly* to tends to make it evident to the subject that *there is something that appears red to him.*" In other words, if a person is appeared redly to, then it is evident to him that there *is* something that appears red to him—provided he considers the question whether something is appearing red to him and provided he has no reason to suppose that it is *not* the case that something appears red to him.

Our general principle is this:

> P4 For every x, if there is a way of appearing such that (i) it is self-presenting and (ii) x is appeared to in that way, then the following is evident for x provided it is epistemically in the clear for him and something that he considers: there is something that is appearing that way to him.

Being thus appeared to puts one in contact, so to speak, with external reality. And such initial contact, it would seem, can only be *via* appearances.

Several Senses of Perception

"Perception," in its ordinary sense, is an epistemic term. If I can be said, in this ordinary sense, to perceive that a sheep is in the field, then it is *evident* to me that a sheep is in the field. Since our present concern is with the question, "How is transcendent evidence possible?", we shall not begin with this epistemic sense of perception. Instead, we will try to disentangle the epistemic and nonepistemic features of perception and then single out those processes *in virtue of which* we can be said, in this ordinary epistemic sense, to perceive—those processes on which perceptual evidence may be said to supervene. We will ask: What is there about those processes that makes transcendent evidence possible? And then, having an answer to this question, we can turn to the ordinary sense of perception.

The objective reference that is involved in perception does not differ in principle from what we have considered already. As we have said, perception may be characterized as a special type of direct attribution—one that essentially involves the concept of *appearance*. But several senses of perception must be distinguished.

An explicit formulation of a perceptual judgment will always make a reference to the perceiver himself. What one perceives is not merely something red or something round, but that something red or something round stands in a certain relation to *oneself*. What would the relation be? If I perceive a thing, then, of course, the thing is related to me as being one of the objects of my perception. And presumably, for each thing that I perceive, I perceive it in *some* way or other that distinguishes my perception of *that* thing at that time from my perception of any other thing at that time. But *this* cannot be the identifying relation that is involved in perception. What one *perceives* is not, in the first instance, that one perceives an object in a certain way. The fact of perception is not a part of the content of perception.

The identifying relation that is involved in perception pertains, rather, to the concept of *appearing*. If I perceive a thing, then I judge that just one thing is appearing to me in a certain way. I may judge, for example, that something appears red to me. If many things are such that each one is appearing red to me, then for each of them there will be a further way of appearing such that that thing is the sole thing that is appearing to me in *that* way. One thing might appear red and round, another thing red and square, and so on.

Our first sense of perception, then, may be characterized as follows:

(I) The property of being F is such that x perceptually takes y to have it =Df. There is a way of appearing such that y and only y appears in that way to x; and the property of being F is a sensible property that x indirectly attributes to y, as the thing that appears to him in that way.

What is intended by the expression "sensible property" may be suggested by the following list: such *visual* properties as blue, green, yellow, red, white, black; such *auditory* properties as sounding or making a noise; such *somesthetic* properties as rough, smooth, hard, soft, heavy, light, hot, cold; such *gustatory* properties as sweet, sour, salty, bitter; and such *olfactory* properties as fragrant, spicy, putrid, burned. Sensible properties would also include such "common sensibles" as movement, rest, number, figure, and magnitude. And we may understand "sensible property" sufficiently broadly so that relations of resemblance and difference among sensible properties may also be counted as sensible properties.

It should be noted that the final clause of our definition (I) exhibits such perception as a type of indirect attribution. We will call this the *primary* sense of perception. It is a very broad sense, for it does not imply evidence or veridicality. From the fact that one thus perceptually takes a thing to be F, it does not follow that the thing *is* F, nor does it follow that the perceiver has *evidence* that the thing is F.

Given this primary sense of perception, we may now define the expression, "x perceives y." Let us say:

(II) x perceives y =Df. There is a property such that x perceptually takes y to have it.

Let us call this the *nonpropositional* sense of perception. I assume that the subspecies of such perception—seeing, hearing, tasting, feeling—can be described by reference to the kinds of ways of being appeared to that they involve.[15] Still other senses of perception ("She heard the concert," "She saw the shadow move") could readily be singled out.[16] But these are not relevant to our present concern.

The two senses of perception just defined presuppose what we may call the *self-presenting* sense of perception:

(III) The property of being F is such that x perceptually takes there to be something that has it =Df. The property of being F is a sensible property such that x is appeared to in such a way that he directly attributes to himself the property of being appeared to in that way by something that is F.

The definiendum may also be read as "x perceptually takes there to be something that is F."

Although perception, in this third sense, implies that the subject is being appeared to in a certain way, it does not imply that anything is *appearing* to him in that way. This last fact is our excuse for using the awkward locution, "he perceptually takes *there to be* something that has it," instead of the simpler "he perceptually takes something to have it."

The several senses of perception here distinguished do not yet include the familiar "perceives that" locution of ordinary language—as in "she perceives that someone is approaching," or "she perceives someone to be approaching." We will be in a position to explicate this ordinary sense of perception after we have formulated certain further epistemic principles.

The Principles of Perceptual Evidence

A simple principle of perceptual evidence would be illustrated by the following: If a person perceptually takes there to be a sheep in the field before him, then it is *evident* to him that a sheep is in the field. Thus Meinong had held, in effect, that the fact that we *think* we perceive confers "presumptive evidence [Vermutungsevidenz]" on the proposition or state of affairs that is the object of our ostensible perception.[17] And H. H. Price has said that the fact that we "perceptually accept" a certain proposition is sufficient to confer some positive epistemic status on that proposition. Price put this point as follows: "We want to be able to say: the fact that a material thing is perceptually presented to the mind is *prima facie evidence* of the thing's existence and of its really having that sort of surface which it ostensibly has; or, again, that there is *some presumption in favor of* this, not merely in the sense that we do as a matter of fact presume it (which of course we do) but in the sense that we are entitled to do so."[18] But such principles, as they stand, are somewhat overpermissive, epistemically.

Using the concept of the "epistemically unsuspect," or of that which is "epistemically in the clear," we might say that certain perceptual attributions are beyond reasonable doubt—*provided* they are epistemically unsuspect. In this way we could formulate a principle that is less permissive than those proposed by Meinong and Price. But we could add that, if such an attribution is a member of a set of properties, which mutually support each other and each of which is beyond reasonable doubt, then the attribution is evident.

What, then, is the requisite sense of "mutual support"? We may say that the members of a set of two or more properties "mutually support" each other for a subject S provided each of the properties is such that (1) the conjunction of all the others confirms it for S, and (2) it is confirmed for S by a self-presenting property that does not confirm any of the others for S. (The concept of confirmation and the relation of mutual support will be discussed in more detail in the following essay.)

This, then, is our perceptual principle:

P5 For every x, if (i) x perceptually takes there to be something that is F, and if (ii) his perceiving an F is epistemically in the clear for x, then it is beyond reasonable doubt for x that he perceives something that is F. If, moreover, his perceiving something that is F is a member of a set of properties, which mutually support each other and each of which is beyond reasonable doubt for x, then it is evident for x that he perceives something that is F.

Let us note certain features of this principle. The first part of the antecedent of the first part of the principle ("x perceptually takes there to be something that is F") refers to the "self-presenting sense of perception" singled out above. The second part of the antecedent ("his perceiving an F is epistemically in the clear") pertains to the class of things we singled out by means of principle P3. The consequent of the first part of the principle refers to the "nonpropositional sense of perception" also singled out above. The property of being F will be what we have called a sensible property.

The consequent of the first part of the principle reads: "It is evident for x that he *perceives something that is F.*" We should remind ourselves that one can perceive something that is F without thereby perceiving *that* the thing *to be* F—without thereby perceiving *that* the thing is F. Thus if the person that I see is a thief, then I perceive something that is a thief. But even if I know that he is a thief, it is not likely that I *perceive* him to be a thief—it is not likely that, in any sense, I perceive *that* he is a thief.

Our principle P5 states certain conditions under which we may say of a person that it is evident or beyond reasonable doubt for him that he perceives something that is F. It does not enable us to say, *do re*, of that person and any external object y, that it is beyond reasonable doubt for the person that he perceives that *that* particular thing y is F. In other words, our principle entitles us to say "x perceives that there is a y such that y is F," but not "There exists a y such that S perceives that y is F." It may be self-presenting for x that he is *being appeared to* in a certain way (that he *senses* in a certain way). But it cannot be self-presenting for him that there *is* something that *is appearing* to him in that way (i.e., it cannot be self-presenting to him that an external stimulus object *causes* him to sense in that way).

By means of what principle, then, can the person pass from a way of appearing to a particular physical thing that "transcends" that way of appearing? We are looking for a principle that enables us to say with respect to two things, x and y, that it is evident to x that y is F. We can find such a principle if we look to that which is self-presenting and also to that which is epistemically in the clear.

I propose, then, the following principle:

P6 For every x and y, if (i) x perceptually takes y and only y to be F, and if (ii) it is epistemically in the clear for x that he perceives something that is F, then y is such that it is beyond reasonable doubt for x that it is F; and if it is evident for x that he perceives something that is F, then y is such that it is evident for x that it is F.

In the first clause of the antecedent we refer to the primary sense of perception and in the second to the nonpropositional sense of perception.

This final perceptual principle introduces the de re epistemic locution: "y is such that it is evident to x that it is F." Therefore the principle is, in a certain respect, less pure than the preceding principle, P5. For, in theory at least, one can ascertain merely by reflection whether or not the antecedent condition of P5 obtains. But the present principle, P6, is not applicable unless there is an external physical thing causing the subject to sense in the way that he does. This fact cannot be ascertained merely by reflection. It cannot be self-presenting to the subject that there *is* a certain thing that he perceives to be F; it can be self-presenting only that he *perceptually takes* there to be something that is F. Hence we might call P6 a "quasi-epistemic principle."

It may be noted that the final clause of the definition begins with the condition, "if it is evident for x that he perceives something that is F." But we have not yet specified the conditions under which it *can* be evident to a person that he perceives something that is F. These conditions are discussed in the essay, "Knowing that One Knows," which follows.

Our perceptual principles are instances of the more general truth: "It is reasonable to trust the senses until one has positive reason for distrusting them."[19]

"But it's at least logically possible that our senses as well as our memories always deceive us. If that were in fact the case, *then* would it be reasonable to trust the senses?" The answer will be suggested by a comparable question: "It is logically possible that all our inductive conclusions (strictly speaking, those that are logically contingent) are false. In such a case, would it be reasonable to follow the principles of induction?" I am convinced that, in such a case, it *would* be reasonable to follow them.

The Ordinary Epistemic Sense of Perception

We are now in a position to explicate the ordinary epistemic sense of perception, as expressed in such locutions as "x perceives that y is F" and "x perceives y to be F." It is this:

(IV) x perceives y to be F =Df y is F; x perceptually takes y to be F; and it is evident to x that y is F.

Alternative readings of the definiendum are "x perceives that y is F" and "the property of being F is such that x perceives y to have it."

The second clause in the definiens—"x perceptually takes y to be F"
—refers to what we called the primary sense of perception. This primary sense was defined by reference to appearing and indirect attribution. The final clause in the definiens—"it is evident to x that y is F"—has been defined in terms of epistemic preferability. And we have seen in principles P5 and P6 the conditions under which the final clause may be said to be true.[20]

Is This Foundationalism?

In order to see the sense in which the present view may be said to be a version of "foundationalism," let us now list the six epistemic principles we have formulated:

P1 If the property of being F is self-presenting, then, for every x, if x has the property of being F and if x considers his having that property, then it is certain for x that he is then F.

P2 For every x, if (i) x directly attributes to himself the property of being F, and if (ii) x being F is not explicitly contradicted by the set of properties that x directly attributes to x, then his being F has some presumption in its favor for x.

P3 For every x, and for every property H, the direct attribution of H is acceptable for S if and only if it is not disconfirmed by the set of all those properties having some presumption in their favor for S.

P4 For every x, if there is a way of appearing such that (i) it is self-presenting and (ii) x is appeared to in that way, then the following is evident for x provided it is epistemically in the clear for him and something that he considers: there is something that is appearing that way to him.

P5 For every x, if (i) x perceptually takes there to be something that is F, and if (ii) his perceiving an F is epistemically in the clear for x, then it is beyond reasonable doubt for x that he perceives something that is F. If, moreover, his perceiving something that is F is a member of a set of properties, which mutually support each other and each of which is beyond reasonable doubt for x, then it is evident for x that he perceives something that is F.

P6 For every x and y, if (i) x perceptually takes y to be F, and if (ii) it is epistemically in the clear for x that he perceives something that is F, then y is such that it is beyond reasonable doubt for x that it is F; and if it is evident for x that he perceives something that is F, then y is such that it is evident for x that it is F.

We may now consider certain philosophical questions.

1) Are there *self-justifiers*—attributions or propositions that may be said to constitute their own justification?

The self-presenting would seem to be the closest we can come to that which constitutes its own justification. That one has a self-presenting property does not itself make it evident that one has that property. But that one has it and also *considers* one's having it does make it evident that one has it. Self-presenting properties, moreover, are distinctive in the following respect: it can be evident to one that one has the property even though one has no nondeductive—no merely inductive—grounds for attributing that property to oneself. In other words, a self-presenting property is a property such that it can be *evident* that one has it even though the only things that *make* it evident that one has it are things that entail it.

2) Is there a sense in which the self-presenting may be said to justify that which is not directly evident? Principles P4 and P5 state conditions under which the self-presenting may make evident certain attributions that are not direcly evident. For in the case of each of these principles, antecedent (i) refers to what is self-presenting and the consequent refers to something that is not directly evident. But application of the principles does not require that it be *evident* to the subject that he has the self-presenting properties in question—for they do not require that he *consider* his having them. It is the self-presenting, then, and not the directly evident, that may be said to justify that which is not directly evident.

3) Is everything that is epistemically justified justified *by* that which is self-presenting? Or is there a sense in which something other than that which is self-presenting can be said to serve as a ground or foundation of our knowledge?

Examination of our principles makes clear that, according to them, our knowledge is not a function *merely* of what is self-presenting. Principle P2 refers to what I have called "the uncontradicted"; this involves the logical relations that one attribution may bear to others. If these relations obtain, that they obtain will not be self-presenting. But, I would say, one can always ascertain by reflection whether or not they obtain. Similar observations hold of "the epistemically unsuspect" (that which is "epistemically in the clear"), referred to in principles P3, P4, and P5.

But the de re principle, P6, is an exception. For antecedent (i)— "if x perceives y to be F"—is not something that can be ascertained merely by reflection. The requisite sense of "perceives," as we have defined it, involves a causal relation between the object of perception and the perceiver. And one cannot determine by reflection whether or not such a relation obtains. Hence I suggested that P6 might be called a "quasi-epistemic principle."

I had written in the second edition of *Theory of Knowledge*:

What, then, of our justification for those propositions that are indirectly evident? We might say that they are justified in three different ways. (1) They may be justified by certain relations that they bear to what is *directly* evident. (2) They may be justified by certain relations that they bear to *each other*. And (3) they may be justified *by their own nature*, so to speak, and quite independently of the relations that they bear to anything else.[21]

I would now replace "the directly evident" above by "the self-presenting"; otherwise, I would say, the passage describes the present version of foundationalism.

4) Can we say that, according to our principles, the self-presenting constitutes the *basis* or *foundation* or *grounds* we have for the other things we know?

We could say that the attribution of E is a *basis* for the attribution of H provided only that E is necessarily such that, if its attribution is evident to a given subject, then the attribution of H is evident to that subject. Taking "basis" or "foundation" this way, we may affirm the following foundational thesis: everything that is evident for any particular subject has a basis or foundation that is entailed by some property that is self-presenting to that subject.

5) Can we say that, according to our principles, the self-presenting constitutes the justification for whatever it is that one is justified in believing? Here the answer must be negative.

I have said that there are two moments of epistemic justification— one that is foundational and the other that is not. The nonfoundational element is provided by principles P2 and P3. Principle P2 tells us that if an attribution is uncontradicted by the set of the subject's *other* attributions, then that attribution has some presumption in its favor. Principle P3 tells us that, if an attribution is not disconfirmed by the set of all those attributions having some presumption in their favor, then that attribution is epistemically acceptable.

The justification for such attributions is not a function merely of that which is self-presenting.

These considerations also apply to a priori knowledge. Thus we might define an *axiom* as a proposition that is necessarily such that (i) it obtains and (ii) whoever conceives it accepts it. Then we could affirm a principle analogous to P1: "If the proposition that p is an axiom, then, for every x, if x conceives the proposition that p, it is certain for x that p." (Here "p" is schematic, replaceable by any English sentence.) Then we could say that that self-presenting state, which is the subject conceiving the proposition that p, is the basis or foundation for his knowledge that p.

Here it might be objected: "You are saying that logic and mathematics are grounded in certain *subjective* states. That is psychologism of the worst sort!" We are saying only that even our knowledge of logic and mathematics begins with experience. We are not saying that logic and mathematics are about that which is subjective. The objection confuses the *ratio essendi* with the *ratio cognoscendi*.

Other Senses of Justification

The issues in theory of knowledge between "foundationalists" and "nonfoundationalists," so far as I have been able to ascertain, are mostly the result of misunderstanding. Foundationalism, I believe it is agreed, is a theory about the *justification* of belief. But apparently those who accept it take "justify" in one way and those who reject it take "justify" in another way.[22]

The foundationalists take "justify" in the *epistemic* sense. This interpretation of justification is illustrated, at least, by the concepts of epistemic preferability I have tried to explicate. And the nonfoundationalists take "justify" in one or another of several nonepistemic senses—some of which seem to presuppose some *further* sense of "justify" and some of which do not. From the fact that foundationalism is false, if "justify" is taken in one of its nonepistemic senses, it does not follow, of course, that it is false if "justify" is taken in its epistemic sense.

If you present one account of justification and I present another, is the difference between us merely verbal? Not if our respective counts are intended to be adequate to the same preanalytic data. And there is a set of data to which most versions of foundationalism and nonfoundationalism are intended to be adequate. Such data imply that there is a valid distinction between knowledge and true belief that isn't knowledge.

The term "justification," in its preanalytic sense, may be thought of as being the term for that which distinguishes knowledge from true belief that isn't knowledge. The terms "warrant" and "grounds" are other possibilities, as are variants of "evidence" and "evident." Still other possibilities are certain broader concepts in terms of which our ordinary evidential concepts can be defined, such as "credible" or "reasonable." Thus I would prefer to make use of terms that can be defined by reference to the comparative concept, *more reasonable than*. But for the present let us use "justification." (In considering these questions, we will do well to keep in mind that such words as "perceive" and "remember" are generally used in a way that implies knowing, and therefore that the danger of circularity arises if we attempt to explicate knowing in terms of perceiving and remembering.)

We presuppose, then, that there *is* a valid distinction between knowledge and true belief that isn't knowledge. In other words, we presuppose that it is possible to have true belief with respect to a certain topic without having knowledge with respect to that topic. Let us cite certain examples of this distinction. For then we will be able to ask whether various proposed analyses of the distinction are adequate to the examples. I shall describe three different cases.

a) We contrast the astronomer who believes that there are at least nine planets with the man who arrived at that belief solely on the basis of an examination of tea-leaves.

b) Consider a case of the sort discussed by Brentano. I happen to have a headache and you believe, solely on the basis of an exaggerated pessimism, that someone in the room has a headache; then you have mere true belief with respect to a topic concerning which I have knowledge.

c) The possible cases need not be restricted to empirical knowledge. Suppose I believe, solely on heresay, that a certain mathematical or logical theorem is true; and suppose the theorem is one that certain mathematicians or logicians have *proved* to be true. Then I will have true belief with respect to the theorem and they will have knowledge.

Here, then, we have three examples of the distinction between true belief that isn't knowledge and true belief that is knowledge. These examples are readily describable in the terminology of epistemic preferability that we have introduced. Let us now consider how they would fare under alternative conceptions of the justification of belief.

1) Sometimes it is said: "A belief is justified if and only if it is arrived at by a *reliable* method." The word "reliable" may then be characterized either by reference to truth alone or by reference to some other sense of justification. If we take it the first way, then we could form a simple version of the "reliable method" theory by saying: "A belief is justified if and only if the method by means of which it was arrived at is, more often than not, a method that leads to beliefs that are true and not to beliefs that are false."

Given such a simple interpretation of "reliable method," it is very difficult to distinguish this sense of "justify" from that which might be put by saying that a belief is justified if and only if it is true. (Such a theory, of course, would not be adequate to our three examples.) If I *have* arrived at a true belief, however accidentally, then I have followed a method that, on this occasion, *has* led to a true belief. Consider, once again, our three examples of true belief that isn't knowledge. It does not take much ingenuity to formulate, for each case, a general procedure that has been followed and that is such that, *whenever* it is followed, it leads to true belief. We need mention only our first case: the man whose decision that there were nine planets was a result of his reading the tea-leaves in a certain way. If this reading took place, say, on a Friday afternoon at 2:17 and if, previously and subsequently, the man never consulted the tea-leaves about the number of planets at that hour on a Friday afternoon, then he followed a procedure that *always* leads to truth — one he could describe by saying, "Whenever I want to find out anything about the number of planets, I should consult the tea-leaves at 2:17 on a Friday afternoon."

The simple version of the "reliability theory," then, does not enable us to distinguish knowledge from true belief that isn't knowledge. Hence one must place certain restrictions on the simple formula I have proposed. It remains to be seen whether this can be done without importing some other sense of justification.[23]

2) "Justify" might be taken to refer to the procedures of decision theory, or game theory. In applying such procedures one may reach conclusions of the following sort: "A course of action is justified (or reasonable) for a particular individual at a particular time, if and only if, in relation to the goals of that individual at that time and in relation to the evidence he has, it is more reasonable for him to pursue that course of action than not to pursue it." How would we apply

such procedures to the acquisition of belief? One might say: "A belief is justified for a particular individual at a particular time, if and only if, in relation to the goals of that individual at that time and to the *evidence* he then has, it is more reasonable for him to have that belief than not to have it." Here, once again, we have a sense of "justify" that presupposes the epistemic sense, for it refers to the *evidence* that the individual has.

"But might not this evidence in turn be characterized by reference to the procedures of decision theory?" The answer is that the kind of regress that would then be involved will not begin in the right place. ("If there are recordings of musical performances, then there must have been at least one actual performance at some time or other." "No; for all our recordings were made from *other* recordings of musical performances.")

"It isn't necessary that we characterize decision procedure epistemically. We can say that the subject should base her beliefs, not on the *evidence* that she has, but merely on the *other beliefs* that she has." We can, of course, formulate decision theory in such a way. But how would reference to such procedures help us to analyze our three examples?[24]

3) Sometimes justification is characterized by reference to "science" as in: "A belief is justified if and only if it has as its object one of the statements of science." This says both too much and too little, for it is inadequate both to our first example and also to our second example. Consider first the case involving the planets. The man who followed the tea leaves *did* accept one of the statements of science — namely, that there are nine planets. The second example knows that he has a headache and therefore that someone in the room has a headache. In what sense was the object of his belief one of the "statements of science"?

If, now, we say, "A belief is justified for a given person if and only if he arrives at it by means of a scientific procedure," then we have once again the difficulties we encountered with "the reliable method" theory.

4) Sometimes, it would seem, "justification" is characterized in terms of *coherence*: a belief or a statement is said to be justified in this sense provided it coheres in a certain way with certain other beliefs or statements. One may ask "In what way?" and, more important, "With *what* other beliefs or statements?" The answer, once again, would seem to presuppose some further sense of justification. Thus I

have made reference to mutual support in principle P5 above; and I shall propose a more general concurrence principle in the following essay. But principle P5 makes use of our basic epistemic concept. What would be an alternative to such a principle? Here, too, programs have been formulated, but not with such detail that we can apply any of them to our present problem.[25]

5) Justification has also been characterized by reference to *probability*. Keith Lehrer has held, for example, that a belief may be said to be completely justified provided only that the believer thinks it has a greater chance of being true than any of its competitors.[26]

What is meant by saying of a belief that it has a "chance of being true"?

One interpretation of "chance" would be statistical. Then to say of a given F that it has a "good chance" of being a G could be taken to mean something like this: the particular F is a member of a set of things most of the members of which are G. But if a belief *is* true, then, ipso facto, it is a member of a set of beliefs most of which are true. And if it is false, then, ipso facto, it is a member of a set of beliefs most of which are false. Hence, taken this way, the probability theory of justification would seem to have the same limitations as does the reliability theory.

But probability may also be taken epistemically. Then, to say of a proposition that it has a "good chance" of being true is to that it is *confirmed* by what is *evident*. But if we take the probability theory this way, then we are presupposing the epistemic concept of justification.

6) In recent years, it has also been contended that a belief or a statement is justified provided only it has a certain *explanatory* power.[27] But it would seem to be impossible to characterize the requisite sense of *explanation* without presupposing some other sense of justification. Normally, a hypothesis is not said to be an explanation for a particular formula unless the hypothesis has *some* positive epistemic status—unless, say, it has some presumption in its favor: "the acceptability of an explanation must be assessed on the basis of the degree to which the explanans as a whole is supported by factual evidence."[28] Moreover, if the suggestion is to be applied to our three examples, then, presumably, we will need an explication, not merely of the logical locution, "E explains O," but of the relativized locution "E explains O for S."[29] How, then, are we to characterize the relativized locution? We will be back where we started if we say merely

"S has an explanation for O." Suppose E explains O, in the logical sense of "explains." And suppose S has true belief, but not knowledge, with respect to E and with respect to O. Will he then "have an explanation" for O? In *one* sense of "have an explanation," the tea leaf man who believes that there are nine planets "has an explanation" for many astronomical phenomena. But this sense of "have an explanation" has no relevance to the distinction between knowledge and true belief that isn't knowledge.

It would seem, once again, that we are considering, not a theory, but a program that needs to be worked out.

7) "Justify" may be taken in a strictly ethical sense, as when one says "I have a right to believe whatever I want, provided no one else is affected by my beliefs." This ethical sense of "justify" does not seem to be relevant to the issues that separate foundationalists and nonfoundationalists.[30] Certainly this concept does not help us in any obvious way with our three examples of the distinction between knowledge and true belief that isn't knowledge. But I shall leave open the possibility that the epistemic sense of justification can be explicated in purely ethical terms.

Chapter 2
Confirmation and Concurrence

Introduction

The proposition that most swans are white may be said to confirm the proposition that all swans are white. Confirmation, so considered, is a relation that holds necessarily between propositions and is therefore comparable to logical implication and to entailment. But we may also speak of the *application* of this absolute relation—of the confirmation that one proposition provides another *for* a particular person S.

Let us use the expression, "e tends to confirm h," to refer to the absolute or logical relation that holds between propositions. And let us use "e confirms h for S" to express the application of this relation to the epistemic situation of a particular person.

An intuitive characterization of confirmation in the first sense would be this: if a proposition e tends to confirm a proposition h, then anyone who knows e to be true has, ipso facto, a reason for accepting h. Can we put the matter more precisely?

One might attempt to define "e tends to confirm h" by saying this: necessarily, for every x, if e is x's total evidence (i.e., if e is evident for x and if everything that is evident for x is entailed by e), then h has some presumption in its favor for x.[1] The epistemic concepts used in this definition—that of being evident and that of having some presumption—are readily definable in terms of epistemic preferability. I had used such a definition in *Theory of Knowledge*. But the definition, as it stands, is not adequate.

The difficulty with the definition is this. It restricts confirming propositions to those that are capable of becoming someone's total evidence. But certain propositions that are *incapable* of being anyone's total evidence—for example, the propositions that most swans are white—are such that we want to be able to say of them that they *are* capable of confirming other propositions. That is to say, the proposition that most swans are white may confirm the proposition that the next swan to be observed is white. But the proposition that most swans are white cannot be anyone's total evidence; there cannot be anyone who is such that the *only* thing she knows is the proposition that most swans are white.

We shall then, refine on this preliminary definition. Then we shall consider certain other epistemic relations—in particular, the relation of making evident and that of concurrence or mutual support.

If, as I have contended, believing and knowing take *properties* rather than propositions as their primary objects, these epistemic relations should be thought of as holding in the first instance between properties. But for simplicity I shall discuss them as they hold of propositions. What I shall say about propositions in this connection is readily adaptable to properties. Thus one property may be to confirm, or to tend to confirm, the attribution of another property; or, to put the matter somewhat differently, one property may be such that it confirms, or tends to confirm, that whatever has it has the other property.

The Absolute Sense of Confirmation

Making use of the epistemic concepts presupposed by the preliminary definition, we first introduce the concepts of an *evidential totality* and of an *evidential basis*. We will then be in a position to define the requisite sense of confirmation.[2]

D1 e is an evidential totality =Df is possibly such that there is something for whom it is evident and for whom everything is evident is entailed by e.

D2 b is a ground of e =Df. Every evidential totality entailing b entails e.

Instead of saying "b is a ground of e," we could say: "b indefeasibly makes e evident."

Every proposition is a ground of itself, according to these definitions. Some but not all propositions are necessarily such that they have grounds that are other than themselves. Some propositions have grounds that do not imply them. We may say in such cases that their grounds are nondeductive.

We next introduce the concept of a *minimal e totality*.

D3 t is a minimal e totality =Df t is an evidential totality entailing a ground of e and not properly entailing any evidential totality entailing a ground of e.

We use "h properly entails i" to abbreviate "h entails i, and i does not entail h."

We may now replace the condition "if e is x's total evidence," which appeared in our original definition of confirmation, by a reference to a minimal e totality:

D4 e tends to confirm h =Df. Every minimal e totality is necessarily such that anyone for whom it is the total evident is someone for whom h has some presumption in its favor.

When we say that one proposition thus *tends to confirm* another, we are affirming a relation between the two propositions that holds necessarily and quite independently of the knowledge or beliefs of any particular subject. The relation in question is sometimes put by saying that the second proposition *is probable in relation to* the first.

An Objection Considered

To understand the concept just introduced, consider the following objection to our definition: "There are propositions that are such that it is impossible that there is someone for whom they are evident and that, therefore, cannot be entailed by any evidential totality. For example, consider a certain proposition to the effect that there are exactly n electrons, where n is some very large number. There is no one for whom that proposition can be evident. Hence it vacuously satisfies the antecedent of D4 and therefore, by D4, it tends to confirm any proposition whatever. But, clearly, the proposition in question tends to confirm some propositions and does not tend to confirm others."

From the fact that there is no one for whom a certain proposition e can be evident, it does not follow that e is necessarily such that there is no one for whom it can be evident. A general postulate of the theory of evidence should be this—that unless a proposition is a priori false, or unless it entails its own nonevidence, then it is possibly such that there is someone for whom it is evident.[3]

"But consider these two propositions: (e) nothing is evident to anyone and 55% of As are Bs and John is an A; and (h) nothing is evident to anyone and John is a B. It is clear that e tends to confirm h. Yet neither e nor h can be evident to anyone. Therefore your definition is not adequate to this case."

From the fact that a proposition is evident it does not follow that that proposition is *true*. There is no contradiction in saying that it is evident to someone that nothing is evident to anyone. There is no reason to suppose, therefore, that the e and the h of the example are necessarily such that they cannot be evident.

Two Logical Points

There are two logical points to be made about the absolute sense of confirmation.

The first point is that the relation of tending to confirm is not transitive. In other words, there are propositions e, h, and i, which are mutually compatible and which are such that (i) e tends to confirm h, (ii) h tends to confirm i, and (iii) e does not tend to confirm i. We may suggest an example by reference to the following proposition (j): 55% of As are Bs and 55% of Bs are Cs. Suppose there are 100 As, 55% of which are Bs, and there are 1,000 Bs, 550 of which are Cs. The conjunction of j and "John is an A" tends to confirm the conjunction of j and "John is a B"; the conjunction of j and "John is a B" tends to confirm the conjunction of j and "John is a C"; but the conjunction of j and "John is an A" does *not* tend to confirm the conjunction of j and "John is a C."[4]

The second logical point to be made about this absolute sense of confirmation is this: such confirmation is *defeasible*. That is to say, it is possible that there are three mutually compatible propositions, e, h, and i, which are such that (i) e tends to confirm h and (ii) the conjunction of e and i does not tend to confirm h. An example is: (e) 55 of the 100 As are Bs, and John is an A; (h) John is a B; and (i) 39 of the 40 As that are Cs are not Bs, and John is a C." In such a case we may say that i *defeats* e's tendency to confirm h. (This defeat may itself be defeated—by a k such that the conjunction of e and i and k does tend to confirm h.)

And so we may speak of two fallacies.

"The transitivity fallacy" would be this: from premises saying (i) that e tends to confirm h and (ii) that h tends to confirm i, one concludes (iii) that e tends to confirm i.

And the "application fallacy" would be this: from premises saying (i) that e is evident for a certain subject S and (ii) that e tends to confirm h, one concludes (iii) that e has some presumption in its favor for that particular subject S. The latter inference ignores the possibility that there might be some proposition i such that i is evident for S and i defeats the confirmation that e tends to provide for h.

The Applied Sense of Confirmation

The absolute concept expressed by "e tends to confirm h" must be distinguished, then, from the *applied* concept expressed by "e confirms h *for S*." The latter concept may be defined as follows:

D5 e confirms h for S =Df e tends to confirm h; e is evident for S; and there is no f such that f is evident for S, and the conjunction of e and f does not tend to confirm h.

The final clause could be said to tell us this: there is no f such that f is evident for S and f *defeats* e's tendency to confirm h.

The absolute relation of tending to confirm is such that, if it holds between two propositions e and h, then it holds eternally between e and h. But the applied relation, expressed by "e confirms h for S," does not hold eternally. It holds only if e is evident for S. And it is possible that, although e confirms h for S today, S will acquire additional evidence tomorrow that will defeat e's tendency to confirm h. In such a case, e will no longer be such as to confirm h for S.

Other Epistemic Relations

In analogy with D4, we may introduce this definition:

D6 e tends to make h evident =Df. Every minimal e totality is necessarily such that anyone for whom it is the total evidence is one for whom h is evident.

The analogue of D5 now becomes:

D7 makes h evident for S =Df e is evident for S; e tends to make h evident; and there is no f such that f is evident for S and the conjunction of e and f does not make h evident.

The final clause could be said to tell us this: there is no f such that f is evident for S and f *defeats* e's tendency to make h evident.

We could introduce analogous definitions of "tends to make acceptable" and "tends to make reasonable."

When one says of a proposition e that it *epistemically justifies* a proposition h, one may mean either (i) that e tends to confirm h, or (ii) that e tends to make h acceptable, or (iii) that e tends to make h reasonable, or (iv) that e tends to make h evident. Our four relations, then, might be said to represent four different degrees of epistemic justification. (And, as we shall see in the second essay that follows, still another sense of justification is presupposed by the traditional doctrine according to which knowledge may be defined as justified true belief.)

In the case of each of these justifying relations, it is important to note that the relation may be *deductive* or *nondeductive*: it is deductive when the first proposition entails the second, and otherwise it is nondeductive. Were it not for the fact that one proposition may thus nondeductively make another proposition evident, we would be unable to extend the sphere of the evident beyond that which is entailed by the self-presenting and the a priori.

What I have called the "transitivity fallacy" and the "application fallacy" have their analogues in the case of each of the four types of justifying relation. Each such relation is defeasible.

But the relation expressed by "e is a ground of h" is not defeasible —even though it may be nondeductive. An alternative reading of "e is a ground of h" could therefore be: "e indefeasibly makes h evident." If e is a ground of h, then e is also such as to tend to make h evident. But one proposition may tend to make another evident without thereby being a ground of the other proposition.

Suppose that a certain proposition h is made evident for me by another proposition e, and that I then *add* to my evidence base a certain further proposition i such that i defeats e's tendency to make h evident. In such a case my original grounds for h will no longer be evident to me (for if they were, then, given our definition of ground, h would still be evident to me). One may ask: "How can this be if I have merely added to my evidence base?" The answer is that it is not possible to *add* anything to one's evidence base without at the same time *subtracting* some other thing. To take as simple an example as possible, suppose we try to alter someone's evidence base merely by adding a certain belief—the belief, say, that some birds are red. If we succeed, we will then subtract from that evidence base the property of *not* believing that some birds are red.[5] Presumably negative propositions are included in every nondeductive evidence base.

What is the relation, then, between those things that *make evident* a certain proposition for me and those things that, as bases, *indefeasibly* make that proposition evident for me? I think we may assume that, whenever a proposition e makes evident for me a proposition h, then a certain negative proposition n obtains, such that the conjunction of e and n indefeasibly makes h evident for me. If e's tendency to make h evident is subsequently defeated by some additional evidence that I acquire, then the proposition n becomes false and is therefore subtracted from my evidence base.

Concurrence

In the second edition of *Theory of Knowledge*, I set forth (p. 83) the following definition and the following general principle:

A is a set of *concurrent* propositions =Df. A is a set of two or more propositions each of which is such that the conjunction of all the others tends to confirm it and is logically independent of it.

Any set of concurring propositions, each of which has some presumption in its favor for S, is such that each of its members is beyond reasonable doubt for S.

The following is an example (somewhat oversimplified) of concurrence: "(1) A cat is on the roof of my house today; (2) One was there yesterday; (3) One was there the day before that; and (4) there has been a cat on the roof of my house at least four days this week." These propositions stand in the relation of concurrence or mutual support; therefore, according to our principle, if each is such as to have some presumption in its favor, then the entire conjunction may be said to be beyond reasonable doubt.

Richard Foley has pointed out that a set of propositions may satisfy the definition of concurrence without satisfying the general principle.[6] He cites the following example, pertaining to the role of a fair die with one hundred sides.

a = (1 or 2 or 3 or 4 . . . or 51) will come up
b = (2 or 3 or 4 or 5 . . . or 52) will come up
c = (3 or 4 or 5 or 6 . . . or 53) will come up

y = (25 or 26 or 27 . . . or 76) will come up
z = (26 or 27 or 28 . . . or 77) will come up

Foley observes that "in this kind of example, the number of members contained in the coherent set can be increased indefinitely by increasing the number of sides of the die and altering a, b, c and so on accordingly" (p. 57).

The definition of concurrence, as formulated above, requires that the members of a concurrent set be *logically* independent of each other. The example suggests that we should say, instead, that the members of a concurrent set are *epistemically* independent of each other. For it is difficult to conceive the example without supposing that S has the same ultimate bases for the different members of the set.

To characterize epistemic independence, then, we may appeal to the foundational concept of a *basic proposition*:

D8 b is a basic proposition for s =Df b is evident for S; and everything that makes b evident for S entails b.

It may be assumed that every such basic proposition is concerned with what is self-presenting. We may now say that two propositions are *epistemically independent* for a given subject S provided only that each is confirmed for S by a basic proposition that does not confirm the other for S.

Our definition of *concurrence*, then, may be put this way:

D9 A is a set of propositions that are concurrent for S =Df. A is a set of two or more propositions each of which is said that (i) the conjunction of all the others tends to confirm it for S and (ii) each is such that there is a basic proposition for S that confirms it and does not confirm any of the others for S.

Then the general principle would become:

Any conjunction of concurrent propositions for S, each of which is epistemically acceptable for S, is beyond reasonable doubt for S.

This principle, presumably, is not satisfied by the above example involving the die. For the members of that set are *not* each such that there is a basic proposition that confirms it and does not confirm any of the others.

Is the Concurrence Principle Dispensable?

Foley also argues that the use of any type of concurrence principle is unnecessary, and that the function performed by such a principle may be performed by the ordinary principles of inductive logic. Let us consider the question in application to our example:

(1) A cat is on the roof of my house today; (2) A cat was on the roof yesterday; (3) a cat was on the roof the day before that; and (4) there has been a cat on the roof of my house at least four days this week.

Each of these propositions may be said to be confirmed for me by a directly evident basis. Let us assume (oversimplifying in respects that don't matter, I believe) that these bases are something like the following:

(e^1) I seem to see a cat on the roof today; (e^2) I seem to remember having seen one there yesterday; (e^3) I seem to remember having seen one there the day before that; and (e^4) I seem to be assured by another person who is a reliable observer that there has been a cat on the roof at least four days this week.

This example satisfies the conditions I have formulated: S's evidence for (4) is epistemically independent of his evidence for the conjunction of (1) and (2) and (3).

We assume, then, that (e^4) tends to confirm (4), and that (4) tends to confirm (1). May we infer that, for the subject of the example, (e^4) may be said to confirm (4)? If what I have said about the nature of confirmation is correct, such an inference would exemplify the "transitivity fallacy" as well as the "application fallacy."

If (e^4) tended to make (4) *evident* and if this tendency were not defeated, then, since (4) tends to confirm (1), we *could* say that (e^4) tends to confirm (1). But the presupposition is only that e tends to *confirm* h—i.e., tends to make h such as to have *some presumption in its favor*. In this case, it seems to me, the fact that tending to confirm is not generally transitive warrants our saying that (e^4) does not confirm (1) for S.

It may be helpful to consider the point in application to some nonfoundational proposition that confirms (4)—but does not make (4) evident. Let the nonfoundational proposition be: (g) 51 percent of the houses in town have had a cat on the roof on four different days this week. If this proposition were *evident* for me, then it might confirm for me the proposition that a cat is on my roof today. But it is only such that it has *some presumption* in its favor for me. I would say, therefore, that it does not confer positive epistemic status on the proposition in question. Although (g) tends to confirm (4) and (4) tends to confirm (1), we may not say that (g) confirms (1).

The problem requiring the introduction of the concurrence principle had been this: how are we to raise the epistemic status of propositions that, according to the epistemic principles I had formulated, are merely such as to have some presumption in their favor—and to raise this status to that of being beyond reasonable doubt? To do this, I believe, we must appeal to a general *epistemic* principle.[7] And some form of the concurrence principle is adequate for this purpose.

Chapter 3

Knowledge as
Justified True Belief

Introduction

According to one traditional view, knowledge may be defined as follows:

> S knows that p =Df p; S believes that p; and S is justified in believing that P.

If in this definition, we take "S is justified in believing that p," as many of us have done, to mean the same as "It is evident for S that p," then the definition is not adequate. For E. L. Gettier has shown that, unless we are willing to be skeptics, we must concede that there is evident true belief that isn't knowledge.[1] Hence, if we understand the traditional definition this way, we are faced with the problem of replacing it. But we could also take Gettier's results as showing that "h is justified for S," as it is to be interpreted in the traditional definition, cannot be taken to mean the same as "h is evident for S." Then we would be faced with the task of finding another analysis of "h is justified for S."

Let us view the problem in the second way. For simplicity, we will assume that all justified true belief is propositional.

Gettier Cases

When might one have a true belief in what is evident without that belief being an instance of knowing? This may happen when a false

---

I am indebted to Earl B. Conee for criticisms of earlier versions of this essay.

evident proposition makes evident a proposition that is true.[2] In one of Gettier's examples, we consider a conjunction e of propositions ("Jones keeps a Ford in his garage; Jones has been seen driving a Ford; Jones says he owns a Ford and he has always been honest and reliable in the past . . . "). This proposition is said to make evident for a certain subject S a false proposition f ("Jones owns a Ford").[3] This false proposition f, in turn, makes evident for S a true proposition h ("Jones owns a Ford or Brown is in Barcelona"). The latter proposition has an evident disjunct that is not true ("Jones owns a Ford") and a true disjunct that is not evident ("Brown is in Barcelona"). Moreover, the true disjunct, we may suppose, is not a proposition that S accepts. The disjunction, then, could be said to derive its truth from its nonevident disjunct and to derive its evidence from its false disjunct. Suppose now that S accepts this disjunctive proposition, h, having inferred it from its first disjunct and having no beliefs with respect to the second disjunct. Then he will be accepting a true proposition that is evident to him. But this circumstance hardly warrants our saying that he *knows* the proposition to be true.

But not all "Gettier type" problems thus involve disjunctions. Consider a second example, proposed by Keith Lehrer.[4]

Smith knows something to be true that he expresses as follows: (e) "Nogot is in my office; she told me she owns a Ford; she has always been honest and reliable in the past; I have just seen her stepping out of a Ford. . . ." This e makes evident the following proposition: (f) "Nogot is in my office and owns a Ford." And Smith sees that f makes evident for him the following proposition: (h) "Someone in my office owns a Ford." We suppose that all three propositions are accepted by Smith.

Now suppose further that Nogot has lied on this occasion—and therefore that f is false. Suppose also that, entirely unsuspected by Smith, a third person in his office—Havit—*does* own a Ford. The e, f, and h of this example will be related as are the e, f, and h of the first example: e will be a proposition that is known by Smith, but h —although it is true, evident, and accepted—will not be a proposition that is known by Smith. In place of the disjunction of the first example, we have in this case an existential generalization, which could be said to derive its truth from an instance of it that is not accepted and to derive its evidence from an instance of it that is accepted but false.

Hence, if we retain the traditional definition of knowledge, we cannot interpret "h is justified for S" to mean that h is evident for S.

Diagnosis of the Difficulty

We will consider the problem only in reference to the first of the two examples. What we will say holds, *mutatis mutandis*, of the second and of all other "Gettier type" cases.

The difficulty arises in part because, as we have noted, the relation of making evident may be nondeductive. That is to say, it is possible for a proposition e to make evident a proposition f even though e is true and f is false. The false f may then, in turn, make evident a proposition h that happens to be true. And this true proposition h, in the Gettier cases, is the one that makes difficulties for the traditional definition of knowing.

Could we deal with Gettier's example, then, by stipulating that one proposition cannot make another proposition evident for a given subject unless the first proposition *entails* the second? This move would rule out the h of Gettier's example; we would no longer have to say that S *knows* that either Jones owns a Ford or Brown is in Barcelona. But such a move would also have the consequence that S knows very little about the world around him. In fact it would restrict the evident—and therefore what is known—to those Cartesian propositions that are self-presenting and to what can be apprehended a priori.

A more precise diagnosis of the problem would seem to be this: the proposition h is based on evidence that nondeductively makes evident a false proposition. So to repair the traditional definition, we may be tempted to say, in effect, that belief in an evident true proposition constitutes knowledge *provided* that the basis for that proposition does *not* make evident any false proposition. But this would have the consequence that the e of Gettier's example would not be known. And this is an undesirable consequence. Although the h of Gettier's example—"Jones owns a Ford"—should not be counted as knowledge, we *should* say that the conjunction e of propositions constituting S's evidence for h—i.e., "Jones keeps a Ford in his garage; Jones has been seen riding in a Ford . . . ."—is a proposition that S knows to be true. Yet it is based on evidence that makes evident a proposition that is false.

Our definition, then, should have the following consequences in application to Gettier's example:

1) The h of that example ("Jones owns a Ford or Brown is in

Barcelona'') is *not* known by the subject S—even though h is evident, true, and accepted by S.

2) The conjunction of propositions e ("Jones keeps a Ford in his garage; Jones has been seen riding in a Ford; and . . . "), which Gettier cites as S's evidence for e, *is* a proposition that is known by S.

3) The conjunction b of directly evident propositions constituting S's ultimate *basis* for e is also a proposition that is known by S.[5]

We can satisfy these conditions by introducing the concept of that which is *defectively evident*. Roughly speaking, we will say (1) that a proposition is defectively evident for a given subject S provided the propositions on which it is based make evident a proposition that is false and (2) that what is known must be evident but not defectively evident. But it will be necessary to characterize the defectively evident somewhat more precisely. To fulfill the desiderata listed above, we shall say that *some* defectively evident propositions—those of a certain sort that we will specify—*can* be known.

Proposed Solution

To deal with the Gettier problem we need three definitions: that of a *basic proposition*; that of the *defectively evident*; and that of *justification*.

In the previous essay we defined the concept of a basic proposition as follows:

> b is a basic proposition for S =Df b is evident for S; and everything that makes b evident for S entails b.

We next define the defectively evident:

> h is defectively evident for S =Df (i) There is a basic proposition for S that makes h evident for S and does not logically imply h; and (ii) every such basic proposition makes evident a proposition that is false.

Now we are in a position to define the type of justification presupposed by the traditional definition of knowledge:

> S is justified in believing that p =Df (i) It is evident for S that p; and (ii) if it is defectively evident for S that p, then the proposition that p is entailed by a conjunction of propositions each of which is evident but not defectively evident for S.

And so we retain the traditional definition of knowledge:

S knows that p =Df p; S believes that p; and S is justified in believing that p.

We now return to the three desiderata listed above.

1) The proposition h of Gettier's example ("Jones owns a Ford or Brown is in Barcelona") will not be counted as known. It is defectively evident for S—since it is made evident by a basic proposition that makes evident a proposition ("Jones owns a Ford") that is false. It does not satisfy the second condition of the definition of justification.

2) The evident proposition e that was cited as S's evidence for h ("Jones keeps a Ford in his garage; and . . . ") is defectively evident by our definition. But it is justified for S, since it is entailed by a conjunction of propositions each of which is made evident for S by a basic proposition that does not make evident a proposition that is false.

3) And that proposition b which is S's directly evident basis for e is not defectively evident, for it fails to satisfy condition (i) of the definition of the defectively evident. There is no basic proposition that nondeductively makes b evident for s.

But the proposed solution has one difficulty: our definitions are not adequate to the possibility that S may *know that he knows*. If we think that this possibility is a real one (I shall defend this view in the following essay), then we must modify our account.

An Alternative Solution

Consider once again the defectively evident e of Gettier's example ("Jones keeps a Ford in his garage; and . . . "). Can S *know that he knows* this proposition? In such a case, the object of his knowledge would be

(1) S knows that e.

This is equivalent to the following conjunction

(2) e; and S believes that e; and S is justified in believing that e.

Now we have noted that, although e is defectively evident, it is entailed by a conjunction of propositions—let us call this conjunction "m & n"—each of which is evident but not defectively evident. Hence (2) is entailed by

(3) m; and n; and S believes that e; and S is justified in believing that e.

The first three conjuncts of (3) are such that they are evident but not defectively evident for S. What of the last conjunct—"S is justified in believing that e"?

If the proposition expressed by "S knows that e" is itself an object of S's knowledge, then the proposition expressed by "S is *justified* in believing that e" must be evident for S. And if the latter proposition *is* evident for S, then it is made evident at least in part by e and by the basic proposition b that makes e evident. (This point is discussed in further detail in the following essay, "Knowing that One Knows.") Therefore "S is justified in believing that e" will be defectively evident for S. But, since it is not entailed by a conjunction of nondefectively evident propositions, we cannot say—given our definition of justification—that S is *justified* in believing it. And therefore we cannot say that S knows that he knows that e. Hence, if we are to say that S *can* know that he knows that e, we must qualify our definitions of justification.

Can we find a special mark that is satisfied just by the final conjunct of (3)—by "S is justified in believing that e"? I think we can. "S is justified in believing that e" implies with respect to one of the *other* conjuncts—the first as well as the second—that it is evident for S. Hence we may modify our definition of justification this way:

> S is justified in believing that p =Df (i) It is evident for S that p; and (ii) if it is defectively evident for S that p, then the proposition that p is entailed by a conjunction of propositions each of which is either (a) evident but not defectively evident for S or (b) a proposition implying with respect to of one of the other conjuncts that it is evident for S.

Conclusion

With these definitions, I believe we have adequately dealt with Gettier's example. What we have said may also be applied to the second example, as well as to the other cases of evident true belief that are not cases of knowing. In all such cases, the object of the evident true belief is a proposition that is defectively evident: it is a proposition such that every proposition, which is basic for that subject and which makes h evident for him, also makes evident for him a proposition that is false. And, unlike Gettier's e and its basis b, it is not a proposition that is entailed by a conjunction of evident propositions each of which is nondefectively evident.

In recent philosophical literature, many "Gettier cases" have been formulated—many examples purporting to be cases of evident true belief that are not cases of knowing. If the examples are indeed cases of evident true belief that are not cases of knowing, then our definitions should insure that they are not counted as cases of knowing. But the reader may find that, in application to *some* of the examples that have been offered, application of the definitions will *not* have this result.[6] I recommend that, in such cases, she look to the proposition corresponding to the e of the original example—the proposition that is supposed to make h evident to the subject in question. She will then find, if I am not mistaken, that e does *not* make h evident. The relation that e bears to h will be some weaker epistemic relation —that, say, of making h beyond reasonable doubt, or perhaps merely that of making h such as to have some presumption in its favor. If this is the case, then the example in question will not be an example of *evident* true belief.

Chapter 4
Knowing That One Knows

Whenever we know something, we either do, or at least can,
by reflecting, directly know that we are knowing it.
                                        H. A. Prichard[1]

Introduction

In discussing the problem of the criterion, I have distinguished two
general questions. These are: *"What* do we know?" and *"How* are we
to decide in any particular case *whether* we know?"[2] The first question could also be put by asking, "What is the *extent* of our knowledge?" and the second by asking, "What are the *criteria* of knowing?"

I assumed it was reasonable to begin our investigations with an
answer—or at least a provisional answer—to the first of these questions. It would also seem reasonable to apply a similar procedure to
an investigation of what it is that we *know that we know* and of what
it is that we are justified in believing about what it is that we are justified in believing.

For example, I had said, with Moore, that we are justified in believing that the earth has existed for hundreds of years past. I would
now add, then, that we are *justified in believing that we are justified
in believing* that the earth has existed for hundreds of years past—
and indeed that we *know that we know* that the earth has existed for
hundreds of years past.

50

I assume, therefore, that one does not need to be an epistemologist to know that one knows. This assumption is in the spirit of Prichard's remark quoted above.

What, then, is the nature of this higher order justification? If one is not an epistemologist, *how* does one know that one knows?

The Interpretation of the Justification Condition

Consider a person who believes something that is true. If we are to say that that person also *knows*, will it be enough to add that she is justified in believing—or must we add that she is also aware of the *nature* of this justification?

The question points to a distinction of what might be called *degrees* —*levels*—of knowing. The distinction may be illustrated this way:

x has first order knowledge that $p(K^1 p)$ =Df p; x believes that p; and there is an e such that e justified x in believing that p.

x has second order knowledge that p $(K^2 p)$ =Df p; x believes that p; and an e that justifies her in believing that p is such that x believes that it justifies her in believing that p.

x has third order knowledge that p $(K^3 p)$ =Df p; x believes that p; and an e that justifies her in believing that p is such that x has first order knowledge that it justifies her in believing that p.

We may note that "$K^3 p$" implies "$K^2 p$" and not conversely, and that "$K^2 p$" implies "$K^1 p$" and not conversely. We will not ask whether it is useful to single out still higher degrees or levels of knowing.

These distinctions have obvious bearing on the concept of *knowing that one knows*. If there are these three degrees or levels of knowing, then there are the following senses of "knowing that one knows that p":

$K^1 K^1 p$

$K^1 K^2 p$

$K^1 K^3 p$

$K^2 K^1 p$

$K^2 K^2 p$

$K^2 K^3 p$

$K^3 K^1 p$

$K^3 K^2 p$

$K^3 K^3 p$

In what follows, we will be primarily concerned only with the first level of knowing that one knows ($K^1 K^1 p$). But we should keep in mind that what is essential for the higher degrees of knowing that one knows need not be essential for the lower. Thus knowing what one's justification is is essential for third order knowing (K^3), but it is not essential for first order knowing (K^1). Nor is it essential for first order knowledge of first order knowledge ($K^1 K^1$).

Suppose one accepts a true proposition p. Then, if there is something that justifies one's belief that p, one has first order knowledge that p. What more is now needed for one to have first order knowledge *that* one has first order knowledge that p? Only (i) that one believe that one knows that p and (ii) that there be something that makes it evident that there *is* something that makes it evident that p. In what follows, we will be concerned with the second of these two conditions.

Substrates and Objectives of Normative States

Let us introduce a terminology that will help us in discussing these matters. We will distinguish *normative states*, their *objectives* and their *substrates*.

An instance of a *normative state* would be this: its being beyond reasonable doubt for me that there are sheep.

The *objective* of this normative state is the proposition that there are sheep. And the *substrate* of this normative state is the nonnormative state (say, the occurrence of certain perceptual takings) on which the normative state supervenes.[3] The substrate, in other words, is a nonnormative state that is necessarily such that, if it obtains, then the normative state obtains. (Suppose it is beyond reasonable doubt for you, but not for me, that there are sheep. Then there will be something *in virtue of which* the fact is beyond reasonable doubt for you, but nothing in virtue of which it is beyond reasonable doubt for me. This something, in your case, will be the substrate of your normative state.)

The substrate of a normative state is necessarily such that, if it obtains, then the normative state obtains. But the relevant necessity is not analytic. This complex point may be summarized as follows: we cannot exhibit the relation between the substrate and the normative state in a sentence that can be seen to be true "in virtue of its form."

Let us say that a *material epistemological principle* tells us what the substrate is of a given normative state.

Ordinarily the substrate and the objective of a normative state are logically independent of each other. But in the case of self-presenting attributions (for example, my judgment that I seem to see a sheep), there will be a normative state (it being certain for me that I seem to see a sheep) that is such that its objective and its substrate will coincide (both will be my seeming to see a sheep).

The three concepts—normative state, objective, and substrate—may be generalized in obvious ways so as to apply to every epistemic situation.

We may also speak of *normative judgments* and of their substrates and objectives.

Epistemological Principles

I have said that a material epistemological principle is a proposition that cites substrates for epistemic normative facts. I have assumed that, wherever there is knowledge, some general epistemological principle is instantiated. But I do not assume that, to know that one knows, one must know the truth of such a principle. (I don't assume that only epistemologists can know.)

In this respect, as in others, it is instructive to consider the analogy between epistemic and moral situations. The moral philosopher also attempts to make generalizations relating certain normative situations to their substrates. But he does not require that, for an act to be morally justified, the agent must be aware of such philosophical principles.

Yet, if knowing that one knows does not require the knowledge of general epistemological principles, it does require that one *know* that one is justified in believing. What, then, of the nature of this knowledge?

The Nonobjective Conception of Epistemic States

Could we develop a theory of knowledge *without* presupposing an objectivistic theory of the truth and falsity of normative states?

If normative epistemic states are neither true nor false and if knowledge implies truth, then there cannot be knowledge of particular epistemic states—such states as might be expressed in locutions of the form "e is evident for S" or "e has some presumption in its favor for S."

But if there cannot be knowledge of such particular epistemic facts, then no one can know that he knows. For if "p is known by S" implies "p is evident for S" as well as "p is true," and if "p is evident for S" is neither true nor false, then no one—including S—can know that p is known by S or indeed that anything is known by anyone.

It is doubtful, therefore, that a nonobjective—or "no truth"—conception of epistemic principles can be seriously maintained.

The Problem of Higher Order Normative States

If knowledge is justified true belief, then one cannot know that one knows a given proposition p unless one is justified in believing that one is justified in believing p. Therefore, if one believes that it is possible for one to know that one knows, one should also believe that such higher order justification is possible. Yet, so far as I know, most philosophers who have discussed knowing that one knows have not discussed the nature of this higher order justification. Let us try to fill in this gap.

Let us say that a *higher order normative state* is a normative state that has a normative state as its objective. An example would be: it being beyond reasonable doubt for me that it is beyond reasonable doubt for me that I see a sheep.

We will assume that the substrate for the *lower order* epistemic normative state of our example consists of certain perceptual takings. They are what justify me in believing that sheep exist.

What, then, of the substrate for the higher order epistemic state— the state that it is beyond reasonable doubt for me that it is beyond reasonable doubt for me that sheep exist? What kind of nonepistemic state—what kind of substrate—would justify me in believing *that*?

If perceptual acceptance, say, is the substrate for its being beyond reasonable doubt for me that sheep exist, what would the substrate be for the higher order epistemic judgment—for the judgment that it is beyond reasonable doubt for me that sheep exist?

Doubtless the failure to find any *additional* substrate for the higher order normative judgment tempts one to the conclusion that the higher order state *has* no substrate and therefore is not itself capable of justification.

But there is no need to accept this conclusion.

Solution of the Problem

I suggest that the substrate for this higher order epistemic state is the *same* as that for that lower order epistemic state which is its objective. In other words, those nonnormative states (the perceptual takings) that justify me in believing that sheep exist *also* justify me in believing that I am justified in believing that sheep exist.

The higher order epistemic state, then, will be true if and only if its objective is true—where its objective is a lower order epistemic state.

This point may be thought of as an instance of a more general principle about epistemic preferability. The more general principle may be summarized in the following formula:

A1 pPq ↔ [B(pPq) P W(pPq)]

The principle may be spelled out as follows:

> For any subject x and any time t, performing a certain act p is more reasonable for x at t than performing a certain act q, if and only if the following condition obtains: believing that, performing p is then more reasonable for him than performing q, is more reasonable for x at t than withholding the belief that his then performing p is more reasonable than performing q.

The "acts" here in question will be believings, withholdings, and any other intentional activities that may stand in relations of epistemic preferability.

Given this principle, we may say that, although truth does not generally imply justification, the truth of a normative state justifies the believer in attributing that state to himself.

Let us now add a second epistemic principle. The locution "Jp" will abbreviate "S is justified in believing that p"; "Kp" will abbreviate "S knows that p"; and "Bp" will abbreviate "S believes that p."

A2 (Jp & BKp) → JKp

(The letter "p" in our formulation, unlike the letters "p" and "q" in the formulation of the previous principle, is not a variable but a schema and thus may be replaced by any well-formed English sentences.)

Given principle A2, it is easy to prove the following principle: if one knows that p and also believes that one knows that p, then one knows that one knows that p.

The principle may be abbreviated as follows: $(Kp \& BKp) \rightarrow KKp$. We presuppose the following schematic definition:

D1 $Kp =_{Df} Bp \& Jp \& p$

That is to say, "S knows that p," is by definition: "S believes that p; x is justified in believing that p, and p." (It may be noted that the expression "true" does not appear in this definition.)

Assume: (1) Kp
(2) BKp
(3) $(Jp \& BKp) \rightarrow JKp$

Then: (4) $Jp \& BKp$ 2, 1, D1
(5) JKp 4, 3
(6) $BKp \& JKp \& Kp$ 2, 5, 1
(7) KKp 6, D1

And so we have an answer to our question: "If one is not an epistemologist, then *how* does one know that one knows?" The answer is: by knowing and by believing that one knows.

Some Objections Considered

"What if one knows but is mistaken about the nature of his justification for believing that he knows that he knows?"

The question pertains to knowing that one knows, but it has the following analogue for knowing *simpliciter*: "What if a person has adequate evidence for a proposition, but she is mistaken about the nature of this evidence. She has a basis, say, for p, but she thinks that something else is her basis for p. In such a case, can she be said to know that p is true?" In such a case, we can say that the believer has first order knowledge that p but not that she has second or third order knowledge that p. (We may affirm "K^1p," but neither "K^3p" nor "K^2p."). The believer in question has made a mistake—but she has not made a mistake with respect to p. She has made an *epistemological* mistake—a mistake about what it is that justifies what. So, too, in the case of knowing that one knows: from the fact that one makes a mistake about the *nature* of the grounds that one·has, it does not follow that one does not *have* those grounds. To know that I know that I know that p, I need not know *what* the propositions are that constitute my basis for p.

"Are you saying that it is impossible to believe falsely that one is justified in believing a certain proposition?" No; it is possible for one to have a mistaken epistemology and therefore it is possible for one to believe falsely that one is justified in believing a certain proposition. What I am saying is rather this: the justification that I have for believing any given proposition is *not* dependent on any belief I may have about the nature of this justification.

"A person can be confused or mistaken about what constitutes his evidence for a particular belief. Given that, the person may unjustifiably believe that his evidence is sufficient to yield knowledge. If his evidence is sufficient then he will have knowledge but not be justified in believing, and thus not know, that he knows."[4]

The objection confuses the question of whether (a) a person can have knowledge that he has first order knowledge that p ($K^1 K^1 p$) with the question whether (b) a person can have first order knowledge that he has second or third order knowledge that p ($K^1 K^2 p$ or $K^1 K^3 p$). The fact that the person is confused or mistaken about the evidence he has shows that he doesn't have second or third order knowledge, but this fact is quite consistent with saying that he has first order knowledge that he has first order knowledge.

There are two essential points to keep in mind. The first is that "justify" must here be taken in the strong sense set forth in the previous essay. And the second is that normally, when one has evidence e that justifies one in believing something p, one does not have, outside of e, *additional* evidence that justifies one in believing that one is justified in believing p.

Appendix: The Justification of Epistemological Principles

I have contended that, to be justified in believing, one need not have knowledge of any of those epistemological principles that formulate the conditions under which one *is* justified in believing. One may ask, however: *Can* we be justified in accepting such principles? And, if this is so, *how* is it possible?

Such principles are necessary, but they are not *axioms*. That is to say, no such principle could be said to be a proposition of this sort: when it is considered by a person, then it has the character of being certain for that person. For one to be *justified* in accepting an axiom, it is enough that one considers it. But it would seem that our epistemological principles, even if they are necessary, are *not* necessarily such that whoever considers them accepts them. For there are some philosophers who have considered them and rejected them.

If epistemological principles are not axiomatic, in what sense can we be said to be justified in accepting them?[5]

Consider the epistemological situation envisaged above: it is beyond reasonable doubt for you but not for me that sheep exist. This means that there is a certain epistemological principle that is instantiated by you and not by me, and hence that there is a certain epistemological substrate that you fulfill and I do not. So to *explain* the difference between us—why it is that a certain thing is beyond reasonable doubt for you but not for me—one may appeal to the general principle and to the substrate.

To be sure, if the general principle is to be used as part of an explanation, then it must have at least some presumption in its favor. How does it acquire this positive epistemic status? Perhaps the one for whom it has such a status knows that the principle is simpler than any of the alternatives that are known to him.

Part II

Chapter 5
The Problem of the Criterion

1

"The problem of the criterion" seems to me to be one of the most important and one of the most difficult of all the problems of philosophy. I am tempted to say that one has not begun to philosophize until one has faced this problem and has recognized how unappealing, in the end, each of the possible solutions is. I have chosen this problem as my topic for the Aquinas Lecture because what first set me to thinking about it (and I remain obsessed by it) were two treatises of twentieth century scholastic philosophy. I refer first to P. Coffey's two-volume work, *Epistemology or the Theory of Knowledge*, published in 1917.[1] This led me in turn to the treatises of Coffey's great teacher, Cardinal D. J. Mercier: *Critériologie générale ou théorie générale de la certitude*.[2]

Mercier and, following him, Coffey set the problem correctly, I think, and have seen what is necessary for its solution. But I shall not discuss their views in detail. I shall formulate the problem; then note what, according to Mercier, is necessary if we are to solve the problem; then sketch my own solution; and, finally, note the limitations of my approach to the problem.

2

What is the problem, then? It is the ancient problem of "the diallelus"—the problem of "the wheel" or "the vicious circle." It was put very neatly by Montaigne in his *Essays*. So let us being by para-paraphrasing his formulation of the puzzle. To know whether things really are as they seem to be, we must have a *procedure* for distinguishing appearances that are true from appearances that are false. But to know whether our procedures is a good procedure, we have to know whether it really *succeeds* in distinguishing appearances that are true from appearances that are false. And we cannot know whether it does really succeed unless we already know which appearances are *true* and which ones are *false*. And so we are caught in a circle.[3]

Let us try to see how one gets into a situation of this sort.

The puzzles begin to form when you ask yourself, "What can I really know about the world?" We all are acquainted with people who think they know a lot more than in fact they do know. I'm thinking of fanatics, bigots, mystics, various types of dogmatists. And we have all heard of people who claim at least to know a lot less than what in fact they do know. I'm thinking of those people who call themselves "skeptics" and who like to say that people cannot know what the world is really like. People tend to become skeptics, temporarily, after reading books on popular science: the authors tell us we cannot know what things are like really (but they make use of a vast amount of knowledge, or a vast amount of what is claimed to be knowledge, to support this skeptical conclusion). And as we know, people tend to become dogmatists, temporarily, as a result of the effects of alcohol, or drugs, or religious and emotional experiences. Then they claim to have an inside view of the world and they think they have a deep kind of knowledge giving them a key to the entire workings of the universe.

If you have a healthy common sense, you will feel that something is wrong with both of these extremes and that the truth is somewhere in the middle: we can know far more than the skeptic says we can know and far less than the dogmatist or the mystic says that he can know. But how are we to decide these things?

3

How do we decide, in any particular case, whether we have a genuine item of knowledge? Most of us are ready to confess that our beliefs far transcend what we really know. There are things we believe that we don't in fact know. And we can say of many of these things that we know that we don't know them. I believe that Mrs. Jones is honest, say, but I don't know it, and I know that I don't know it. There are other things that we don't know, but they are such that we don't know that we don't know them. Last week, say, I thought I knew that Mr. Smith was honest, but he turned out to be a thief. I didn't know that he was a thief, and, moreover, I didn't know that I didn't know that he was a thief; I thought I knew that he was honest. And so the problem is: How are we to distinguish the real cases of knowledge from what only seem to be cases of knowledge? Or, as I put it before, how are we to decide in any particular case whether we have genuine items of knowledge?

What would be a satisfactory solution to our problem? Let me quote in detail what Cardinal Mercier says:

If there is any knowledge which bears the mark of truth, if the intellect does have a way of distinguishing the true and the false, in short, *if there is* a criterion of truth, then this criterion should satisfy three conditions: it should be *internal, objective,* and *immediate.*

It should be *internal.* No reason or rule of truth that is provided by an *external authority* can serve as an ultimate criterion. For the reflective doubts that are essential to criteriology can and should be applied to this authority itself. The mind cannot attain to certainty until it has found *within itself* a sufficient reason for adhering to the testimony of such an authority.

The criterion should be *objective.* The ultimate reason for believing cannot be a merely *subjective* state of the thinking subject. A man is aware that he can reflect upon his psychological states in order to control them. Knowing that he has this ability, he does not, so long as he has not made use of it, have the right to be sure. The ultimate ground of certitude cannot consist in a subjective feeling. It can be found only in that which, objectively, produces this feeling and is adequate to reason.

Finally, the criterion must be *immediate.* To be sure, a certain conviction may rest upon many different reasons some of which are subordinate to others. But if we are to avoid an infinite regress, then we must find a ground of assent that presupposes no other. We must find an *immediate* criterion of certitude.

Is there a criterion of truth that satisfies these three conditions? If so, what is it?[4]

4

To see how perplexing our problem is, let us consider a figure that Descartes had suggested and that Coffey takes up in his dealings with the problem of the criterion.[5] Descartes' figure comes to this.

Let us suppose that you have a pile of apples and you want to sort out the good ones from the bad ones. You want to put the good ones in a pile by themselves and throw the bad ones away. This is a useful thing to do, obviously, because the bad apples tend to infect the good ones and then the good ones become bad, too. Descartes thought our beliefs were like this. The bad ones tend to infect the good ones, so we should look them over very carefully, throw out the bad ones if we can, and then—or so Descartes hoped—we would be left with just a stock of good beliefs on which we could rely completely. But how are we to do the sorting? If we are to sort out the good ones from the bad ones, then, of course, we must have a way of recognizing the good ones. Or at least we must have a way of recognizing the bad ones. And—again, of course—you and I do have a way of recognizing good apples and also of recognizing bad ones. The good ones have their own special feel, look, and taste, and so do the bad ones.

But when we turn from apples to beliefs, the matter is quite different. In the case of the apples, we have a method—a criterion—for distinguishing the good ones from the bad ones. But in the case of the beliefs, we do not have a method or a criterion for distinguishing the good ones from the bad ones. Or, at least, we don't have one yet. The question we started with was: How *are* we to tell the good ones from the bad ones? In other words, we were asking: What is the proper method for deciding which are the good beliefs and which are the bad ones—which beliefs are genuine cases of knowledge and which beliefs are not?

And now, you see, we are on the wheel. First, we want to find out which are the good beliefs and which are the bad ones. To find this out we have to have some way—some method—of deciding which are the good ones and which are the bad ones. But there are good and bad methods—good and bad ways—of sorting out the good beliefs from the bad ones. And so we now have a new problem: How are we to decide which are the good methods and which are the bad ones?

If we could fix on a good method for distinguishing between good and bad methods, we might be all set. But this, of course, just moves the problem to a different level. How are we to distinguish between a good method for choosing good methods? If we continue in this way, of course, we are led to an infinite regress and we will never have the answer to our original question.

What do we do in fact? We do know that there are fairly reliable ways of sorting out good beliefs from bad ones. Most people will tell you, for example, that if you follow the procedures of science and common sense—if you tend carefully to your observations and if you make use of the canons of logic, induction, and the theory of probability—you will be following the best possible procedure for making sure that you will have more good beliefs than bad ones. This is doubtless true. But how do we know that it is? How do we know that the procedures of science, reason, and common sense are the best methods that we have?

If we do know this, it is because we know that these procedures work. It is because we know that these procedures do in fact enable us to distinguish the good beliefs from the bad ones. We say: "See—these methods turn out good beliefs." But *how* do we know that they do? It can only be that we already know how to tell the difference between the good beliefs and the bad ones.

And now you can see where the skeptic comes in. He'll say this: "You said you wanted to sort out the good beliefs from the bad ones. Then to do this, you apply the canons of science, common sense, and reason. And now, in answer to the question, 'How do you know that that's the right way to do it?', you say 'Why, I can see that the ones it picks out are the good ones and the ones it leaves behind are the bad ones.' But if you can *see* which ones are the good ones and which ones are the bad ones, why do you think you need a general method for sorting them out?"

5

We can formulate some of the philosophical issues that are involved here by distinguishing two pairs of questions. These are:

A) "*What* do we know? What is the *extent* of our knowledge?"
B) "How are we to decide *whether* we know? What are the *criteria* of knowledge?"

If you happen to know the answers to the first of these pairs of questions, you may have some hope of being able to answer the second. Thus, if you happen to know which are the good apples and which are the bad ones, then maybe you could explain to some other person how he could go about deciding whether or not he has a good apple or a bad one. But if you don't know the answer to the first of these pairs of questions—if you don't know what things you know or how far your knowledge extends—it is difficult to see how you could possibly figure out an answer to the second.

On the other hand, *if*, somehow, you already know the answers to the second of these pairs of questions, then you may have some hope of being able to answer the first. Thus, if you happen to have a good set of directions for telling whether apples are good or bad, then maybe you can go about finding a good one—assuming, of course, that there are some good apples to be found. But if you don't know the answer to the second of these pairs of questions—if you don't know how to go about deciding whether or not you know, if you don't know what the criteria of knowing are—it is difficult to see how you could possibly figure out an answer to the first.

And so we can formulate the position of *the skeptic* on these matters. He will say: "You cannot answer question A until you have answered question B. And you cannot answer question B until you have answered question A. Therefore you cannot answer either question. You cannot know what, if anything, you know, and there is no possible way for you to decide in any particular case." Is there any reply to this?

6

Broadly speaking, there are at least two other possible views. So we may choose among three possibilities.

There are people—philosophers—who think that they do have an answer to B and that, given their answer to B, they can then figure out their answer to A. And there are other people—other philosophers—who have it the other way around: they think that they have an answer to A and that, given their answer to A, they can then figure out the answer to B.

There don't seem to be any generally accepted names for these two different philosophical positions. (Perhaps this is just as well. There are more than enough names, as it is, for possible philosophical views.) I suggest, for the moment, we use the expressions "methodists" and "particularists." By "methodists," I mean, not the followers of John Wesley's version of Christianity, but those who think they have an answer to B, and who then, in terms of it, work out their answer to A. By "particularists" I mean those who have it the other way around.

7

Thus John Locke was a methodist—in our present, rather special sense of the term. He was able to arrive—somehow—at an answer to

B. He said, in effect: "The way you decide whether or not a belief is a good belief—that is to say, the way you decide whether a belief is likely to be a genuine case of knowledge—is to see whether it is derived from sense experience, to see, for example, whether it bears certain relations to your sensations." Just what these relations to our sensations might be is a matter we may leave open, for present purposes. The point is: Locke felt that if a belief is to be credible, it must bear certain relations to the believer's sensations—but he never told us *how* he happened to arrive at this conclusion. This, of course, is the view that has come to be known as "empiricism." David Hume followed Locke in this empiricism and said that empiricism gives us an effective criterion for distinguishing the good apples from the bad ones. You can take this criterion to the library, he said. Suppose you find a book in which the author makes assertions that do not conform to the empirical criterion. Hume said: Commit it to the flames: for it can contain nothing but sophistry and illusion."

8

Empiricism, then, was a form of what I have called "methodism." The empiricist—like other types of methodist—begins with a criterion and then he uses it to throw out the bad apples. There are two objections, I would say, to empiricism. The first—which applies to every form of methodism (in our present sense of the word)—is that the criterion is very broad and far-reaching and at the same time completely arbitrary. How can one *begin* with a broad generalization? It seems especially odd that the empiricist—who wants to proceed cautiously, step by step, from experience—begins with such a generalization. He leaves us completely in the dark so far as concerns what *reasons* he may have for adopting this particular criterion rather than some other. The second objection applies to empiricism in particular. When we apply the empirical criterion—at least, as it was developed by Hume, as well as by many of those in the nineteenth and twentieth centuries who have called themselves "empiricists"—we seem to throw out, not only the bad apples but the good ones as well, and we are left, in effect, with just a few parings or skins with no meat behind them. Thus Hume virtually conceded that, if you are going to be empiricist, the only matters of fact that you can really know about pertain to the existence of sensations. "'Tis vain," he said, "To ask whether there be body." He meant you cannot know whether any physical things exist—whether there are trees, or houses, or bodies, much less whether there are atoms or other such microscopic particles. All you can know is that there are and have been certain sensations. You cannot know whether there is any you who experiences those sensations—much less whether any other people exist who experience sensations. And I think, if he had been consistent in his empiricism, he would also have said you cannot really be sure whether there have been any sensations in the past; you can know only that certain sensations exist here and now.

9

The great Scottish philosopher, Thomas Reid, reflected on all this in the eighteenth century. He was serious about philosophy and man's place in the world. He finds Hume saying things implying that we can know only of the existence of certain sensations here and now. One can imagine him saying: "Good Lord! What kind of nonsense is this?" What he did say, among other things, was this: "A traveller of good judgment may mistake his way, and be unawares led into a wrong track; and while the road is fair before him, he may go on without suspicion and be followed by others but, when it ends in a coal pit, it requires no great judgment to know that he hath gone wrong, nor perhaps to find out what misled him."[6]

Thus Reid, as I interpret him, was not an empiricist; nor was he, more generally, what I have called a "methodist." He was a "particularist." That is to say, he thought that he had an answer to question A, and in terms of the answer to question A, he then worked out kind of an answer to question B.[7] An even better example of a "particularist" is the great twentieth century English philosopher, G. E. Moore.

Suppose, for a moment, you were tempted to go along with Hume and say "The only thing about the world I can really know is that there are now sensations of a certain sort. There's a sensation of a man, there's the sound of a voice, and there's a feeling of bewilderment or boredom. But that's all I can really know about." What would Reid say? I can imagine him saying something like this: "Well, you can talk that way if you want to. But you know very well that it isn't true. You know that you are there, that you have a body of such and such a sort and that other people are here, too. And you know about this building and where you were this morning and all kinds of other things as well." G. E. Moore would raise his hand at this point and say: "I know very well this is a hand, and so do you. If you come across some philosophical theory that implies that you and I cannot know that this is a hand, then so much the worse for the theory." I think that Reid and Moore are right, myself, and I'm inclined to think that the "methodists" are wrong.

Going back to our questions A and B, we may summarize the three possible views as follows: there is skepticism (you cannot answer either question without presupposing an answer to the other, and therefore the questions cannot be answered at all); there is "methodism" (you begin with an answer to B); and there is "particularism" (you begin with an answer to A). I suggest that the third possibility is the most reasonable.

10

I would say—and many reputable philosophers would disagree with me—that, to find out whether you know such a thing as that this is a hand, you don't have to apply any test or criterion. Spinoza has it right. "In order to know," he said, "there is no need to know that we know, much less to know that we know that we know."[8]

This is part of the answer, it seems to me, to the puzzle about the diallelus. There are many things that quite obviously, we do know to be true. If I report to you the things I now see and hear and feel—or, if you prefer, the things I now think I see and hear and feel—the chances are that my report will be correct; I will be telling you something I know. And so, too, if you report the things that you think you now see and hear and feel. To be sure, there are hallucinations and illusions. People often think they see or hear or feel things that in fact they do not see or hear or feel. But from this fact—that our senses do sometimes deceive us—it hardly follows that your senses and mine are deceiving you and me right now. One may say similar things about what we remember.

Having these good apples before us, we can look them over and formulate certain criteria of goodness. Consider the senses, for example. One important criterion—one epistemological principle—was formulated by St. Augustine. It is more reasonable, he said, to trust the senses than to distrust them. Even though there have been illusions and hallucinations, the wise thing, when everything seems all right, is to accept the testimony of the senses. I say "when everything seems all right." If on a particular occasion something about *that* particular occasion makes you suspect that particular report of the senses, if, say, you seem to remember having been drugged or hypnotized, or brainwashed, then perhaps you should have some doubts about what you think you see, or hear, or feel, or smell. But if nothing about this particular occasion leads you to suspect what the senses report on this particular occasion, then the wise thing is to take such a report at its face value. In short the senses should be regarded as innocent until there is some positive reason, on some particular occasion, for thinking that they are guilty on that particular occasion.

One might say the same thing of memory. If, on any occasion, you think you remember that such-and-such an event occurred, then the wise thing is to assume that that particular event did occur—unless something special about this particular occasion leads you to suspect your memory.

We have then a kind of answer to the puzzle about the diallelus. We start with particular cases of knowledge and then from those we generalize and formulate criteria of goodness—criteria telling us what it is for a belief to be epistemologically respectable. Let us now try to sketch somewhat more precisely this approach to the problem of the criterion.

11

The theory of evidence, like ethics and the theory of value, presupposes an objective right and wrong. To explicate the requisite senses of "right" and "wrong," we need the concept of *right preference* — or, more exactly, the concept of one state of mind being *preferable*, epistemically, to another. One state of mind may be *better*, epistemically, than another. This conept of epistemic preferability is what Cardinal Mercier called an *objective* concept. It is one thing to say, objectively, that one state of mind is *to be preferred* to another. It is quite another thing to say, subjectively, that one state of mind is in fact preferred to another—that someone or other happens to prefer the one state of mind to the other. If a state of mind A is to be preferred to a state of mind B, if it is, as I would like to say, intrinsically preferable to B, then anyone who prefers B to A is *mistaken* in his preference.

Given this concept of epistemic preferability, we can readily explicate the basic concepts of the theory of evidence. We could say, for for example, that a proposition p is *beyond reasonable doubt t* provided only that believing p is then epistemically preferable for S to withholding p—where by "withholding p" we mean the state of neither accepting p nor its negation. It is evident to me, for example, that many people are here. This means it is epistemically preferable for me to believe that many people are here than for me neither to believe nor to disbelieve that many are people here.

A proposition is *evident* for a person if it is beyond reasonable doubt for that person and is such that his including it among the propositions upon which he bases his decisions is preferable to his not so including it. A proposition is *acceptable* if withholding it is *not* preferable to believing it. And a proposition is *unacceptable* if withholding it *is* preferable to believing it.

Again, some propositions are not beyond reasonable doubt but they may be said to have *some presumption in their favor*. I suppose that the proposition that each of us will be alive an hour from now is one that has some presumption in its favor. We could say that a proposition is of this sort provided only that believing the proposition is epistemically preferable to believing its negation.

Moving in the other direction in the epistemic hierarchy, we could say that a proposition is *certain*, absolutely certain, for a given subject at a given time, if that proposition is then evident to that subject and if there is no other proposition that is such that believing that other proposition is then epistemically preferable for him to believing the given proposition. It is certain for me, I would say, that there seem to be many people here and that 7 and 5 are 12. If this is so, then each of the two propositions is evident to me and there are no other propositions that are such that it would be even better, epistemically, if I were to believe those other propositions.

This concept of epistemic preferability can be axiomatized and made the basis of a system of epistemic logic exhibiting the relations among these and other concepts of the theory of evidence.[9] For present purposes, let us simply note how they may be applied in our approach to the problem of the criterion.

12

Let us begin with the most difficult of the concepts to which we have just referred—that of a proposition being *certain* for a man at a given time. Can we formulate *criteria* of such certainty? I think we can.

Leibniz had said that there are two kinds of immediately evident proposition—the "first truths of fact" and the "first truths of reason." Let us consider each of these in turn.

Among the "first truths of fact," for any man at any given time, I would say, are various propositions about his own state of mind at that time—his thinking certain thoughts, his entertaining certain beliefs, his being in a certain sensory or emotional state. These propositions all pertain to certain states of the man that may be said to manifest or present themselves to him at that time. We could use Meinong's term and say that certain states are "self-presenting," where this concept might be marked off in the following way.

A man's being in a certain state is *self-presenting* to him at a given time provided only that (i) he is in that state at that time and (ii) it is necessarily true that if he is in that state at that time then it is evident to him that he is in that state at that time.

The states of mind just referred to are of this character. Wishing, say, that one were on the moon is a state that is such that a man cannot be in that state without it being evident to him that he is in that state. And so, too, for thinking certain thoughts and having certain sensory or emotional experiences. These states present themselves and are, so to speak, marks of their own evidence. They cannot occur unless it is evident that they occur. I think they are properly called the "first truths of fact." Thus St. Thomas could say that "the intellect knows that it possesses the truth by reflecting on itself."[10]

Perceiving external things and remembering are not states that present themselves. But thinking that one perceives (or seeming to perceive) and thinking that one remembers (or seeming to remember) *are* states of mind that present themselves. And in presenting themselves they may, at least under certain favorable conditions, present something else as well.

Coffey quotes Hobbes as saying that "the inn of evidence has no sign-board."[11] I would prefer saying that these self-presenting states are sign-boards—of the inn of indirect evidence. But these sign-boards need no further sign-boards in order to be presented, for they present themselves.

13

What of the first truths of reason? These are the propositions that some philosophers have called "a priori" and that Leibniz, following

Locke, referred to as "maxims" or "axioms." These propositions are all necessary and have a further characteristic that Leibniz described in this way: "You will find in a hundred places that the Scholastics have said that these propositions are evident, *ex terminis*, as soon as the terms are understood, so that they were persuaded that the force of conviction was grounded in the nature of the terms, i.e., in the connection of their ideas."[12] Thus St. Thomas referred to propositions that are "manifest through themselves."[13]

An axiom, one might say, is a necessary proposition such that one cannot understand it without thereby knowing that it is true. Since one cannot know a proposition unless it is evident and one believes it, and since one cannot believe a proposition unless one understands it, we might characterize these first truths of reason in the following way:

A proposition is *axiomatic* for a given subject at a given time provided only that (i) the proposition is one that is necessarily true and (ii) it is also necessarily true that if the person then believes that proposition, the proposition is then evident to him.

We might now characterize the *a priori* somewhat more broadly by saying that a proposition is a priori for a given subject at a given time provided that one or the other of these two things is true: either (i) the proposition is one that is axiomatic for that subject at that time, or else (ii) the proposition is one such that it is evident to the man at that time that the proposition is entailed by a set of propositions that are axiomatic for him at that time.

In characterizing the "first truths of fact" and the "first truths of reason," I have used the expression "evident." But I think it is clear that such truths are not only evident but also certain. And they may be said to be *directly*, or *immediately*, evident.

What, then, of the indirectly evident?

14

I have suggested in rather general terms above what we might say about memory and the senses. These ostensible sources of knowledge are to be treated as innocent until there is positive ground for thinking them guilty. I will not attempt to develop a theory of the indirectly evident at this point. But I will note at least the *kind* of principle to which we might appeal in developing such a theory.

We could *begin* by considering the following two principles, M and

P; M referring to memory, and P referring to perception or the senses.

M) For any subject S, if it is evident to S that she seems to remember that *a* was F, then it is beyond reasonable doubt for S that *a* was F.

P) For any subject S, if it is evident to S that she thinks she perceives that *a* is F, then it is evident to S that *a* is F.

"She seems to remember" and "she thinks she perceives" here refer to certain self-presenting states that, in the figure I used above, could be said to serve as sign-boards for the inn of indirect evidence.

But principles M and P, as they stand, are much too latitudinarian. We will find that it is necessary to make qualifications and add more and more conditions. Some of these will refer to the subject's sensory state; some will refer to certain of her other beliefs; and some will refer to the relations of confirmation and mutual support. To set them forth in adequate detail would require a complete epistemology.[14]

So far as our problem of the criterion is concerned, the essential thing to note is this. In formulating such principles we will simply proceed as Aristotle did when he formulated his rules for the syllogism. As "particularists" in our approach to the problem of the criterion, we will fit our rules to the cases—to the apples we know to be good and to the apples we know to be bad. Knowing what we do about ourselves and the world, we have at our disposal certain instances that our rules or principles should countenance, and certain other instances that our rules or principles should rule out or forbid. And, as rational beings, we assume that by investigating these instances we can formulate criteria that any instance must satisfy if it is to be countenanced and we can formulate other criteria that any instance must satisfy if it is to be ruled out or forbidden.

If we proceed in this way we will have satisfied Cardinal Mercier's criteria for a theory of evidence or, as he called it, a theory of certitude. He said that any criterion, or any adequate set of criteria, should be internal, objective, and immediate. The type of criteria I have referred to are certainly *internal*, in his sense of the term. We have not appealed to any external authority as constituting the ultimate test of evidence. (Thus we haven't appealed to "science" or to "the scientists of our culture circle" as constituting the touchstone of what we know.) I would say that our criteria are *objective*. We have formulated them in terms of the concept of epistemic preferability—where the location "*p* is epistemically preferable to *q* for S" is taken to refer to an objective relation that obtains independently of the actual preferences of any particular subject. The criteria that we formulate, if they are adequate, will be principles that are necessarily true. And they are also *immediate*. Each of them is such that, if it is applicable at any particular time, then the fact that it is then applicable is capable of being directly evident to that particular subject at that particular time.

15

But in all of this I have presupposed the approach I have called "particularism." The "methodist" and the "skeptic" will tell us that we have started in the wrong place. If now we try to reason with them, then, I am afraid, we will be back on the wheel.

What few philosophers have had the courage to recognize is this: we can deal with the problem only by begging the question. It seems to me that, if we do recognize this fact, as we should, then it is unseemly for us to try to pretend that it isn't so.

One may object: "Doesn't this mean, then, that the skeptic is right after all?" I would answer: "Not at all. His view is only one of the three possibilities and in itself has no more to recommend it than the others do. And in favor of our approach there is the fact that we *do* know many things, after all."

Chapter 6
The Foundation
of Empirical Statements

I shall suggest answers to the following questions which were among those raised in the original prospectus of the Warsaw Colloquy:

It seems to belong to the very content of a scientific statement that it is one which is founded, justified, or valid (*ein begründeter Satz*), and a suggestion that there are scientific statements that are unfounded, gratuitous conjectures seems to imply a contradiction. Yet some methodologists of inductive sciences maintain that neither their basic statements nor their general laws have any foundation (*Begründung*).

What is the object of foundation (justification, validation, legitimization)? Is it the statement itself or possibly its assertion?

If the object of foundation is the assertion of a statement (and thus a kind of human behavior, similar to decision making), could the problem of foundation of statements be viewed in a way similar to the problem of rational decision making?

In what sense, if any, may one speak of the foundation of basic statements in the empirical sciences?

Must the foundation of a statement consist in its derivation from other statements, or may it also consist in its derivation from something that is not a statement (e.g., from a perception)?

Must the concept of a founded statement be thought of as relative or may it be thought of as absolute?

The above quotation contains only part of what was stated in the original prospectus, and I have changed the order of the questions.

1

"What is the object of foundation (justification, validation, legitimization)? Is it the statement itself or possibly its assertion?"

The term "justify" suggests that, if we say a *statement* is justified, what we mean is that a certain kind of human behavior or activity with respect *to* that statement is justified. But what kind of behavior or activity? Not the *assertion* of the statement—if "assertion" is taken to mean the overt utterance, affirmation, or avowal of the statement. For there are many justified statements that we are not justified in overtly asserting; and perhaps there are unjustified statements that, at times, we are justified in overtly asserting. When we say that a statement is justified, what we mean, surely, is that its *acceptance* is justified.

What is the relevant sense of "justify"? Making use just of the concept of *more reasonable than*, we may distinguish several different senses in which a statement may be said to be justified. A statement is *acceptable* for a given subject provided only that withholding that statement (neither accepting it nor accepting its negation) is not more reasonable for him than accepting it; it is *probable* for that subject provided only that accepting it is more reasonable for him than withholding it; and it is *evident* for that subject provided only that his including that statement among those on which he bases his decisions is more reasonable for him than is his not so including it.

2

"If the object of foundation is a kind of human behavior, similar to decision making, could the problem of the foundation of statements be viewed in a way similar to the problem of rational decision making?"

We must solve the problem of the foundation of statements in the *way* in which we must solve the problem of rational decision making; but proper *application* of rational decision theory presupposes proper application of the theory of the justification of statements.

If it were possible to formulate a complete set of rules for rational decision making, these rules would tell us, perhaps among other things, how to decide at any particular time: (1) whether, for any two states of affairs, one would be *better* than the other; (2) whether a given statement is one that, for us, is *evident,* or *probable*, or *acceptable*, or none of these, at that time; (3) whether, with respect to any two statements, the evidence at our disposal at that time (i.e., the set of all those statements that for us are evident at that time) *confirms* one to a higher degree than it confirms the other; and, finally, (4) what we ought to do. Such a set of rules would constitute a hierarchy in that, to apply those that come later on the list, a reasonable man would need first to apply those that come earlier. We may say that ethics or moral philosophy is concerned with (1), epistemology or the theory of knowledge with (2), inductive logic or confirmation theory with (3), and rational decision theory with (4). The *way in which* we should go about formulating these sets of rules is similar in each case: we suppose ourselves able to recognize certain cases that would conform to the rules we are attempting to formulate, and certain other cases that do not conform to them; then, from these sets of cases, we "extract" in Socratic fashion the rules we desire.

3

"In what sense, if any, may one speak of the foundation of basic statements in the empirical sciences?"

First, we must ask: What is a basic statement, and how are we to decide whether there are any? To answer these questions, we must consider what it would be to formulate "rules of evidence."

If we wish to formulate, or make explicit, our rules of evidence, we should proceed as we do in logic when we formulate rules of inference, or in ethics when we formulate rules of action. We suppose that we have at our disposal certain instances that the rules should countenance and other instances that the rules should forbid; and we suppose that by investigating these instances we can formulate criteria that any instance must satisfy if it is to be countenanced, and criteria that any instance must satisfy if it is to be forbidden. To obtain the instances we should need if we were to formulate rules of evidence, I suggest that we should proceed in the following way.

We should consider certain statements—or beliefs, or hypotheses— that are of the sort that we want to call evident. And we should "examine" these statements by considering, with respect to each of them, what would be a reasonable answer to the following question: "What justification do you have for counting this statement (belief, hypothesis) as one that is evident?" or "What justification do you have for thinking you know this statement is true?" And similarly for statements thought to be merely probable, and statements thought to be merely acceptable.

There are philosophers who will point out, with respect to some statements that are quite obviously true, that questions concerning their justification or evidence "do not arise," for (they will say) to express a doubt concerning such statements is (somehow) to "violate the rules of our language." To these philosophers we may point out that our questions need not be taken to express any doubts or to indicate an attitude of skepticism. They are not challenges and they do not imply or presuppose that there is any ground for doubting, or for suspecting, the statements with which they are concerned; they seek only to elicit information.[1] When Aristotle considered an invalid mood and asked himself "What is wrong with this?" he was trying to learn; he need not have been suggesting to himself that perhaps nothing was wrong with the mood.

It should also be noted that when we ask, concerning some evident statement, "What justification do you have for counting this statement as one that is evident?" or "What justification do you have for thinking you know that this statement is one that is true?" we are not asking what procedures might *further confirm* the statement. We are supposing that the statement is one that is evident, and we are attempting to discover the nature of its evidence.

In many instances the answers to our questions could take the following form: "What justifies me in counting it as evident that a is F is that (i) it is evident that b is G and (ii) if it is evident that b is G then it is evident that a is F." (Or, "What justifies me in saying that I know that a is F is that (i) I know that b is G and (ii) if I know that b is G, then I know that a is F.") For example, "What makes it evident that he has that disorder is that it is evident that he has these symptoms, and if it is evident that he has these symptoms then it is evident that he has that disorder." Such a reply has two parts. First, we say that our justification for counting one statement as evident is that a certain other statement is evident. And secondly, we offer what may be called a "rule of evidence"; for we make a statement that says that if a statement of the second sort is evident then a statement of the first sort is also evident. One could say, of the rule, that it tells us that one statement *confers evidence* upon another statement.

Such a reply to our questions would shift the burden of justification from one statement to another. For we may now ask, "What justifies you in counting it as evident that b is G?" (or "What justifies you in thinking you know that b is G?").[2] And to this question we may receive again an answer of the first sort: "What justifies me in counting it as evident that b is G is that (i) it is evident that c is H and (ii) if it is evident that c is H then it is evident that b is G." ("What justifies me in counting it as evident that he has these symptoms is that it is evident that his temperature is high, his face is flushed. . . . ") How long can we continue in this way?

Let us note that our replies may take a slightly different form from that just considered. The phrase "it is evident that" may be omitted from the first part, and from the first part of the second part, of the reply, leaving us with: "What justifies me in counting it as evident that a is F, is that (i) b is G and (ii) if b is G then it is evident that a is F." In some cases, we may say that the fact that it is *evident* that b is G is implicit in such a reply, but in others, according to what I take to be the views of some philosophers, it may not be.

If we say, as I think we should, that there are some statements that are evident and that the interrogation just described should involve neither a vicious circle nor an infinite regress, then we are committed to saying that there are "basic statements."

Let us suppose that, in the course of describing the justification of some statement, we have made a statement, "a is F," and we are now confronted with the question: "What justification do you have for counting the statement that a is F as one that is evident?" I suggest that the statement that a is F could be said to be a "basic statement" if it would be reasonable to answer the question in either of the following ways:

1) "What justifies me in counting it as evident that a is F is simply the fact that a is F."
2) "The statement that a is F cannot properly be said to be evident (or to be nonevident) and therefore the question 'What is your justification for counting it as evident that a is F?' cannot arise."

In the first case, we have a statement that is made evident by the fact that it is true; and in the second, we have a statement that is not itself evident (or that "cannot properly be said" to be evident) but that may, all the same, confer evidence upon other statements. Thus the first suggests a prime mover that moves itself, the second a prime mover unmoved. In the present case, I believe, the two descriptions differ only in terminology. The issues involved in saying this may be seen if we consider certain particular "basic statements."

One advantage in describing "basic statements" in one or the other of the present two ways is that our discussion neither touches on "certainty" and "incorrigibility" nor becomes entangled in the issues to which these misleading terms sometimes give rise.

4

"Must the foundation of a statement consist in its derivation from other statements, or may it also consist in its derivation from something that is not a statement (e.g., from a perception)?"

Let us first ask: Are perceptual statements—statements expressing what we perceive—"basic" in either of the senses just described?

To justify the statement that Mr. Smith is here, one may say "I see that he is here." But "I see that he is here" is not a "basic statement" in either sense described. In reply to the question, "What is your justification for counting it as evident that it is Mr. *Smith* whom you see?" a reasonable man would *not* say, "What justifies me in counting it as evident that it is Mr. Smith is simply the fact that it *is* Mr. Smith." Nor would he say, "The statement that it is Mr. Smith whom I see is not a statement that can properly be said to be evident." He would say, instead, something like this: "(It is evident that:) Mr. Smith is a tall man with dark glasses; I see such a man; no one else satisfying that description would be in *this* room now . . . etc." Each of these statements in turn, including "I see such a man," would be defended by appeal to still other statements. Similarly for any other perceptual statement. If this is so, perception does not yield any "basic statements" in either of the two senses of that term we have described.

There are philosophers who might say, "What justifies me in counting it as evident that Mr. Smith is here (or that I see Mr. Smith) is simply my present experience; but the experience itself cannot be said to be evident, much less to have evidence conferred upon it." With this reply they have supposed themselves able to circumvent some of the more difficult questions of the theory of knowledge.[3] Yet the reply seems clearly to make room for further questioning. Thus one may ask, "What justifies you in counting it as evident that your experience is of such a sort that experiences of that sort make it evident to you that Mr. Smith is here, or that you see that Mr. Smith is here?" And to this question, one could reasonably reply in the way described above.

It must be conceded, I think, that the only empirical "basic statements," in our present sense of the term, are certain psychological statements about oneself. For example, any one of the following statements *may* be so interpreted that it is "basic" in one or the other of our two senses: "I seem to remember having seen that man before," "That looks green," "This tastes bitter," "I believe that Socrates is mortal," and "I hope that the peace will continue." Let us consider the first of these.

The statement "I seem to remember having seen that man before," is one to which we may appeal in justifying some other statement. Thus part of my justification for counting it as evident that I have been among these people before may be that I seem to remember having seen that man before; and if *you* say "I seem to remember having seen him before," part of my justification for counting it as evident that you and I seem to remember the same thing is that *I* seem to remember having seen him before. How, then, shall we deal with the question "What justification do you have for counting it as evident that you have seen that man before?" It seems clear to me that we must choose between the two alternatives I have described, and hence that the statement in question is one that is "basic."

1) We may say, "What justifies me in counting it as evident that I seem to remember having seen that man before is simply that I *do* seem to remember having seen him before." In this case, we have justified a statement simply by reiterating it. This type of justification, if I am not mistaken, is never appropriate to empirical statements that are not psychological; and if what I have said above is correct, it is never appropriate to ordinary perceptual statements. We should also note that such a justification presupposes that the statement justified is a *true* statement.

2) We may say what many philosophers would now prefer to say: "The fact that I seem to remember having seen that man before is not something that can properly be said to be *evident*; hence the question 'What justifies you in counting it as evident?' is not a question that can arise."

In defense of the second way of putting the matter, one may point out that, ordinarily, people never do apply such terms as "evident" to such statements as "I seem to remember having seen that man before."[4] (But from this fact alone, it would be a mistake to infer that "evident" cannot correctly be applied to such statements.)

One may also point out that seeming to remember is not accompanied by a second-order consciousness, or insight, that "illuminates" one's seeming to remember.[5] (But to infer from this that it cannot be said to be evident to me that I seem to remember would be to presuppose that a statement cannot be said to be evident unless it concerns something that is revealed by a special kind of consciousness or illumination; and, according to what was said at the end of Section 1 above, such a presupposition is gratuitous.) It seems clear to me that this second way of formulating our basic statements differs only verbally from the first.[6]

If the "basic statements" of empirical knowledge are psychological statements about oneself, then the "basic statements" of the empirical sciences must be found among those statements that, for each empirical scientist, are basic for him. How are we to show that "objective" science can thus be "subjectively" based? Only, I think, by formulating rules of evidence that will state the conditions under which statements that are subjective may be said to confer evidence upon statements that are not. I can state possible examples of such rules; but the task of deciding whether these, or any other, rules are adequate has yet to be carried out.

Let us recall that we have distinguished the concepts of a statement being *evident*, a statement being *probable* (more probable than not), and a statement being *acceptable*. If a statement is evident it is probable, but not conversely; and if a statement is probably it is acceptable, but not conversely.

Rules taking the following form might be described as epistemically liberal, or latitudinarian:

"For any subject S, if it is evident to S that she seems to remember that *a* was *F*, then it is evident to S that *a* was *F*."

"For any subject S, if it is evident to S that she thinks she perceives that *a* is *F*, then it is evident to S that *a* is *F*."

If we are to decide to formulate our "basic propositions" in the second of the two ways described, then we should omit the first occurrence of "it is evident to S that" in each of these rules.

The rules may be made more rigid by replacing the second occurrence of "evident" in each of them by "probable," and even more rigid by replacing it by "acceptable." And if the rules turn out to be still too liberal, as perhaps they may, we can consider such possibilities as these:

"For any subject S, if it is evident to S that she seems to remember that *a* was *F*, then it is evident (probable, acceptable) to S that *a* was *F*, provided that the statement that she *does* remember that *a* was *F* is not disconfirmed by the set of all the other statements expressing what it is evident to S that she seems to remember."

"For any subject S, if it is evident to S that she thinks she perceives that *a* is *F*, then it is evident (probable, acceptable) to S that *a* is *F*, provided that the statement that she *does* perceive that *a* is *F* is not disconfirmed by the set of all the other statements expressing either what it is evident to S that she seems to remember or what it is evident to S that she seems to perceive."

Perhaps the expression "other statements" is better replaced by "statements not logically implied by the statement that *a* is *F*."

The rules of inductive logic, or confirmation theory, may be construed in this way, as telling us the conditions under which sets of evident statements may be said to confer probability upon statements that are not evident. We may find that there are certain statements in the empirical sciences that we wish to count as evident, but that we cannot count as evident unless inductive logic includes, in addition to rules of probability, certain rules of evidence. An inductive rule of evidence would be a rule specifying conditions under which confirmation by a set of evident statements could confer evidence upon a statement that is not entailed by that set.

We can say of our "basic statements" that if they are evident they are also true. But our rules do not guarantee, with respect to other statements, that if *they* are evident, then they, too, are true.

5

"Must the concept of a founded statement be thought of as relative, or may it be thought of as absolute?"

The foundation of statements may be said to be "relative" in the sense that, for any statement *b*, it is possible for *b* to be evident (or probable, or acceptable) for one man and not for another. But our rules may be said to be "absolute" in the sense that they formulate conditions of being evident (or probable, or acceptable) that hold for all men. Thus we have used the phrase "for any subject S."

What if someone were to propose an alternative set of rules—by beginning with cases quite different from those with which we began? And suppose we find that we can reach no agreement with him concerning any of those cases that, at the outset, are to be counted as instances of what is evident, or probable, or acceptable. Shall we say that at most one of two such sets of conflicting rules is valid or correct? I am afraid I cannot answer this ancient question—beyond saying that what may be said about the correctness or validity of rules of evidence should also hold, mutatis mutandis, of the rules of logic, ethics, and the theory of rational decision.

Chapter 7

Verstehen: The Epistemological Question

Introduction

By "the doctrine of *Verstehen*," I shall mean the thesis according to which a certain type of apprehension—sometimes called· "Verstehen," sometimes called "intuitive understanding"—is essential to our knowledge of other minds. I shall try to formulate, as clearly as I can, what the problem is that the doctrine is intended to solve; then I shall try to say just what it is that the doctrine is intended to be; and I shall conclude that some form of the doctrine is true.

For some years now philosophers have refused to recognize the problems of the theory of knowledge. But once one does recognize these problems, one sees that the question of other minds has its analogues in the case of external perception and memory. Thus it may be asked: by means of what principles can we proceed from what is directly evident to propositions about external things and to propositions about the past? The first steps, of course, are by way of perception and by way of memory.

Three Types of Justifying Principle

Making use of the concept of self-presentation, we may say that a person's *evidence base* at any given time comprises the set of all those propositions that are self-presenting to that person at that time. Any proposition entailed by the conjunction of the members of the evidence base may then be said to be *directly evident* for that person.

There are three different ways in which a given hypothesis may be related to a body of evidence e. What we say will be true of that body of evidence e that is one's evidence-base at any time, as this concept has just been defined. It will also be true of any body of evidence that is not thus restricted to the directly evident.

1) The hypothesis h is a *deductive* consequence of the body of evidence e.

2) The hypothesis h is an *inductive* consequence of the body of evidence e. This point may be put somewhat more precisely as follows: application of the principles of inductive logic to e will yield the result that e tends to confirm h.

3) The hypothesis h is an *epistemic* consequence of the body of evidence e. In other words, there are certain valid principles of evidence of the following sort: they are not themselves principles of inductive logic, but they are such that the application of them and the principles of inductive logic to e will yield the result that e tends to confirm h. (There is, of course, a problem of deciding just which principles are principles of inductive logic and which ones are epistemic principles. One way to make the distinction is this: if it is essential to the principle that it make reference to the state of mind of a person [saying, for example, that this state of affairs confers positive epistemic status upon some proposition], then the principle is epistemic and not logical.)

Obviously this third possibility is of interest only if we have reason to believe that there *are* valid principles of evidence other than the principles of deductive and inductive logic. How, then, do we decide *whether* such principles exist?

First, we assume that what one knows at any time is justified by reference to what is in one's evidence base at that time. Second, we assume that we know various things that are not included in our evidence base—for example, certain propositions about external physical things, certain propositions about the past, and certain propositions about "other minds." And, third, we then attempt, in a Socratic manner, to formulate principles of evidence that are such that in application to our evidence base they will yield the propositions that are thus known and they will not yield any propositions that are not thus known.

If we do find such principles, and if we *also* find that the principles of inductive and deductive logic do not suffice to yield the knowledge in question, then we have a reason to suppose that valid principles of evidence exist other than the principles of deductive and inductive logic.

We may illustrate this process, somewhat schematically, in connection with the knowledge that is attributed to perception and memory. Then we may discuss its application to our knowledge of "other minds." This illustration will constitute a defense of at least one version of a thesis that might well be called the doctrine of Verstehen.

We first consider the above distinctions in application to "our knowledge of the external world." Let us suppose that h is a proposition about an external thing—perhaps a proposition that one might express by saying "A sheep is in the field" or "A cat is on the roof." Let us assume that this is a proposition that our subject S knows to be true.

I believe it can be shown that from directly evident premises— premises expressing our awareness of sensations and of our own states of mind—neither induction nor deduction will justify any proposition affirming the existence of an external thing.[1] If this is correct, then any such proposition that the subject then knows to be true is neither a deductive nor an inductive consequence of his evidence base. Now since our subject does have the knowledge and since, we are assuming, whatever he knows may be justified by reference to his evidence base, it follows that the proposition is an *epistemic* consequence of S's evidence base. This means that, in addition to the logical principles of deduction and induction, there are valid principles of evidence that, in application to directly evident premises (for example, premises about what we may call "thinking that one perceives"), will confer evidence on propositions about external things. Thus Meinong had held, in effect, that our *thinking* that we perceive confers "presumptive evidence (*Vermutungsevidenz*)" on the proposition or state of affairs that is the object of our ostensible perception.[2] And H. H. Price has said that the fact that we "perceptually accept" a certain proposition is sufficient to confer some positive epistemic status on that proposition. Price put this point as follows: "We want to be able to say: the fact that a material thing is perceptually presented to the mind is *prima facie evidence* of the thing's existence and of its really having that sort of surface which it ostensibly has: or, again, that there is *some presumption in favor of* this, not merely in the sense that we do as a matter of fact presume it (which of course we do) but in the sense that we are entitled to do so."[3]

It is, of course, a task of epistemology to formulate principles more precisely, to say precisely what types of directly evident premises we here appeal to and to say precisely what types of conclusion are made by such premises. The principles, then, will enable us to *extend* our directly evident evidence base by adding certain perceptual propositions to it. Hence we may speak of a perceptually extended evidence base. This concept may be characterized as follows:

> e is the perceptually extended evidence base for S at t =Df e is the conjunction of all those states of affairs that are such that either they are directly evident for S at t or they are perceptual propositions that are evident for S at t.

Another example of an epistemological problem is provided by the relation between certain propositions about the past and that self-presenting state which is "seeming to remember." But this problem—at least as it is commonly understood—presupposes a solution to the problem of our knowledge of external things. And where the problem of our knowledge of external things concerns the relation of certain propositions to one's evidence base, in the strict sense of the expression "evidence base," the problem of memory has to do with the relation of certain propositions about the past to what may be called one's "perceptually extended evidence base."

The "problem of memory," then, is analogous to "the problem of the external world," but instead of relating to one's strict evidence base, it relates to one's perceptually extended evidence base. It is not difficult to see, with respect to certain propositions that we know about the past, that those propositions are neither deductive nor inductive consequences of our perceptually extended evidence base. Hence we will conclude that such propositions are epistemic consequences of our perceptually extended evidence base. This means that valid principles of evidence exist that, in application to our perceptually extended evidence base, will confer evidence on propositions about the past. Thus Meinong had held that certain facts about what we might call "thinking that one remembers" confer "presumptive evidence" on what it is that we thus think we remember.[4] And C. I. Lewis has held, in effect, that a certain proposition's being an object of ostensible memory is itself sufficient to confer some positive epistemic status on that proposition. He put this point as follows: "Whatever is remembered, whether as explicit recollection or merely in the form of our sense of the past, is *prima facie* credible because so remembered."[5]

What, now, of the "problem of other minds"?

The Problem of Other Minds

Each of us knows various things about the thoughts, feelings, and purposes of other people; we may be able to say, for example, "I know that that person wants us to leave" or "I know that he is feeling somewhat depressed," or "It is evident that he is embarrassed."

The problem of "other minds" is related to memory in the way in which the problem of memory is related to our knowledge of external things. Assuming that certain mnemic propositions may be said to be evident for S at t, we now introduce the concept of a *perceptually and mnemically extended evidence base*:

> e is the perceptually and mnemically extended evidence base for s at t =Df e is the conjunction of all those states of affairs that are such that either they are directly evident for S at t or they are perceptual or mnemic propositions that are evident for S at t.

I take the problem of other minds to be this: Does one's perceptually and mnemically extended base provide justification for propositions about the psychological states of people other than ourselves? And I take the doctrine of Verstehen to be, in part, the following: in addition to the principles of inductive and deductive logic, and to the principles of perceptual evidence and the principles of mnemic evidence, there are also principles of evidence such that, in application to one's perceptually and mnemically extended evidence base, they will justify certain propositions about other minds.

Let us first ask, then, whether application of the principles of deductive and inductive logic to one's perceptually and mnemically extended evidence will yield any conclusions about the thoughts and feelings of other people.

One may be tempted to answer this question by appealing to an enumerative induction. "More often than not, when a man makes a gesture of such and such a sort, he is feeling depressed; this man is now making a gesture of that sort; therefore, in all probability, he is depressed." Or, "More often than not, when people behave in ways like that; they want to be alone; that's the way that he is behaving; therefore, in all probability, he wants to be alone." But this type of answer obviously does not solve our philosophic problem. For the instances to which we appeal when we make our induction ("He made this gesture yesterday when he was depressed" or "The last person we saw behaving like that wanted to be alone") presuppose the general type of knowledge-claim we are now trying to justify ("What is your justification for thinking you know that he *was* depressed—or that he *did* want to be alone—at that particular time?")

If we are not to presuppose the type of knowledge-claim that we are trying to justify, then our argument must be an instance of "hypothetical induction." The "hypothesis" that the person in question is now depressed, or that he wants to be alone, will be put forward as the most likely *explanation* of certain other things we know—presumably, certain facts about his present behavior and demeanor. But to construct an inductive argument in which the hypothesis that the person is depressed, or that he wants to be alone, *is* thus to be confirmed, we must have access to a premise telling us what some of the consequences of his depression, or some of the consequences of his wanting to be alone, are likely to be. And how are we to justify *this* premise?

One may suppose that the premise thus required by our hypothetical induction may be justified by still another induction—this time an argument from *analogy*. For example, we might argue: "That person and I have such and such physical characteristics in common; usually, as a result of being depressed, I will speak in such and such a tone of voice; therefore, in all probability, if he is depressed he will also speak in that tone of voice; and he *is* speaking in that tone of voice." Or we might argue: "That person and I have such and such physical characteristics in common; most of the time, when I want to be alone, I will say 'Yes' if stimulated by the words 'Do you want to be alone?'; and therefore, in all probability, his wanting to be alone would predispose *him* to say 'Yes' if he were stimulated by such words. Now the person has been stimulated by those words and he *does* say 'Yes'." The first premise in each of these arguments appeals to a certain positive analogy obtaining between the other person and me. But we must not forget that whoever the other person may be, there is also an impressive negative analogy—difference in background, environment, heredity, physique, and general physiology—and that one could go on *ad infinitum* enumerating such differences. If our evidence base doesn't already include premises referring to another person's states of mind, it will be very difficult indeed to assess the relative importance of the various points of analogy and disanalogy. Any such analogical argument, therefore, is certain to be weak. It would seem that, if this procedure is the best that we have, then there is very little, if anything, that we can be said to *know* about other peoples' states of mind.

We are thus led to the characteristic argument of the proponent of Verstehen. Perception, memory, and "self-presentation," he will tell us, do not suffice to justify what it is that we know about the states of mind of other people, for no deductive or inductive argument based on the data of perception, memory, and "self-presentation" will warrant any claim to such knowledge; hence, there must be additional epistemic principles. He will then formulate these principles by reference to Verstehen, or "intuitive understanding." The point would not be merely that in Verstehen, or intuitive understanding, we have a fruitful *source* of hypotheses about the mental states of other people; the point has to do with the *justification* of hypotheses. Thus, one may contend, for example, that the fact that a statement expresses one's Verstehen will confer some positive epistemic status upon that statement.

What are the Principles of Verstehen?

To *what* epistemic principles, then, will the proponent of the doctrine of Verstehen appeal? If we look to the writings of those who have emphasized the term, "Verstehen," we may be somewhat disappointed. Although the doctrine of Verstehen is usually associated with Wilhelm Dilthey, what Dilthey says does not seem to be sufficiently clear to afford us an answer to our question and I will not speculate as to how he might have answered it.[6]

One fairly good statement is the following exposition, by Alfred Schuetz, of Max Scheler's theory of the perception of other minds (*"Wahrnehmungstheorie des fremden Ich"*):

But what else shall we perceive of the other than its body and its gestures? Scheler thinks that we certainly perceive in the other's smile his joy, in his tears his suffering, in his blushing his shame, in his joined hands his praying, in the sounds of his words his thought—all this without empathy and without any inference by analogy. We start reasoning only if we feel induced to distrust our perceptions of the other's experiences—as, e.g., if we feel we have misunderstood him or if we discover that we have to deal with an insane individual. But even those "inferences" are based on perceptions of the other which are rather complicated. In looking at him I not only perceive his eyes, but also that he looks at me, and even that he does so as if he would prevent my knowing that he looks at me. If we really ask what the object of our perception of the other is, we have to answer that we perceive neither the other's body nor his Soul or Self or Ego, but a totality, undivided into objects of outer and inner experiences. The phenomena arising out of this unity are psycho-physically indifferent. They might be analyzed as color-qualities, form-units, units of movements, or changes in the position of his bodily organs. But by no worse reasoning might they be interpreted as "expressions" of the other's thought which cannot be broken down into parts of expressive character, but show the structure of a unit (for instance, a physiognomical unit).[7]

But by far the best statement of what I mean by the doctrine of Verstehen may be found in the writings of Thomas Reid. Reid does not explicitly formulate any rules of evidence, but he cites the following "first principle":

That certain features of the countenance, sounds of the voice, and gestures of the body, indicate certain thoughts and dispositions of the mind.[8]

Reid's view is, in part, a view about the genesis of our knowledge (he refers, for example, to the way in which children acquire their beliefs). But it is also a theory of evidence—an account of what it is that confers evidence on statements about other minds:

When we see the sign, and see the thing signified always conjoined with it, experience may be the instructor, and teach us how that sign is to be interpreted. But how shall experience instruct us when we see the sign only, when the thing signified is invisible? Now, this is the case here: the thoughts and passions of the mind, as well as the mind itself, are invisible, and therefore their connection with any sensible sign cannot be first discovered by experience; there must be some earlier source of this knowledge.

Nature seems to have given to men a faculty or sense, by which this connection is perceived. And the operation of this sense is very analogous to that of the external senses.

When I grasp an ivory ball in my hand, I feel a certain sensation of touch. In the sensation there is nothing external, nothing corporeal. The sensation is neither round nor hard; it is an act of feeling of mind, from which I cannot by reasoning, infer the existence of any body. But, by the constitution of my nature, the sensation carries along with it the conception and belief of a round hard body really existing in my hand.

In like manner, when I see the features of an expressive face, I see only figure and colour variously modified. But by the constitution of my nature, the visible object brings along with it the conception and belief of a certain passion or sentiment in the mind of the person.

In the former case, a sensation of touch is the sign, and the hardness and roundness of the body I grasp is signified by that sensation. In the latter case, the features of the person is the sign, and the passion of sentiment is signified by it.[9]

I would endorse these remarks—except that, where Reid appeals to a genetic concept ("the constitution of our nature"), I would appeal to an epistemic concept ("a principle of evidence").

It is interesting to compare, in this context, the following observation by Wittgenstein: "Think of the recognition of *facial expressions*. Or of the description of facial expression—which does not consist in giving the measurements of the face. Think, too, how one can imitate a man's face without seeing one's own in a mirror."[10]

We have asked: are the principles of induction, of perceptual evidence, and of mnemic evidence sufficient to justify what we know about other minds? Let us consider the way that Reid puts this question—and the way he answers it.

That many operations of the mind have their natural signs in the countenance, voice, and gesture, I suppose every man will admit . . . the only question is, whether we understand the signification of these signs by the constitution of our nature, by a kind of natural perception similar to the perceptions of sense; or whether we gradually learn the signification of such signs from experience, as we learn that smoke is a sign of fire, or that the freezing of water is a sign of cold? I take the first to be the truth.[11]

In speaking of perception, Meinong and Price had said, in effect, that a certain type of perceptual taking confers positive epistemic status on the proposition or state of affairs that is the object of that taking. In speaking of memory, Meinong and Lewis had said, in effect, that a certain kind of ostensible memory, what one might call "mnemic taking," confers positive epistemic status on the proposition or state of affairs that is the object of that taking. We may now appropriate the words of Reid to formulate the theory of Verstehen in an analogous way: that we take "certain features of the countenance, sounds of the voice, and gestures of the body" to indicate certain psychological properties of the person whose body it is confers positive epistemic status on the proposition that the person in question does have those psychological properties.

Unfortunately, we have used only the expression "certain features," without specifying more precisely just *what* features confer evidence on *what* propositions. To spell this out more precisely, it would be necessary for epistemology and descriptive psychology (or "phenomenology") to join forces. Let us hope that this is a real possibility.[12]

Chapter 8
What is a Transcendental Argument?

1. Introduction

If we are to be faithful to the use that the expression "transcendental argument" has come to have in recent philosophy, we may follow one or the other of two different procedures in attempting to formulate a definition. (a) We could consider certain arguments that have been called "transcendental" and we could try to state what is common and peculiar to these arguments. Then we could discuss the question whether transcendental arguments, as defined, are valid. Or (b) we could try to characterize transcendental arguments ideally as a type of valid argument that Kant and others may have thought they characterized their reasoning as transcendental. Then there would be no question about the validity of transcendental arguments, but we could ask, with respect to arguments that have been called transcendental whether in fact they are transcendental. And, indeed, we could ask whether anyone has ever formulated a transcendental argument. I will follow the second of these procedures.

2. A Preliminary Statement

A transcendental argument could be said to be an argument formulating the results of a certain procedures—a "transcendental procedure." In carrying out such a procedure, one first notes certain general features of a given subject-matter; then, by reflecting on these general features, one arrives at certain principles concerning the conditions necessary for the existence of that subject-matter; then by applying these principles to the description of the subject-matter, one deduces certain consequences; and finally, one concludes that the propositions thus deduced have thereby been shown to be justified.

Let us first consider a simple example. Then by reference to it we may be able to formulate more precisely the nature of the transcendental procedure.

The following example has the form of a transcendental argument. But whether it is in fact a transcendental argument depends on whether or not we are justified in affirming the premises—a question to which I shall return below. There are, then, two premises and a conclusion:

1) We have learned to use and understand a language of the following sort: it contains certain color-terms (a color-term being an expression having a certain color as its sense); some of these color terms may be defined by reference to the others, but it is not possible to define them all.
2) It is impossible to learn to use and understand a language containing terms that are not all definable unless some of these terms designate certain objects (which objects will then exemplify the senses of the terms).
3) Therefore there are colored objects.

On the basis of such an argument one may claim to have justified the proposition that there are colored objects. And perhaps one will also claim to have refuted those forms of skepticism that call such justification into question.

3. The Transcendental Procedure

We may now try to characterize the transcendental procedure more exactly.

1) In carrying out the transcendental procedure, one begins with the contemplation of a certain subject-matter. This subject-matter may be a set of propositions constituting a certain corpus of knowledge. Or it may be something quite different from a set of propositions; for example, it might be "experience," or perception, or thought, or language. But whether or not the initial subject-matter is itself a

body of propositions, the transcendental procedure makes use of certain propositions about this subject-matter. I will say that these propositions constitute the *preanalytic data* of the transcendental procedure.

In our example above, the preanalytic data are set forth in the first premise.

2) As a result of reflecting on the preanalytic data, one is able to apprehend certain necessary principles about the conditions under which it is possible for the initial subject-matter to exist (or about the conditions under which it is possible for the preanalytic data to be true). Since these principles are necessary and since (it is assumed) they are known to be true, they may be said to be known a priori. I will say that the second step of the transcendental procedure consists in the apprehension of certain *transcendental principles*.[1]

One may object: "But in many of the arguments that have been said to be transcendental, the general principle corresponding to your second step is not set forth is an a priori principle. It has, rather, the status of a possible explanatory hypothesis." The reply is that a principle having the status only of a possible explanatory hypothesis cannot be used as a step in a direct proof. And one is not justified in using such a principle as a premise in a philosophical argument.

3) The transcendental principles are then conjoined with the propositions constituting the prenalytic data and certain consequences are deduced from the result. Given that the premises of the transcendental arguments are justified, the significance of the argument will be a function of the significance of these consequences. Presumably, as in the case of the conclusion of our example above, they will be propositions that have been held to be at best problematic and that may have been challenged by skeptics or agnostics.

The proponent of the transcendental procedure may also claim that skeptics or agnostics in question have been refuted.

4. The Significance of the Transcendental Procedure

What are we to say about the significance of this procedure?

We should note first that the procedure is hardly likely to provide us with a way of *refuting* the skeptic. For such a refutation would not be possible unless the skeptic could be persuaded to accept the premises of the argument.

Thus there may be skeptics who are not prepared to accept the preanalytic data. It may well be, in the case of our example, that those skeptics who question the proposition that there are things that are colored will also question the proposition that we have learned to use and to understand a language containing certain color-terms. We could hardly claim to have refuted such skeptics by means of the argument of our example.

Nor can we refute those skeptics who deny the possibility of a priori knowledge. (Some philosophers, who are convinced that a priori knowledge is impossible, appeal to this supposed fact to show that transcendental arguments are impossible.)

And, obviously, if our transcendental principle has the status only of a possible explanatory hypothesis, then we can hardly appeal to it to show that the skeptic is mistaken.

But we should remind ourselves that there is no point in trying to *refute* a skeptic. For the true skeptic will refrain from asserting anything. He will restrict himself to the mechanical reiteration of the question, "But how do you prove that . . . ?" And the contention that a certain proposition is in fact epistemically justified does not imply that every skeptical challenge that may be made with respect to that proposition is capable of being met. (If the skeptic thinks otherwise, then he presupposes the following dogmatic principle: "For every proposition p, if p is justified, then it is possible to meet every challenge that may be made with respect to the justification of p." How would the skeptic defend this dogmatic principle?)

If we cannot refute the skeptic by means of a transcendental argument, we may at least be able to use such an argument to justify certain propositions that the skeptic has held to be problematic. Has this ever been done? Most transcendental arguments—at least all of those that are known to me—share the defects of the example I have set forth. The preanalytic data of such arguments may well consist of premises that are known to be true or are at least beyond reasonable doubt. And the arguments can be constructed in such a way that the conclusion can be seen to follow logically from the premises. But in almost every case, the second premise—what I have called the transcendental principle—is a proposition that is highly problematic. It is not a proposition known a priori to be true; it is at best a possible explanatory hypothesis.

The latter point may be illustrated by the supposed transcendental principle constituting the second premise of our example above. "It is impossible to learn and understand a language containing terms that are not all definable unless some of these terms designate certain objects . . . ''). There is, we may suppose, a certain psychological process that is brought about when a subject is confronted with colored objects and this process enables the subject to acquire the concept of color and thus to be able to use and understand color-terms. But how are we to prove that the confrontation with colored objects is essential to this process? Might not the process also be brought about by certain types of illusory experience? Surely there is no a priori answer to such questions.

Obviously any application of the transcendental procedure will be dependent on the initial credibility of the preanalytic data and on the justification of the transcendental principles that are thought to be apprehended as a result of reflecting on such data. But such questions about justification and initial credibility presuppose a solution to the traditional problems of the theory of knowledge. And it is most unlikely that these problems can be solved by constructing transcendental arguments.

Chapter 9
The Paradox of Analysis: A Solution

Roderick M. Chisholm
and Richard Potter

Introduction

We present an intentionally oriented theory of properties and show how this theory may solve what has been called "the paradox of analysis." This so-called "paradox" is not primarily a problem about language, as is commonly thought, but is rather a problem about certain intentional attitudes and the objects of those attitudes.

The problem concerns those definitions that are intended to be "philosophical analyses of concepts." The definiens, or analysans, is intended to be "an analysis of" the definiendum, or analysandum. (Of course, not every philosophical definition is thus intended as an analysis. Some are simply notational abbreviations. Others are presented as a part of a system of definitions in which, so to speak, one entire subject-matter is reduced to another.) We take the following to be paradigmatic cases of analysis:

Man is a rational animal.

A cube is a regular solid with six equal square sides.

We shall be concerned with the interpretation of the word "is" in these statements.

The so-called paradox arises because of the existence of what appear to be conflicting *desiderata* for an adequate philosophical analysis. These desiderata are three.

1) The analysans and the analysandum should be so related that

the analysans—the analyzing concept—conveys everything that is conveyed by the analysandum. Moreover, it should be logically impossible for anything to exemplify the one without also exemplifying the other. The latter point is sometimes put—somewhat incautiously —by saying that the analysans must be "identical with" the analysandum.

2) A good philosophical analysis must be an analysis that extends our knowledge. The analysans must be, in some sense, conceptually richer than the analysandum. Therefore, strictly speaking, the analysans cannot be identical with the analysandum.

3) The analysans must not be obtained merely by adding to or expanding on the analysandum. We would not be analyzing "man," for example, if we said that a "man" is a "man that is rational." This third condition may be put by saying that the analysis should not be circular. It might also be put by saying that the analysandum is in no sense a proper part of the analysans.

The problem is: how are we to fulfill all three conditions at once?

If the analysans and the analysandum are logically equivalent, as the first condition requires, then how is it possible for the analysans to be conceptually richer than the analysandum, as the second condition requires? How could the analysans contain anything that the analysandum does not contain? In short, how could the analysis be said to extend our knowledge?

Again, if the analysans is conceptually richer than the analysandum, as the second condition requires, then the analysans must contain everything that the analysandum does and something else as well. But, if this is so, then the analysans must somehow contain the analysandum as a proper part. How is this possible without violating the third condition—the condition that the analysis must not be circular?

It is tempting to view the problem as a problem about language. Yet the problem, as we have stated it, is not a problem about language. No considerations about language, so far as we know, have been sufficient to solve it.

The problem, we suggest, is a problem about those abstract objects that are *properties*, and certain elementary considerations about properties will enable us to solve it.

A Conception of Properties

In setting forth a theory of properties, we make use of the following undefined concepts: exemplification; de re necessity (as in "x is necessarily such that it exemplifies H"); conceiving; and attributing. Conceiving and attributing are intentional attitudes and both may take properties as their objects.

We will here understand a *property* as being anything that is capable of exemplification—anything that is possibly such that there is something that exemplifies it.

One property may be said, in the following sense, to *imply* another:

P implies Q =Df P is necessarily such that if it is exemplified then Q is exemplified.

The property "being a wife" may be said, in this sense, to imply the property "being a husband," and conversely. For each is necessarily such that, if it is exemplified, then the other is exemplified. But the thing that exemplifies the one is not identical with the thing that exemplifies the other.

We next introduce an important intentional relation that obtains between various properties: one property may be said to *involve* another.

P involves Q =Df P is necessarily such that whoever conceives it conceives Q.

The property of being *both* red *and* round *involves* the property of being round and it also *implies* the property of being round. The property of being *either* red *or* round also involves the property of being round (for one cannot conceive the property of being either red or round without conceiving the property of being round), but it does *not* imply the property of being round. So, too, for the property of being nonround: it involves but does not imply the property of being round. Thus many properties involve properties they do not imply.

And many properties imply properties they do not involve. "Being red," for example, implies—but does not involve—"being either red or round;" it also implies but does not involve the property of "being either round or nonround." We might describe the relationship between "being red" and "being either round or nonround" by saying that they are "entirely diverse in content" from one another. This is in virtue of the fact that the only properties that they both involve are "universal" (that is, properties that everything has, such as *being a thing*).

We shall single out the important relation of *Diversity in Content* by means of implication and involvement:

P is entirely different in content from Q =Df For any R, if P involves R and if Q involves R, then R is involved by every property; P does not involve Q, and Q does not involve P.

We add, finally, the following relation of property *entailment*. We define it by reference to *attribution* (as in "He attributes the property of wisdom to himself"):

P entails Q =Df P is necessarily such that whoever attributes it attributes Q.

For we assume that, if P entails Q, then P implies and inolves Q.[1]

The relations between properties that we have just described—implication, involvement, content-diversity, and entailment—have their analogues, obviously, for relations. The relevant distinctions may readily be extended to *propositions*. (The reference to exemplification in the definition of implication would be replaced by a reference to truth; and the reference to attribution in the definition of entailment would be replaced by a reference to believing.[2]

An Analysis of Analysis

Let us now consider, once again, the three desiderata that gave rise to our problem.

1) We said that the analysans must "convey everything that is conveyed by" the analysandum and also that the analysans and the analysandum must be "logically equivalent." We may now put this first condition precisely as follows:

If Q is analyzed by P, then P entails Q and Q implies P.

This requirement, that P entail Q and that Q imply P, insures that P conveys everything that Q conveys. It also insures that the analysans and the analysandum are logically equivalent; for it tells us that they imply each other and therefore that each is necessarily such that if it is exemplified then the other is exemplified.

2) We said that the analysans must be, in some sense, "conceptually richer" than the analysandum. We can now say what that sense is:

> If Q is analyzed by P, then P entails a nonuniversal property that
> is entirely diverse is content from Q.

We say "nonuniversal property," since the greater conceptual richness
of the analysans should pertain just to properties that are implied by
the analysandum and not to properties that *everything* has. Normally,
it would not improve an analysis to include in the analysans such
properties as "being either red or nonred" or "being such that there
are no round squares."

Thus, for example, "being a rational animal" entails "being rational," and "being rational" shares no nonuniversal content in common with "being a man." Hence the property, "being a rational
animal," is conceptually richer than the property, being a man.

"If 'being a rational animal' is conceptually richer than being a
man, then 'being an individual that is a rational animal' is conceptually
richer than 'being a rational animal.' But, surely, of the latter two
properties, the first cannot be said to be an analysis of the second."
The latter point is well taken, but what we have said does not imply
that being an individual that is a rational animal is an analysis of rational animal, or of man. For any such analysis would violate our third
condition—the one pertaining to "circularity."

3) We said that the analysis should not be "circular" and that the
analysans should not contain the analysandum "as a proper part.'
We can now say what this means.

The analysans entails and therefore involves the analysandum. But
the analysandum does not involve the analysans, inasmuch as the
analysans is conceptually richer than the analysandum. Let us say
that the analysans *properly involves* the analysandum. (We use
"properly involves" in analogy with "proper part"; if A properly
involves B, then A involves B but B does not involve A.)

In saying that the analysis should not be circular and that "no
proper part of it contains the analysandum," we mean this: although the analysans properly involves the analysandum, the analysandum does not properly involve anything that itself properly
involves the analysandum. Hence we may put our third point this
way:

> If Q is analyzed by P, then P does not properly involve anything
> that properly involves Q.

Thus "being an individual that is a rational animal" does not analyze "being a man," for it properly involves something—namely, "being a rational animal"—that properly involves "being a man."[3]

Our analysis, then, is this:

> Q is analyzed by P =Df (i) P entails Q, and Q implies P; (ii) P entails a property that is entirely diverse in content from Q; and (iii) P does not properly involve anything that properly involves Q.

We have restricted our formulation to those analyses wherein the analysans and the analysandum are properties. But what we have said is readily adaptable to those cases where the analysans and the analysandum are relations, or are propositions.

Thus Russell may be said to have analyzed the proposition, "The golden mountain exists," by reference to the following proposition: There is an x such that x is a mountain and x is golden; and for every y, if y is a mountain and y is golden, then y is identical with x. The analysans, unlike the analysandum, entails the relation "being identical with." (It should be noted that the relation "being identical with," unlike the relation "standing in some relation with," is *not* a universal relation; it is not a relation that is such that, for every x and y, it obtains between x and y.)

Solution to the Problem

We now return to the questions with which we began.

"If the analysans and the anaysandum are logically equivalent, then how is it possible for the analysans to be conceptually richer than the analysandum? What could the analysans contain that the analysandum does not?" The analysans is conceptually richer than the analysandum in that it entails—and therefore involves—something that the analysans does not involve.

"How is it possible for an analysis to extend our knowledge?" The analysis can extend our knowledge by exhibiting certain nonuniversal properties that are implied—but not involved—by the analysandum.

"If the analysans is conceptually richer than the analysandum but logically equivalent to it, then the analysans must contain everything the analysandum contains and something else as well. But if this is so, then the analysans must somehow contain the analysandum as a proper part. How is this possible without violating the third condition—the condition requiring that an analysis not be circular?" The analysans properly involves everything that the analysandum involves, including the analysandum itself. However, the analysandum is not a "mere" proper part of the analysans. Even though the analysans involves the analysandum and "something else as well," the analysans is not "composed" of the analysandum in combination with some other of its "proper parts;" for the analysans does not properly involve anything that properly involves the analysandum.

We also asked about the meaning of the word "is" in such definitions as "Man is a rational animal" and "A cube is a regular solid with six equal square sides." The answer is that it refers to that relation that obtains between two properties, P and Q, when Q may be said to be analyzed by P. Hence the definitions might be put more clearly by saying: "'Being a man' is analyzed by 'being a rational animal'," and "'Being a cube' is analyzed by 'being a regular solid with six equal square sides'."

Part III

Chapter 10

Theory of Knowledge in America

Introduction

Most of the problems and issues constituting the "theory of knowledge" were discussed in detail by Plato and Aristotle and by the Greek skeptics. There is some justification, I am afraid, for saying that the subject has made very little progress in the past two thousand years. Perhaps it is unreasonable, therefore, to expect much to have happened within a thirty-year period in twentieth-century America.

In the late 1920s and early 1930s—the beginning of the period with which this study is concerned—the principal emphasis in American epistemology was metaphysical or cosmological. The problem was that of the status of "appearances" and the controversy concerned the two basic theses of "dualism." These theses, which received their classic statement in A. O. Lovejoy's *The Revolt Against Dualism* (1930), were, first, that our knowledge of reality is derived from the inspection of the "appearances" of reality and, second, that "appearances" are mental entities composed of a different metaphysical stuff from that of physical objects.

The "revolt against dualism," which had taken many forms, became the attempt to reconcile the first of the two dualistic theses with the denial of the second. This involved constructing metaphysical systems in which "appearances" were treated as a part of the stuff of physical reality. In C. A. Strong's *Essays on the Natural Origin of Mind* (1930), physical objects were said to have a "double aspect," one aspect of which was made up of appearances; in Roy Wood Sellars' *The Philosophy of Physical Realism* (1932), physical objects were said to have sensible appearances as their "qualitative dimensions," or, as some put it, as their "metaphysical insides"; and in the "objective relativism" of Arthur Murphy and the "perspective realism" of E. B. McGilvary, the *ways* in which physical objects appear were taken to be a kind of constituent of the objects themselves. "Objective realism" and "perspective realism" had been influenced by similar views, developed in the 1920s by the British philosophers Samuel Alexander and A. N. Whitehead, and also suggested in John Dewey's *Experience and Nature* (1925). Perhaps the last great work of this phase of American epistemology was George Santayana's *The Realms of Being*, first published as a single volume in 1942; Santayana's epistemology was a version of "dualism." But by the end of the 1930s the live issues in epistemology had changed.

The change of interest was due, in part, to "logical positivism," or "logical empiricism," an approach to philosophy generally associated with the Vienna Circle of the late 1920s. The members of the original circle were logicians and philosophers of science who hoped to make philosophical use of the techniques of mathematical logic. The philosophical work of the "logical positivists" was partly constructive and partly destructive. The constructive work was done in mathematical logic, in the logic of probability and confirmation, and in the attempt to describe what an adequate "language of science" would be. Most of this work was not primarily epistemological and hence does not fall within our survey, but it bore on epistemology in various places. Discussions of probability and confirmation, for example, presupposed the concept of *evidence*, or that of a proposition or statement being *evident*; what little that has been said, in these discussions, about the concept of evidence seems to me to be inadequate, but it has served to bring this essentially epistemological concept into clear focus. Investigations of what would constitute an adequate "language of science" touched on the first of the two theses of "dualism" noted above, on the thesis that our knowledge of reality is derived from the inspection of the "appearances" of reality. The status of "the given"—including the "appearances" thought by many to be at the basis of the "edifice of knowledge"—became one of the dominant epistemological questions of the late 1930s and early 1940s. "Logical empiricists" touched on other epistemological questions in discussions of the place of psychology, or "behavioristics," in the system of sciences.

The destructive side of "logical empiricism"—an attempt to dismiss the traditional questions of philosophy as deriving from statements that are "meaningless" or that "make no sense"—is of much less significance, it seems to me. There are now indications that the metaphysical discussion of the late 1920s and early 1930s is being resumed—for example, in recent discussions of the "physical status" of sensations—and that these discussions will be characterized by the clarity, precision, and objectivity typical of the constructive writings of "logical empiricism."

Among the American philosophers who have come to be known as "logical empiricists," some but not all of whom were associated with the original Vienna Circle, are Gustav Bergmann, Rudolf Carnap, Herbert Feigl, C. G. Hempel, and the late Hans Reichenbach. Philosophers having similar interests, but not properly called "logical empiricists," are Nelson Goodman, Ernest Nagel, W. V. Quine, and Wilfrid Sellars. The writings of these philosophers are not primarily concerned with the theory of knowledge. Indeed, not many American philosophers, during the period of this survey, have thought of themselves as being primarily epistemologists, or specialists in the theory of knowledge. Most of the important contributions to the subject have come from philosophers specializing in other areas—in logic, in the philosophy of language, in the philosophy of science, and in metaphysics—and most of these contributions have appeared in works that are concerned with these other areas and that only touch on the theory of knowledge.

The dominant influence in the 1940s and early 1950s came to be the later philosophy of Ludwig Wittgenstein and the writings of Gilbert Ryle, J. L. Austin, and other philosophers teaching at Oxford. Wittgenstein, whose *Tractatus logico-philosophicus* (1922) is one of the most important philosophical writings of the present century, later developed quite different views that, for a while, he preferred not to publish. These views, which were thought to be revolutionary, were first made known to American philosophers through copies of his lectures; through the writings of Max Black, Alice Ambrose Lazerowitz, Morris Lazerowitz, Norman Malcolm, and others; and after 1953 through the publication of Wittgenstein's own work. These writings and those of the Oxford philosophers have made philosophers sensitive to language and have served to sharpen and clarify many philosophical questions. But, if I am not mistaken, they have also led some philosophers to exaggerate the relevance of linguistic facts to philosophy.

"Idealism" and "neo-Kantianism" are represented in the works of Brand Blanshard, W. H. Werkmeister, and others. "Thomistic realism" is represented in John Wild's *Introduction to Realistic Philosophy* (1948), in writings of the members of the Association for Realistic Philosophy, and in the manuals on epistemology that are used in many Catholic universities. There is considerable literature by American philosophers on "phenomenology," "existentialism," and "existential psychiatry," but, as I interpret these works, they are not strictly relevant to the traditional questions of epistemology.

The "pragmatic" tradition in American philosophy persisted through this period, most notably in the writings of John Dewey. Dewey disclaimed being an epistemologist and most of his philosophical work was concerned with what others would call "philosophical anthropology." There are many who believe, however, that his views about human knowledge are relevant to the traditional questions of epistemology. In what follows I shall note where these views do seem to me to be relevant and important. "Pragmatism" is also represented, but only to a limited extent, in the writings of C. I. Lewis, whose first contributions to philosophy were in the field of modal logic. The important "pragmatic" element in his philosophy is his view of the cognitive function of "appearances" and their relation to action. Lewis's *An Analysis of Knowledge and Valuation* (1946) combines the clarity and precision of the positivistic writings with what I believe to be a proper respect for the problems of traditional philosophy.

This essay is itself offered as a contribution to the theory of knowledge, for I have attempted to justify my appraisals of the various works and views I have mentioned. The reader who is not familiar with contemporary philosophy should be told that, for almost every judgment I make here, there is some competent philosopher who would disagree with it, and that any other philosopher would probably discuss works quite different from those that I discuss.

In the first section of this chapter, on "the problem of skepticism," I shall attempt to present one of the basic problems of the theory of knowledge, one may well be incapable of solution; many of the views I shall consider in subsequent chapters can be understood only in terms of this problem. In the second section, on the "myth of the given," I shall consider the controversies about the "basis" of our knowledge; in the third section I shall consider what American philosophers have said about "reason and a priori knowledge"; and in the final section, I shall consider the problem of the relation of "appearances" to our knowledge of reality.

The Problem of Skepticism

1

Two of the traditional questions of the theory of knowledge, or epistemology, have been *"What* do we know?" and "How are we to decide *whether* we know?" The former question may also be put as "What is the *extent* of our knowledge?" and the latter as "What are the *criteria* of knowing?" If we happen to know the answer to either one of these questions, then we can set out to answer the other. If we can specify the *criteria* of knowledge and thus have a procedure for deciding whether we know, we may then be able to decide the extent of our knowledge. Or if we happen to know the *extent* of our knowledge and thus know what the things are that we know, we may then be able to formulate criteria enabling us to mark off the things we do know from those we do not. But if we do not have the answer to the first question, then, it would seem, we cannot determine the answer to the second, and if we do not have the answer to the second, then, it would seem, we cannot determine the answer to the first.

It is characteristic of "empiricism," as a philosophical tradition, to assume that we have certain criteria of evidence, or that we can identify a certain "source" of our knowledge, and then to apply these criteria, or to refer to this source, and thus determine what it is that we can know. It is characteristic of "commonsensism," as an alternative philosophical tradition, to assume that we do know, pretty much, those things that we think we know, and then, having identified this knowledge, to trace it back to its sources and formulate criteria that will set it off from those things that we do not know. And it is characteristic of "skepticism" *not* to assume either that we know or that we have any criteria of evidence. Each of these traditions has been represented in recent American philosophy.

The philosophers with whom we are here concerned have found it difficult to agree about these questions or even to understand each other. The reasons are, in part, that the fundamental questions of epistemology have been approached, as it were, from three different directions; one and the same philosopher may approach one area of knowledge (say, "our knowledge of the external world") from the first of these three points of view, another area (say, logic and mathematics) from the second, and still another (say, ethics) from the third; and many philosophers seem to realize that the approach they take to some of these questions may differ, not only from that which certain other philosophers take to these same questions, but also from that which they themselves take to other questions of a very similar sort.

2

A typical way of answering the second question — "How are we to decide *whether* we know?" — is to refer to the "sources" of our knowledge and say that an ostensible item of knowledge is genuine if and only if it is the product of a properly accredited source. It is traditional to say that there are four such sources:

1) Perception, by means of the external sense organs;
2) Memory;
3) "Inner consciousness," or the apprehension of our own states of mind — for example, our awareness of our own sensations, of our beliefs and desires, of how we feel, of what we are undertaking to do;
4) Reason, as the source of our a priori knowledge of necessity — our knowledge, for example, of some of the truths of logic and mathematics.

The first three sources on the list are sometimes grouped together and called simply "experience"; hence those who believe that our knowledge is restricted to whatever is yielded by these four sources say that our knowledge is "the product of reason and experience."

But if we are concerned with the question "How are we to decide whether we know?" we can hardly be satisfied with the answer that an ostensible item of knowledge is genuine if and only if it is the product of a properly accredited source of knowledge. For we are now led to ask "How are we to decide whether an ostensible source of knowledge *is* properly accredited?" and "How are we to decide just *what* it is that is yielded by a properly accredited source?"

We will best understand these questions if we recall that, according to some, there are three *additional* sources of knowing, other than reason and experience. These are:

5) "Moral consciousness";
6) "Intuitive understanding"; and
7) "Religious consciousness."

Among the things we know (according to philosophers who appeal to these additional sources) are certain facts about ethics, about human society and "other minds," and about God or "the Holy." It is controversial whether any such knowledge is yielded by (1), (2), (3), or (4); hence some of those who believe we do know such facts deduce that there are (5), (6), and (7). Those who are skeptical with respect to the type of fact in question deny that there *are* these additional sources of knowledge. Hence we arrive at the question "How are we to decide whether an ostensible source of knowledge is a source of knowledge?"

Some of those who believe that we do have knowledge about these controversial subjects—ethics, other minds and society, and God—*also* believe that there are no "sources of knowing" in addition to experience and reason, i.e., in addition to (1), (2), (3), and (4). And those who are more skeptical believe that experience and reason do not yield the kind of knowledge that is claimed. Hence we arrive at the question "How are we to decide what it is that we know by means of experience and reason?"

3

Some of the moral philosophers who believe that our sources of knowledge include a "moral consciousness" have reasoned in essentially this way: (P) We do have ethical knowledge; for example, we know that mercy is good and ingratitude is bad, whatever their consequences; but (Q) reason and experience do not yield such knowledge; hence (R) there is a source of knowledge in addition to reason and experience. The reasoning of such philosophers, who have been called "moral intuitionists," may be contrasted with that of certain other philosophers who believe that we have no strictly ethical knowledge and who may therefore be called "moral skeptics." The moral skeptic argues: (Not-R) There is no source of knowledge other than reason and experience; (Q) reason and experience do not yield any strictly ethical knowledge; therefore (not-P) we do not have such knowledge. The intuitionist and the skeptic thus agree with respect to the second premise; the intuitionist takes as his first premise the contradictory of the skeptic's conclusion; and the skeptic takes as *his* first premise the contradictory of the intuitionists's conclusion.

The moral intuitionist may also be called a "moral cognitivist." But it is essential to note that there are moral cognitivists of a somewhat different sort—essential because the distinction will throw light on the epistemological controversies to which our first four "sources" of knowledge give rise. This second type of cognitivist is like the skeptic in that he is *not* liberal with respect to what he will count as a proper source of knowledge; he will say with the skeptic that, for his part, he cannot find the moral intuitions to which the intuitionist appeals. But this second type of cognitivist is unlike the skeptic in that he *is* liberal with respect to what he will count as the legitimate product of a proper source of knowledge. Oversimplifying slightly, we may put his argument as follows: "Whatever we know we know through experience and reason; we know that certain things are morally good and other things morally bad; the only experience that could yield such knowledge is our experience of moral feelings, e.g., of moral approval and disapproval; hence the experience of these moral feelings yields knowledge of what is morally good and morally bad." (This point of view is typical of "value theory" in the Austrian tradition, where our feeling for what is valuable, *das Wertgefühl*, is said to be something we know by means of our "inner consciousness" and to be the source of our knowledge of values.) The skeptic replies, of course, by saying that we do not have such moral knowledge, or knowledge of values, and that the moral cognitivist of our second sort has mistaken certain facts about his own state of mind for a knowledge of ethical truths.

The dispute between the skeptic and the cognitivist of the second sort is thus a dispute, not about the "sources of knowing," but about criteria of evidence; the cognitivist holds that our moral feelings justify us in believing something about the presence of value, or of good or evil; and the skeptic believes that they do not. (It is unfortunate that, in contemporary writings on ethics, the term "intuitionism" is used to designate both types of moral cognitivism. It would be more correctly used to designate only cognitivism of the first type, for some of the objections that hold of the first—e.g., the objection that such "intuitions" are not to be found—do not apply to the second.) The pattern of these disputes, as we shall see, is repeated in many different areas of epistemology.

The problem of religious knowledge, as many conceive it, is similar in essential respects to that of ethical knowledge. George Burch, who has seen the problem clearly, has recently written: "There are three coordinate sources of ordinary knowledge—reason, experience, and revelation. . . . Reason discloses relations among ideas and so shows what conclusions follow from presmises already accepted. Experience, including perception and introspection, discloses the existence of those processes which we actually observe: Revelation, at the minimum, teaches the existence of the substantial deity which is the reality of the world and the substantial self which is the reality of the individual. . . . Experience has illusions, reason has fallacies, and faith has heresies. These errors can be corrected only within the faculty concerned."[1] Thus Burch argues: (P) Some people have metaphysical knowledge about God and the self; but (Q) such knowledge is not yielded by, or significantly confirmed by, reason or experience; hence (R) there is a source of knowledge—revelation—in addition to reason and experience. The "positivists" whom he criticizes argue, on the contrary: (Not-R) Reason and experience are the only sources of knowledge that there are; (Q) reason and experience do not supply, or significantly confirm, any information about God and the self; hence (not-P) no one has metaphysical knowledge about God and the self. The pattern of the argument is like that of the first argument over moral cognitivism: Burch and the positivist agree with respect to the second premise; Burch takes as his first premise the negation of the positivist's conclusion; and the positivist takes as *his* first premise the negation of Burch's conclusion.

But Burch also allows for the possibility of "religious cognitivism" of a second sort—parallel to our second type of moral cognitivism.

The source of revelation is an obscure problem. Quakers believe that God speaks directly to individuals; Protestants and Moslems, that revelation is given once for all in the inspired scripture; Catholics, that it is given continuously in the living Church; Hindus, that it exists eternally in the Veda. The most naturalistic theory is that it has its source in the insight of mystics, men who have abnormal cognitive powers transcending both reason and perception, and who give to the rest of us verbal reports of these ineffable visions, reports which we are then free either to believe or disbelieve. Or it may be that revelation has no origin, but is handed down from an infinite regress of teachers, without any beginning. Ignorance of its source, however, does not affect our knowledge of its existence; we do not deny the moon's existence because we do not know where it came from.[2]

The controversies to which some of these possibilities gave rise are like those of the second type of moral cognitivism we have considered, for they concern criteria of evidence. The religious cognitivist holds that certain facts of common experience are an indication that we know certain truths about religious matters, and the skeptic holds that they are not.

Of the three areas of skeptical controversy that we noted above—our ostensible knowledge of ethics, of religious truths, and of certain social and psychological facts—the third differs in one important respect from the other two. Although we find moral and religious cognitivists of two sorts—the first appealing to "sources" of knowing beyond reason and experience and the second confining themselves to reason and experience but appealing to special criteria of evidence—I think we find only the latter type of cognitivist in the third area. Wilhelm Dilthey and his followers have spoken of *Verstehen* as a "source" of our knowledge of certain psychological and social facts. But this *Verstehen*, or intuitive understanding, is not something unfamiliar to those who are skeptical about such facts; it is a feeling that is said to be familiar to everyone. The social cognitivist believes that the presence of this feeling is an indication of certain facts about societies and "other minds," and the skeptic believes that it is not.

Maurice Mandelbaum has recently defended this type of social cognitivism. He argues, not implausibly, that the knowledge that most of us have of social facts (e.g., the fact that Mr. Jones has overdrawn his account at the bank) cannot be completely expressed in terms of those physical facts that we are ordinarily thought to perceive by means of the external senses. To those who would object that our experience does not yield any knowledge of "societal facts" and who are thus skeptical about such facts on the basis of a particular theory of knowledge, Mandelbaum replies: "Since those who would hold this theory of knowledge would presumably wish to show that we can be said to know something of the nature of human societies, and since they would also wish to hold that our means of gaining this knowledge is through the observation of the repeated patterns of activities of individuals, a proof that their theory of knowledge cannot account for our apprehensions of the nature of individual action is, in the present context, a sufficient disproof of the epistemological type of objection."[3]

We encounter similar controversies in connection with the knowledge that is sometimes attributed to "reason"—number (4) in our list. The "rationalists" of the seventeenth and eighteenth centuries emphasized "reason" as the most important of our sources of knowledge, but philosophers in the "empirical" tradition have tried, in various ways, to show that there is *no* such source of knowledge. Knowledge of metaphysics, as well as of logic and mathematics, has been attributed to reason. Most of those who now reject reason as a possible source of knowledge also deny that we have the kind of knowledge of metaphysics that has been attributed to this source; but instead of denying that we have the knowledge of logic and mathematics that has traditionally been attributed to reason, they attribute this knowledge to some one or another of the other sources listed here. John Stuart Mill tried to show that our knowledge of logic and mathematics is derived by induction from the perception of external things, and he might be interpreted therefore as reducing (4) to (1). Theodore Lipps proposed, in 1880, that "logic is either the physics of thought or nothing at all" and tried to show that the truths of logic are in fact truths about the ways in which people think; the logical statement "If no Greeks are Romans, then no Romans are Greeks" tells us, really, that whoever believes that no Greeks are Romans cannot help believing also that no Romans are Greeks.[4] This "psychologistic" conception of the truths of logic, if it were tenable, would reduce "reason," as a source of knowledge, to our "inner consciousness"—i.e., reduce (4) to (3). Other philosophers proposed a modified "psychologistic" view, according to which the truths of logic and mathematics concern, not the ways in which people *do* think, but the ways in which they *ought* to think. On one interpretation, this modified view could be said to reduce "reason" to our "moral consciousness"—reducing (4) this time to (6)—and moral skepticism would then imply skepticism concerning logic and mathematics.

In recent years, "psychologism," as a view about the subject matter of logic and mathematics, has been replaced by a parallel view, which might be called "linguisticism." This view attempts to construe the statements of logic and mathematics as expressing certain facts about language, and hence might be thought to reduce (4) to (1), (2), and (3), or to some subclass of these. But the "rationalist" may say, as the American logician Alonzo Church has said: "The preference of (say) *seeing* over *understanding* as a method of observation seems to me capricious. For just as an opaque body may be seen, so a concept may be understood or grasped."[5]

The linguistic conception of logic and mathematics, like the "psychologistic" one, may seem also to have an ethical form; for the statements of logic and mathematics have also been associated with "rules" of language and hence might be thought to tell us something about the way in which words *ought* to be used. If this view could be taken literally and were true, then (4) would be reduced, again, to (6); but I believe the view cannot be taken this way and, as it happens, many of the philosophers who have accepted it have also been ethical skeptics. I shall consider some of the details of these questions in Section 3.

4

In discussing the issues of recent American epistemology, I shall assume, with respect to certain beliefs falling within the first four categories on our list, that we are justified in thinking they are instances of knowing; or, what comes to the same thing, I shall assume, with respect to these beliefs, that we have *adequate evidence* for them, or, better, that these beliefs pertain to what is evident. Then, given this assumption, I shall go on to ask certain further questions about the nature of this justification, or evidence.

The man who is more skeptical than we are will feel that we are assuming too much, and the man who is more credulous, that we are assuming too little. The skeptic may say, for example, "You should *not* assume that we have adequate evidence for any belief about the past" and the credulous man may say "You *should* assume that we have adequate evidence for certain beliefs about the relations between God and man." Perhaps we can show the skeptic that certain principles he himself accepts imply that we *do* have adequate evidence for some of our beliefs about the past; and perhaps we can show the credulous man that certain principles that *he* accepts imply that we do *not* have adequate evidence for any beliefs about the relations between God and man. But if we cannot show the skeptic and the credulous man that they themselves have beliefs that imply that our assumptions are true, then we can only be dogmatic and say "We do have evidence for this, and we do not have evidence for that." But the skeptic and the credulous man may be equally dogmatic in their replies. To understand the issues of epistemology, it is essential to realize that there is no way of evaluating these conflicting dogmas until we have made certain assumptions concerning what it is that we know, or what it is that we are justified in thinking we know.

If two philosophers happen to make the same assumption concerning what we are justified in thinking that we know, and if they also find themselves accepting common principles of justification, then they may be able to agree about other things that we can, or cannot, know. If they do not share any assumptions or principles, they may yet be able to agree concerning what each of them, given his own assumptions and principles, is justified in thinking that he knows; but there will be no way to reach an agreement concerning these assumptions or principles themselves. Here, then, we have a typically philosophical predicament.

Philosophers have come to realize—largely as a result of the work of G. E. Moore and Ludwig Wittgenstein—that many of their apparent disagreements are a result of linguistic difficulties, and some have attempted to trace the present predicament to a similar source. Occasionally we can deal with the skeptic merely by correcting his language. One such case of this, in recent American philosophy, is Paul Edwards' treatment of Bertrand Russell's doubts about induction.[6] Somewhat oversimplified, the situation was this: Russell had said that we have no good evidence for any of our beliefs about the future; Edwards pointed out, first, that Russell was using the words "we have no good evidence for any of our beliefs about the future" to mean *merely* that none of our beliefs about the future can be logically deduced from any of our beliefs about the past; he pointed out, second, that Russell's use of these words was hardly their ordinary use, and that when we put in a more correct way what it was that Russell was telling us, we see that his view is not a form of skepticism at all. Perhaps there are credulous men whose statements can be treated similarly: when they say "We have good evidence for believing that certain relations hold between God and man" they *may* mean merely that such beliefs are essential to a certain kind of peace of mind; and in such a case, perhaps, they do not disagree with us at all. But this way of resolving our ostensible disagreements is available only when the disagreements *are* thus verbal ones; if the skeptic, or the credulous man, happens to mean what we mean by "evidence," "knowledge," and "justification," we are still in our predicament. (The importance of "correcting" the language of philosophers was, for a time, exaggerated, it seems to me. Norman Malcolm wrote, in 1942, that "any philosophical statement which violates ordinary language is false."[7] But it should be noted, concerning the example of Russell's supposed skepticism, above, that when Russell's statements, purporting to express doubts about the future, were "corrected" and translated into ordinary language, we learned that what he had been saying, incorrectly, was *true*, not false.)

There have been other "linguistic" attempts to deal with our predicament. One of these—aimed at the philosopher who professes to be skeptical about the existence of material things—may be put as follows. There are linguistic expressions, among them the expression "material thing," that we can understand only because we are acquainted with certain paradigm cases of their correct use; one cannot understand "material thing" unless one has been *shown* a material thing. Hence, from the fact that the expression "material thing" has a correct use, it follows that there are material things.[8] Or, somewhat more precisely: (1) Many people, both skeptics and nonskeptics, understand and are able to use correctly the expression "material thing"; but (2) the meaning and use of this expression could not have been explained to these people in terms merely of other expressions; hence (3) the people could not have learned the meaning and use of the expression unless they had been confronted with instances of what it denotes or truly applies to—i.e., unless they were confronted with some material things; and therefore (4) there are material things.

The weakest point of the argument, obviously, is the step from (2) to (3). For the skeptic—even if he has conceded (1) and (2) —has only to point out that people could learn the meaning and correct use of the expression "material thing" by being shown instances of what, as it happens, they *mistakenly*, though perhaps quite reasonably, *believe* to be material things. (Just as a man might learn the meaning of the word "rabbit" by being shown a toy that he mistakenly believes to be alive.) But if (3) is a non sequitur, then the conclusion (4) has not been established.

Other versions of this argument, which in some of its forms has come to be known as the "paradigm case argument" have been applied in other areas of recent philosophy.[9]

5

In the 1930s, and for a while after, it was thought that a certain doctrine about what kinds of statements are "meaningless," or "make no sense," would help us in dealing with some aspects of the kind of epistemological predicament we have been considering. But, I think, the doctrine itself involved a similar predicament.

During the writing of the *Principles of Mathematics* (1903), Bertrand Russell discovered the following logical paradox. Suppose W is the class of all those classes that are not members of themselves; then the statement "W is *not* a member of itself" implies "W is a member of itself," and "W is a member of itself" implies "W is not a member of itself." To enable logic to escape this and similar paradoxes, Russell proposed the "theory of types." This theory, which was incorporated into Russell and Whitehead's *Principia mathematica*, implied, among other things, that some of the sentences giving rise to the paradoxes belong to a class of sentences that are "meaningless"— in a sense of the term "meaningless" that implies that a "meaningless" sentence is neither true nor false. If a sentence can be shown thus to be "meaningless," then the theoretical difficulties that would be involved in supposing it to be true, or in supposing it to be false, need not be faced. And this suggests the possibility of setting aside many of the traditional problems of philosophy—if we can show that the philosophically puzzling sentences that give rise to these problems are "meaningless," in the present technical sense of the term. But how are we to show, with respect to sentences that sophisticated people think they understand, that the sentences are neither true or false?

One answer to this question had been proposed by Charles Saunders Peirce in an article entitled "How to Make Our Ideas Clear," which first appeared in the *Popular Science Monthly* in 1878—an article that, according to William James, constituted the beginning of "pragmatism" in American philosophy.[10] "Our idea of anything," Peirce said, "is our idea of its sensible effects." Hence to ascertain the meaning, for us, of any particular concept, we have only to apply the following maxim: "Consider what effects, that might conceivably have practical bearings, we conceive the object of our conception to have. Then our conception of these effects is the whole of our conception of the object." If a sentence, purporting to express some concept, tells us nothing about any possible experience, then the sentence does not really express any concept at all. To talk of something, for example, "as having all the sensible characters of wine, yet being in reality blood, is senseless jargon."

This doctrine was set forth in somewhat more precise terms in the 1929 manifesto of the Vienna Circle and defended in various forms by subsequent "logical positivists," or "logical empiricists."[11] The "verifiability theory of meaning," as the doctrine came to be called, was essentially this: (1) the more puzzling sentences of traditional philosophy differ from the sentences of the empirical sciences in that the latter but not the former are *verifiable*; and (2) a sentence (other than one expressing a truth or a falsehood of logic or mathematics) is *meaningful*, and therefore either true or false, if and only if it is *verifiable*. Some philosophers objected that (2) was arbitrary, as of course it was, and that it was implausible.[12] Others noted that the criteria of *verifiability* that had been offered did not in fact preserve the truth of (1): on some of the criteria, the sentences, neither of philosophy nor of the physical sciences, could be counted as verifiable; on others, the sentences *both* of philosophy and the sciences could be counted as verifiable. Which sentences, moreover, *are* sentences of "science"? Some philosophers had hoped to count, among the sentences that are meaningless, those expressing "the neo-vitalist speculations about entelechies or vital forces" and "the 'telefinalist hypothesis' proposed by Lecomte du Nöuy" and hence it was essential to say that these are not sentences of science.[13] But those scientists — or those people believing themselves to be scientists — who accepted such sentences preferred to say that the sentences *are* sentences of science; and hence that if there is a sense in which their sentences are "unverifiable," then there is a sense in which some of the sentences of science are "unverifiable."

The kind of predicament we have encountered in connection with skepticism and its alternatives has its analogues, then, when we attempt to answer such questions as "What sentences are meaningless?" and "What sentences are sentences of science?" (The questions "What sentences are descriptive?" "What sentences are factual?" and "What sentences are capable of being settled by recourse to empirical matters of fact?" involve a similar predicament.) This fact and, more generally, the kind of answer that was available to the question "What reason is there for believing that the sentences of traditional philosophy are neither true nor false?" suggested to many that problems of philosophy could not be so easily set aside.

Other philosophers, influenced by Wittgenstein, believe that certain facts about our language — about how it is acquired and taught and about the ways in which it is ordinarily used — *do* indicate that certain philosophical sentences "make no sense" and hence that some of the problems that these sentences are used to express can be dealt with by reference to linguistic considerations. Here, too, there is a conflict of approaches that seems incapable of being resolved. One philosopher may assume, concerning certain troublesome philosophical sentences, that enough is now known about language for us to infer, from linguistic facts, that the troublesome sentences are neither true nor false and hence that they are not really understood. Another philosopher may assume that not enough is yet known about language to warrant such inferences and that, since the sentences *are* understood and are either true or false, any theory of language implies that they are not is, ipso facto, inadequate.

An interesting example of the first approach is Norman Malcolm's *Dreaming* (Humanities, 1959). Most philosophers, from Aristotle on, have assumed that dreams are "the activity of the mind during sleep" —that is to say, that thinking, judging, fearing, desiring, and the other activities commonly called "mental" take place during our dreams just as they do during our waking life. This view seems obvious enough (consider "In my dream last night I remembered that I had promised to meet you today"), but if we could show it to be false, we could simplify the work both of the theory of knowledge and of the philosophy of mind. The point of Malcolm's book is to show, by reference to certain facts about language, that the view is not only false but "unintelligible" as well.

Malcolm claimed to offer "a proof that thinking in sleep, reasoning in sleep, imagining in sleep, and so on, are all unintelligible notions," a proof that woul also apply, mutatis mutandis, to judging in sleep, to having imagery in sleep, and to feeling emotions such as fear, joy, and anxiety in sleep (p. 45). To illustrate this approach to the problems of philosophy, I shall set forth in a series of separate steps what I take to be Malcolm's proof that judging in sleep is an "unintelligible concept." It should be noted, however, that he does not set forth his reasoning in this explicit fashion and that there is a problem of interpretation concerning what I shall list as the second step of the proof.

The argument, then, seems to be this: (1) It is theoretically impossible for me, or for anyone else, to find out, or to verify, that "the state of myself that I claim to describe by the sentence 'I am asleep' really is the state of being asleep." (2) No one can understand a sentence unless, for the most part, when she utters the sentence what she says is true. Hence (3) no one can understand the sentence "I am asleep" unless "for the most part when she says 'I am asleep' what she says is true." And therefore (4) it is theoretically impossible for anyone to verify the sentence "I am asleep." But (5) if it is theoretically impossible for anyone to verify a given sentence, then that sentence is "without sense and necessarily so." Therefore (6) the sentence "I am asleep" is without sense and necessarily so. Hence (7) the notion of a person judging that she is asleep is absurd. But (8) if it is absurd to speak of a sleeping person judging that she is asleep, then it is also absurd to speak of her making any *other* judgment in her sleep. And therefore (9) judging in sleep is an unintelligible concept.

A similar argument may be applied in the case of those other mental activities that we ordinarily suppose, sometimes take place while we dream.[14]

I have presented the argument in such a way that the conclusion does follow from the premises. Premises (2), (5), and (8) are, of course, the ones that are controversial. In defense of (2), or of something like (2), Malcolm says: "In order for the sentence to have a *correct* use, one would sometimes have to say it when the thing one said was true. . . . You would have no right to say that someone understood the sentence 'He is asleep' unless, for the most part, when he applied those words to some person that person was induced asleep. The same thing would have to hold for the sentence 'I am asleep'" (pp. 36, 10). He also refers to a passage in Wittgenstein's *Philosophical Investigations* that he interprets as saying something similar.[15] Yet Malcolm does not quite commit himself to (2), and it may be doubted whether he would wish to. For (2) implies, implausibly, that no one can understand the sentences "There are people on the moon," "Nixon was President of the United States," and "I am sitting perfectly still."[16] Some version of (2), however, is required in order to justify (3) and therefore (9), but it is extraordinarily difficult to imagine how such a premise might itself be justified. Even if such a premise *could* be found and justified, we could still avoid the implausible conclusion of the argument merely by rejecting (8), or by rejecting that version of the "verifiability theory of meaning" that survives in (5). And this takes us back to the kind of predicament with which we began.

The Myth of the Given

1

The doctrine of "the given" involved two theses about our knowledge. We may introduce them by means of a traditional metaphor:

A) The knowledge that a person has at any time is a structure or edifice, many parts and stages of which help to support each other, but which as a whole is supported by its own foundation.

The second thesis is a specification of the first:

B) The foundation of one's knowledge consists (at least in part) of the apprehension of what have been called, variously, "sensations," "sense-impressions," "appearances," "sensa," "sense-qualia," and "phenomena."

These phenomenal entities, said to be at the base of the structure of knowledge, are what was called "the given." A third thesis is sometimes associated with the doctrine of the given, but the first two theses do not imply it. We may formulate it in terms of the same metaphor.

C) The *only* apprehension that is thus basic to the structure of knowledge is our apprehension of "appearances" (etc.)—our apprehension of the given.

Theses (A) and (B) constitute the "doctrine of the given"; thesis (C), if a label were necessary, might be called "the phenomenalistic version" of the doctrine. The first two theses are essential to the empirical tradition in Western philosophy. The third is problematic for traditional empiricism and depends in part, but only in part, on the way in which the metaphor of the edifice and its foundation is defined and elaborated.

I believe it is accurate to say that, at the time at which our study begins, most American epistemologists accepted the first two theses and thus accepted the doctrine of the given. The expression "the given" became a term of contemporary philosophical vocabulary partly because of its use by C. I. Lewis in his *Mind and the World-Order* (Scribner, 1929). Many of the philosophers who accepted the doctrine avoided the expression because of its association with other more controversial parts of Lewis's book—a book that might be taken (though mistakenly, I think) also to endorse thesis (C), the "phenomenalistic version" of the doctrine. The doctrine itself—theses (A) and (B)—became a matter of general controversy during the period of our survey.

Thesis (A) was criticized as being "absolute" and thesis (B) as being overly "subjective." Both criticisms may be found in some of the "instrumentalistic" writings of John Dewey and philosophers associated with him. They may also be found in the writings of those philosophers of science ("logical empiricists") writing in the tradition of the Vienna Circle. (At an early stage of this tradition, however, some of these same philosophers seem to have accepted all three theses.)

Discussion became entangled in verbal confusions—especially in connection with the uses of such terms as "doubt," "certainty," "appearance," and "immediate experience." Philosophers, influenced by the work that Ludwig Wittgenstein had been doing in the 1930s, noted such confusions in detail, and some of them seem to have taken the existence of such confusions to indicate that (A) and (B) are false.[17] Many have rejected both theses as being inconsistent with a certain theory of thought and reference; among them, in addition to some of the critics just referred to, we find philosophers in the tradition of nineteenth century "idealism."

Philosophers of widely diverging schools now believe that "the myth of the given" has finally been dispelled.[18] I suggest, however, that, although thesis (C), "the phenomenalistic version," is false, the two theses, (A) and (B), that constitute the doctrine of the given are true.

The doctrine is not merely the consequence of a metaphor. We are led to it when we attempt to answer certain questions about *justification*—our justification for supposing, in connection with any one of the things that we know to be true, that it is something that we know to be true.

2

To the question "What justification do I have for thinking I know that *a* is true?" one may reply: "I know that *b* is true, and if I know that *b* is true then I also know that *a* is true." And to the question "What justification do I have for thinking I know that *b* is true?" one may reply: "I know that *c* is true, and if I know that *c* is true then I also know that *b* is true." Are we thus led, sooner or later, to something *n* of which one may say: "What justifies me in thinking I know that *n* is true is simply that *n* is true." If there is such an *n*, then the belief or statement that *n* is true may be thought of either as a belief or statement that "justifies itself" or as a belief or statement that is itself "neither justified nor unjustified." The distinction—unlike that between a Prime Mover that moves itself and a Prime Mover that is neither in motion nor at rest—is largely a verbal one; the essential thing, if there is such an *n*, is that it provides a stopping place in the process, or dialectic, of justification.

We may now reexpress, somewhat less metaphorically, the two theses I have called the "doctrine of the given." The first thesis, that our knowledge is an edifice or structure having its own foundation, becomes (A) "every statement, which we are justified in thinking that we know, is justified in part by some statement that justifies itself." The second thesis, that there are appearances ("the given") at the foundation of our knowledge, becomes (B) "there are statements about appearances that thus justify themselves." (The third thesis—the "phenomenalistic version" of the doctrine of the given—becomes (C) "there are no self-justifying statements that are not statements about appearances.")

Let us now turn to the first of the two theses constituting the doctrine of the given.

3

"Every justified statement is justified in part by some statement that justifies itself." Could it be that the question this thesis is supposed to answer is a question that arises only because of some mistaken assumption? If not, what are the alternative ways of answering it? And did any of the philosophers with whom we are concerned actually accept any of these alternatives? The first two questions are less difficult to answer than the third.

There are the following points of view to be considered, each of which *seems* to have been taken by some of the philosophers in the period of our survey.

1) One may believe that the questions about justification that give rise to our problem are based on false assumptions and hence that they *should not be asked* at all.

2) One may believe that no statement or claim is justified unless it is justified, at least in part, by some other justified statement or claim that it does not justify; this belief may suggest that one should continue the process of justifying *ad indefinitum*, justifying each claim by reference to some additional claim.

3) One may believe that no statement or claim *a* is justified unless it is justified by some other justified statement or claim *b*, and that *b* is not justified unless it in turn is justified by *a*; this would suggest that the process of justifying is, or should be, *circular*.

4) One may believe that at some particular claims *n* the process of justifying should stop, and one may then hold of any such claim *n* either: (a) *n* is justified by something—viz., *experience* or *observation*—that is not itself a claim and that therefore cannot be said itself either to be justified or unjustified; (b) *n* is itself *unjustified*; (c) *n* *justifies itself*; or (d) *n* is *neither justified nor unjustified*.

These possibilities, I think, exhaust the significant points of view; let us now consider them in turn.

4

"The questions about justification that give rise to the problem are based on false assumptions and therefore should not be asked at all."

The questions are *not* based on false assumptions; but most of the philosophers who discussed the questions put them in such a misleading way that one is very easily misled into supposing that they *are* based upon false assumptions.

Many philosophers, following Descartes, Russell, and Husserl, formulated the questions about justification by means of such terms as "doubt," "certainty," and "incorrigibility," and they used, or misused, these terms in such a way that, when their questions were taken in the way in which one would ordinarily take them, they could be shown to be based on false assumptions. One may note, for example, that the statement "There is a clock on the mantelpiece" is not self-justifying—for to the question "What is your justification for thinking you know that there is a clock on the mantelpiece?" the proper reply would be to make some other statement (e.g., "I saw it there this morning and no one would have taken it away"—and one may then go on to ask "But are there any statements that can be said to justify themselves?" If we express these facts, as many philosophers did, by saying that the statement "There is a clock on the mantelpiece" is one that is not "certain," or one that may be "doubted," and if we then go on to ask "Does this doubtful statement rest on other statements that are certain and incorrigible?" then we are using terms in an extraordinarily misleading way. The question "Does this doubtful statement rest on statements that are certain and incorrigible?"—if taken as one would ordinarily take it—does rest on a false assumption, for (we may assume) the statement that a clock is on the mantelpiece is one that is not doubtful at all.

John Dewey, and some of the philosophers whose views were very similar to his, tended to suppose, mistakenly, that the philosophers who asked themselves "What justification do I have for thinking I know this?" were asking the quite different question "What more can I do to verify or confirm that this is so?" and they rejected answers to the first question on the ground that they were unsatisfactory answers to the second.[19] Philosophers influenced by Wittgenstein tended to suppose, also mistakenly, but quite understandably, that the question "What justification do I have for thinking I know this?" contains an implicit challenge and presupposes that one does not have the knowledge concerned. They then pointed out, correctly, that in most of the cases where the question was raised (e.g., "What justifies me in thinking I know that this is a table?") there is no ground for challenging the claim to knowledge and that questions presupposing that the claim is false should not arise. But the question "What justifies me in thinking I know that this is a table?" does not challenge the claim to know that this is a table, much less presuppose that the claim is false.

The "critique of cogency," as Lewis described this concern of epistemology, presupposes that we *are* justified in thinking we know most of the things that we do think we know, and what it seeks to elicit is the nature of this justification. The enterprise is like that of ethics, logic, and aesthetics:

The nature of the good can be learned from experience only if the content of experience be first classified into good and bad, or grades of better and worse. Such classification or grading already involves the legislative application of the same principle which is sought. In logic, principles can be elicited by generalization from examples only if cases of valid reasoning have first been segregated by some criterion. In esthetics, the laws of the beautiful may be derived from experience only if the criteria of beauty have first been correctly applied.[20]

When Aristotle considered an invalid mood of the syllogism and asked himself "What is wrong with this?" he was not suggesting to himself that perhaps nothing was wrong; he presupposed that the mood *was* invalid, just as he presupposed that others were not, and he attempted, successfully, to formulate criteria that would enable us to distinguish the two types of mood.

When we have answered the question, "What justification do I have for thinking I know this?" what we learn, as Socrates taught, is something about ourselves. We learn, of course, what the justification happens to be for the particular claim with which the question is concerned. But we also learn, more generally, what the criteria are, if any, in terms of which we believe ourselves justified in counting one thing as an instance of knowing and another thing not. The truth that the philosopher seeks, when he asks about justification, is "already implicit in the mind which seeks it, and needs only to be elicited and brought to clear expression."[21]

Let us turn, then to the other approaches to the problem of "the given."

5

"No statement or claim would be justified unless it were justified, at least in part, by some other justified claim or statement that it does not justify."

This regressive principle might be suggested by the figure of the building and its supports: no stage supports another unless it is itself supported by some other stage beneath it—a truth that holds not only of the upper portions of the building but also of what we call its foundation. And the principle follows if, as some of the philosophers in the tradition of logical empiricism seemed to believe, we should combine a frequency theory of probability with a probability theory of justification.

In *Experience and Prediction* (U. of Chicago, 1938) and in other writings, Hans Reichenbach defended a "probability theory of knowledge" that seemed to involve the following contentions:

1) To justify accepting a statement, it is necessary to show that the statement is probable.

2) To say of a statement that it is probable is to say something about statistical frequencies. Somewhat more accurately, a statement of the form "It is *probable* that any particular a is b" may be explicated as saying "Most ds are bs." Or, still more accurately, to say "The probability is n that a particular a is a b" is to say "The limit of the relative frequency with the property of being a b occurs in the class of things having the property a is n."

3) Hence, by (2), to show that a proposition is probable it is necessary to show that a certain statistical frequency obtains; and, by (1), to show that a certain statistical frequency obtains it is necessary to show that it is probable that the statistical frequency obtains; and therefore, by (2), to show that it is probable that a certain statistical frequency obtains, it is necessary to show that a certain frequency of frequencies obtains. . . .

4) And therefore "there is no Archimedean point of absolute certainty left to which to attach our knowledge of the world; all we have is an elastic net of probability connections floating in open space" (p. 192).

This reasoning suggests that an infinite number of steps must be taken to justify acceptance of any statement. For, according to the reasoning, we cannot determine the probability of one statement until we have determined that of a second, and we can not determine that of the second until we have determined that of a third, and so on. Reichenbach does not leave the matter here, however. He suggests that there is a way of "descending" from this "open space" of probability connections, but, if I am not mistaken, we can make the descent only by letting go of the concept of justification.

He says that, if we are to avoid the regress of probabilities of probabilities of probabilities . . . , we must be willing at some point merely to make a guess; "there will always be some blind posits on which the whole concatenation is based" (p. 367). The view that knowledge is to be identified with certainty and that probable knowledge must be "imbedded in a framework of certainty" is "a remnant of rationalism. An empiricist theory of probability can be constructed only if we are willing to regard knowledge as a system of posits."[22]

But if we begin by assuming, as we do, that there is a distinction between knowledge, on the one hand, and a lucky guess, on the other, then we must reject at least one of the premises of any argument purporting to demonstrate that knowledge is a system of "blind posits." The unacceptable conclusion of Reichenbach's argument may be so construed as to follow from premises (1) and (2); and premise (2) may be accepted as a kind of definition (though there are many who believe that this definition is not adequate to all of the uses of the term "probable" in science and everyday life.) Premise (1), therefore is the one we should reject, and there are good reasons, I think, for rejecting (1), the thesis that "to justify accepting a proposition it is necessary to show that the proposition is probable." In fairness to Reichenbach, it should be added that he never explicitly affirms premise (1); but some such premise is essential to his argument.

6

"No statement or claim *a* would be justified unless it were justified by some other justified statement or claim *b* that would not be justified unless it were justified in turn by *a*."

The "coherence theory of truth," to which some philosophers committed themselves, is sometimes taken to imply that justification may thus be circular; I believe, however, that the theory does not have this implication. It does define "truth" as a kind of systematic consistency of beliefs or propositions. The truth of a proposition is said to consist, not in the fact that the proposition "corresponds" with something that is not itself a proposition, but in the fact that it fits consistently into a certain more general system of propositions. This view may even be suggested by the figure of the building and its foundations. There is no difference in principle between the way in which the upper stories are supported by the lower, and that in which the cellar is supported by the earth just below it, or the way in which the stratum of earth is supported by various substrata farther below; a good building appears to be a part of the terrain on which it stands and a good system of propositions is a part of the wider system that gives it its truth. But these metaphors do not solve philosophical problems.

The coherence theory did in fact appeal to something other than logical consistency; its proponents conceded that a system of false propositions may be internally consistent and hence that logical consistency alone is no guarantee of truth. Brand Blanshard, who defended the coherence theory in *The Nature of Thought*, said that a proposition is true provided it is a member of an internally consistent system of propositions and *provided further* this system is "the system in which everything real and possible is coherently included."[23] In one phase of the development of "logical empiricism" its proponents seem to have held a similar view: a proposition—or, in this case, a statement—is true provided it is a member of an internally consistent system of statements and *provided further* this system is "the system which is actually adopted by mankind, and especially by the scientists in our culture circle."[24]

A theory of truth is not, as such, a theory of justification. To say that a proposition is true is not to say that we are justified in accepting it as true, and to say that we are justified in accepting it as true is not to say that it is true. (I shall return to this point in the final section.) Whatever merits the coherence theory may have as an answer to certain questions about truth, it throws no light upon our present epistemological question. If we accept the coherence theory, we may still ask, concerning any proposition *a* that we think we know to be true, "What is my justification for thinking I know that *a* is a member of the system of propositions in which everything real and possible is coherently included, or that *a* is a member of the system of propositions that is actually adopted by mankind and by the scientists of our culture circle?" And when we ask such a question, we are confronted, once again, with our original alternatives.

7

If our questions about justification do have a proper stopping place, then, as I have said, there are still four significant possibilities to consider. We may stop with some particular claim and say of it that either:

a) It is justified by something—by experience, or by observation—that is not itself a claim and that, therefore, cannot be said either to be justified or to be unjustified;

b) It is justified by some claim that refers to our experience or observation, and the claim referring to our experience or observation has *no* justification;

c) It justifies itself; or

d) It is itself neither justified nor unjustified.

The first of these alternatives leads readily to the second, and the second to the third or to the fourth. The third and the fourth—which differ only verbally, I think—involve the doctrine of "the given."

Carnap wrote, in 1936, that the procedure of scientific testing involves two operations: the "confrontation of a statement with observation" and the "confrontation of a statement with previously accepted statements." He suggested that those logical empiricists who were attracted to the coherence theory of truth tended to lose sight of the first of these operations—the confrontation of a statement with observation. He proposed a way of formulating simple "acceptance rules" for such confrontation and he seemed to believe that, merely by applying such rules, we could avoid the epistemological questions with which the adherents of "the given" had become involved.

Carnap said this about his acceptance rules: "If no foreign language or introduction of new terms is involved, the rules are trivial. For example: 'If one is hungry, the statement "I am hungry" may be accepted'; or: 'If one sees a key one may accept the statement "there lies a key."'"[25] As we shall note later, the first of these rules differs in an important way from the second. Confining ourselves for the moment to rules of the second sort—"If one sees a key one may accept the statement 'there lies a key'"—let us ask ourselves whether the appeal to such rules enables us to solve our problem of the stopping place.

When we have made the statement "There lies a key," we can, of course, raise the question "What is my justification for thinking I know, or for believing, that there lies a key?" The answer would be "I see the key." We cannot ask "What is my justification for seeing a key?" But we *can* ask "What is my justification for thinking that it is a *key* that I see?" and, if we *do* see that the thing is a key, the question will have an answer. The answer might be "I see that it's shaped like a key and that it's in the lock, and I remember that a key is usually here." The possibility of this question, and its answer, indicates that we cannot stop our questions about justification merely by appealing to observation or experience. For, of the statement "I observe that that is an A," we can ask, and answer, the question "What is my justification for thinking that I observe that there is an A?"

It is relevant to note, moreover, that conditions may exist under which seeing a key does *not* justify one in accepting the statement "There is a key" or in believing that one sees a key. If the key were so disguised or concealed that the man who saw it did not recognize it to be a key, then he might not be justified in accepting the statement "There is a key." If Mr. Jones unknown to anyone but himself is a thief, then the people who see him may be said to see a thief— but none of those who thus sees a thief is justified in accepting the statement "There is a thief."[26]

Some of the writings of logical empiricists suggest that, although some statements may be justified by reference to other statements, those statements involve "confrontation with observation" are not justified at all. C. G. Hempel, for example, wrote that "the acknowledgement of an experiential statement as true is psychologically motivated by certain experiences; but within the system of statements which express scientific knowledge or one's beliefs at a given time, they function in the manner of postulates for which no grounds are offered."[27] Hempel conceded, however, that this use of the term "postulate" is misleading and he added the following note of clarification: "When an experiential sentence is accepted 'on the basis of direct experiential evidence,' it is indeed not asserted arbitrarily; but to describe the evidence in question would simply mean to repeat the experiential statement itself. Hence, in the context of cognitive justification, the statement functions in the manner of a primitive sentence."[28]

When we reach a statement having the property just referred to— an experiential statement such that to describe its evidence "would simply mean to repeat the experiential statement itself"—we have reached a proper stopping place in the process of justification.

8

We are thus led to the concept of a belief, statement, claim, proposition, or hypothesis, that justifies itself. To be clear about the concept, let us note the way in which we would justify the statement that we have a certain belief. It is essential, of course, that we distinguish justifying the statement *that* we have a certain belief from justifying the belief itself.

Suppose, then, a man is led to say "I believe that Socrates is mortal" and we ask him "What is your justification for thinking that you believe, or for thinking that you know that you believe, that Socrates is mortal?" To this strange question, the only appropriate reply would be "My justification for thinking I believe, or for thinking that I know that I believe, that Socrates is mortal is simply that I *do* believe that Socrates is mortal." One justifies the statement simply by reiterating it; the statement's justification is what the statement says. Here, then, we have a case that satisfies Hempel's remark quoted above; we describe the evidence for a statement merely by repeating the statement. We could say, as C. J. Ducasse did, that "the occurrence of belief is its own evidence."[29]

Normally, as I have suggested, one cannot justify a statement merely by reiterating it. To the question "What justification do you have for thinking you know that there can be no life on the moon?" it would be inappropriate, and impertinent, to reply by saying simply "There *can* be no life on the moon," thus reiterating the fact at issue. An appropriate answer would be one referring to certain *other* facts—for example, that we know there is insufficient oxygen on the moon to support any kind of life. But to the question "What is your justification for thinking you know that you believe so and so?" there is nothing to say other than "I *do* believe so and so."

We may say, then, that some statements are self-justifying, or justify themselves. And we may say, analogously, that certain beliefs, claims, propositions, or hypotheses are self-justifying, or justify themselves. A statement, belief, claim, proposition, or hypothesis may be said to be self-justifying for a person, if the person's justification for thinking he knows it to be true is simply the fact that it *is* true.

Paradoxically, these things I have described by saying that they "justify themselves" may *also* be described by saying that they are "neither justified nor unjustified." The two modes of description are two different ways of saying the same thing.

If we are sensitive to ordinary usage, we may note that the expression "I believe that I believe" is ordinarily used, not to refer to a second-order belief about the speaker's own beliefs, but to indicate that the speaker has not yet made up his mind. "I *believe that I believe* that Johnson is a good president" might properly be taken to indicate that, if the speaker *does* believe that Johnson is a good president, he is not yet firm in that belief. Hence there is a temptation to infer that, if we say of a man who is firm in his belief that Socrates is mortal, that he is "justified in believing that he believes that Socrates is mortal," our statement "makes no sense." A temptation also arises to go on and say that it "makes no sense" even to say of such a man, that his *statement* "I believe that Socrates is mortal" is one which is "justified" for him.[30] After all, what would it mean to say of a man's statement about his own belief, that he is *not* justified in accepting it?[31]

The questions about what does or does not "make any sense" need not, however, be argued. We *may* say, if we prefer, that the statements about the beliefs in question are "neither justified nor unjustified." Whatever mode of description we use, the essential points are two. First, we may appeal to such statements in the process of justifying some *other* statement or belief. If they *have* no justification they may yet *be* a justification—for something other than themselves. ("What justifies me in thinking that he and I are not likely to agree? The fact that I believe that Socrates is mortal and he does not.") Second, the making of such a statement does provide what I have been calling a "stopping place" in the dialectic of justification; but now, instead of signaling the stopping place by reiterating the questioned statement, we do it by saying that the question of its justification is one that "should not arise."

It does not matter, then, whether we speak of certain statements that "justify themselves" or of certain statements that are "neither justified nor unjustified," for in either case we will be referring to the same set of statements. I shall continue to use the former phrase.

There are, then, statements about one's own beliefs ("I believe that Socrates is mortal")—and statements about many other psychological attitudes—that are self-justifying. "What justifies me in believing, or in thinking I know, that I *hope* to come tomorrow? Simply that I *do* hope to come tomorrow." Thinking, desiring, wondering, loving, hating, and other such attitudes are similar. Some, but by no means all, of the statements we can make about such attitudes, when the attitudes are our own, are self-justifying—as are statements containing such phrases as "I think I remember" or "I seem to remember" (as distinguished from "I remember"), and "I think that I see" and "I think that I perceive" (as distinguished from "I see" and "I perceive"). Thus, of the two examples Carnap introduced in connection with his "acceptance rules" discussed above viz., "I am hungry" and

"I see a key," we may say that the first is self-justifying and the second is not.

The "doctrine of the given," it will be recalled, tells us (A) that every justified statement, about what we think we know, is justified in part by some statement that justifies itself and (B) that there are statements about appearances that thus justify themselves. The "phenomenalistic version" of the theory adds (C) that statements about appearances are the *only* statements that justify themselves. What we have been saying is that the first thesis, (A), of the doctrine of the given is true and that the "phenomenalistic version," (C), is false; let us turn now to thesis (B).

9

In addition to the self-justifying statements about psychological attitudes, are there self-justifying statements about "appearances"? Now we encounter difficulties involving the word "appearance" and its cognates.

Sometimes such words as "appears," "looks," and "seems" are used to convey what one might also convey by such terms as "believe." For example, if I say "It appears to me that General de Gaulle was successful," or "General de Gaulle seems to have been successful," I am likely to mean only that I believe, or incline to believe, that he has been successful; the words "appears" and "seems" serve as useful hedges, giving me an out, should I find out later that de Gaulle was not successful. When "appear"-words are used in this way, the statements in which they occur add nothing significant to the class of "self-justifying" statements we have just provided. Philosophers have traditionally assumed, however, that such terms as "appear" may also be used in a quite different way. If this assumption is correct, as I believe it is, then this additional use does lead us to another type of self-justifying statement.

In the final chapter we shall have occasion to note some of the confusions to which the substantival expression "appearance" gave rise. The philosophers who exposed these confusions were sometimes inclined to forget, I think, that things do appear to us in various ways.[32] We can alter the appearance of anything we like merely by doing something that will affect our sense organs or the conditions of observation. One of the important epistemological questions about appearance is "Are there self-justifying statements about the ways in which things appear?"

Augustine, refuting the skeptics of the late Platonic Academy, wrote: "I do not see how the Academician can refute him who says: 'I know that this appears white to me, I know that my hearing is delighted with this, I know this has an agreeable odor, I know this tastes sweet to me, I know that this feels cold to me.' . . . When a person tastes something, he can honestly swear that he knows it is sweet to his palate or the contrary, and that no trickery.of the Greeks can dispossess him of that knowledge."[33] Suppose, now, one were to ask "What justification do you have for believing, or thinking you know, that this appears white to you, or that that tastes bitter to you?" Here, too, we can only reiterate the statement: "What justifies me in believing, or in thinking I know, that this appears white to me and that that tastes bitter to me is that this *does* appear white to me and that *does* taste bitter."

An advantage of the misleading substantive "appearance," as distinguished from the verb "appears," is that the former may be applied to those sensuous experiences which, though capable of being appearances of things, are actually not appearances of anything. Feelings, imagery, and the sensuous content of dreams and hallucination are very much like the appearances of things and they are such that, under some circumstances, they could be appearances of things. But if we do not wish to say that they are experiences wherein some external physical thing *appears* to us, we must use some expression other than "appear." For "appear," in its active voice, requires a grammatical subject and thus requires a term that refers, not merely to a way of appearing, but also to *something that appears*.

But we may avoid *both* the objective "*Something* appears blue to me," and the substantival "I sense a blue *appearance*." We may use another verb, say "sense," in a technical way, as many philosophers did, and equate it in meaning with the passive voice of "appear," thus saying simply "I *sense* blue," or the like. Or better still, it seems to me, and at the expense only of a little awkwardness, we can use "appear" in its passive voice and say "I am *appeared to* blue."

Summing up, in our new vocabulary, we may say that the philosophers who talked of the "empirically given" were referring, not to "self-justifying" statements and beliefs generally, but only to those pertaining to certain "ways of being appeared to." And the philosophers who objected to the doctrine of the given, or some of them, argued that no statement about "a way of being appeared to" can be "self-justifying."

10

Why would one suppose that "This appears white" (or, more exactly, "I am now appeared white to") is not self-justifying? The most convincing argument was this: If I say "This appears white," then, as Reichenbach put it, I am making a "comparison between a present object and a formerly seen object."[34] What I am saying *could* have been expressed by "The present way of appearing is the way in which white objects, or objects that I believe to be white, ordinarily appear." And this new statement, clearly, is not self-justifying; to justify it, as Reichenbach intimated, I must go on and say something further — something about the way in which I remember white objects to have appeared.

"Appears white" *may* thus be used to abbreviate "appears the way in which white things normally appear." Or "white thing," on the other hand, *may* be used to abbreviate "thing having the color of things that ordinarily appear white." The phrase "appear white" as it is used in the second quoted expression cannot be spelled out in the manner of the first; for the point of the second can hardly be put by saying that "white thing" may be used to abbreviate "thing having the color of things that ordinarily appear the way in which *white things* normally appear." In the second expression, the point of "appears white" is not to *compare* a way of appearing with something else; the point is to say something about the way of appearing itself. It is in terms of this second sense of "appears white" — that in which one may say significantly and without redundancy "Things that are white may normally be expected to appear white" — that we are to interpret the quotation from Augustine above. And, more generally, when it was said that "appear"-statements constitute the foundation of the edifice of knowledge, it was not intended that the "appear"-statements be interpreted as statements asserting a comparison between a present object and any other object or set of objects.

The question now becomes "Can we formulate any significant 'appear'-statements *without* thus comparing the way in which some object appears with the way in which some other object appears, or with the way in which the object in question has appeared at some other time? Can we interpret 'This appears white' in such a way that it may be understood to refer to a present way of appearing *without* relating that way of appearing to any other object?" In *Experience and Prediction*, Reichenbach defended his own view (and that of a good many others) in this way:

The objection may be raised that a comparison with formerly seen physical objects should be avoided, and that a basic statement is to concern the present fact only, as it is. But such a reduction would make the basic statement empty. Its content is just that there is a similarity between the present object and one formerly seen; it is by means of this relation that the present object is described. Otherwise the basic statement would consist in attaching an individual symbol, say a number, to the present object; but the introduction of such a symbol would help us in no way, since we could not make use of it to construct a comparison with other things. Only in attaching the same symbols to different objects, do we arrive at the possibility of constructing relations between the objects [pp. 176-77].

It is true that, if an "appear"-statement is to be used successfully in communication, it must assert some comparison of objects. Clearly, if I wish *you* to know the way things are now appearing to me, I must relate these ways of appearing to something that is familiar to you. But our present question is not "Can you understand me if I predicate something of the way in which something now appears to me without relating that way of appearing to something that is familiar to you?" The question is, more simply, "Can I predicate anything of the way in which something now appears to me without thereby comparing that way of appearing with something else?" From the fact that the first of these two questions must be answered in the negative it does not follow that the second must also be answered in the negative.[35]

The issue is not one about communication, nor is it, strictly speaking, an issue about language; it concerns, rather, the nature of thought itself. Common to both "pragmatism" and "idealism," as traditions in American philosophy, is the view that to *think* about a thing, or to *interpret* or *conceptualize* it, and hence to have a *belief* about it, is essentially to relate the thing to *other* things, actual or possible, and therefore to "refer beyond it." It is this view—and not any view about language or communication—that we must oppose if we are to say of some statements about appearing, or of any other statements, that they "justify themselves."

To think about the way in which something is now appearing, according to the view in question, is to relate that way of appearing to something else, possibly to certain future experiences, possibly to the way in which things of a certain sort may be commonly expected to appear. According to the "conceptualistic pragmatism" of C. I. Lewis's

Mind and the World-Order (1929), we grasp the present experience, any present way of appearing, only to the extent to which we relate it to some future experience.[36] According to one interpretation of John Dewey's "instrumentalistic" version of pragmatism, the present experience may be used to present or disclose something else but it does not present or disclose itself. And according to the idealistic view defended in Brand Blanshard's *The Nature of Thought*, we grasp our present experience only to the extent that we are able to include it in the one "intelligible system of universals" (vol. 1, p. 632).

This theory of reference, it should be noted, applies not only to statements and beliefs about "ways of being appeared to" but also to those other statements and beliefs I have called "self-justifying." If "This appears white," or "I am appeared white to," compares the present experience with something else, and thus depends for its justification on what we are justified in believing about the something else, then so, too, does "I believe that Socrates is mortal" and "I hope that the peace will continue." This general conception of thought, therefore, would seem to imply that no belief or statement can be said to justify itself. But according to what we have been saying, if there is no belief or statement that justifies itself, then it is problematic whether any belief or statement is justified at all. And therefore, as we might expect, this conception of thought and reference has been associated with skepticism.

Blanshard conceded that his theory of thought "does involve a degree of scepticism regarding our present knowledge and probably all future knowledge. In all likelihood there will never be a proposition of which we can say, "This that I am asserting, with precisely the meaning I now attach to it, is absolutely true."[37] On Dewey's theory, or on one common interpretation of Dewey's theory, it is problematic whether anyone can now be said to *know* that Mr. Jones is working in his garden. A. O. Lovejoy is reported to have said that, for Dewey, "I am about to have known" is as close as we ever get to "I know."[38] C. I. Lewis, in his *An Analysis of Knowledge and Valuation* (Open Court, 1946) conceded in effect that the conception of thought suggested by his earlier *Mind and the World-Order* does lead to a kind of skepticism; according to the later work there *are* "apprehensions of the given" (cf. pp. 182-83)—and thus beliefs that justify themselves.

What is the plausibility of a theory of thought and reference that seems to imply that no one knows anything?

Perhaps it is correct to say that when we think about a thing we think about it as having certain properties. But why should one go on to say that to think about a thing must always involve thinking about some *other* thing as well? Does thinking about the other thing then involve thinking about some third thing? Or can we think about one thing in relation to a second thing without thereby thinking of a third thing? And if we can, then why can we not think of one thing—of one thing as having certain properties—without thereby relating it to another thing?

The linguistic analogue of this view of thought is similar. Why should one suppose—as Reichenbach supposed in the passage cited above and as many others have also supposed—that to *refer* to a thing, in this instance to refer to a way of appearing, is necessarily to relate the thing to some *other* thing?

Some philosophers seem to have been led to such a view of reference as a result of such considerations as the following: We have imagined a man saying, in agreement with Augustine, "It just does appear white—and that is the end of the matter." Let us consider now the possible reply that "It is not the end of the matter. You are making certain assumptions about the language you are using; you are assuming, for example, that you are using the word 'white' or the phrase 'appears white,' in a way in which you have formerly used it, or in the way in which it is ordinarily used, or in the way in which it would ordinarily be understood. And if you state your justification for this assumption, you *will* refer to certain other things—to yourself and to other people, to the word 'white,' or to the phrase 'appears white,' and to what the word or phrase has referred to or might refer to on other occasions. And therefore, when you say 'This appears white' you are saying something, not only about your present experience, but also about all of these other things as well."

The conclusion of this argument—the part that follows the "therefore"—does not follow from the premises. In supposing that the argument is valid, one fails to distinguish between (1) *what* it is that a man means to say when he uses certain words and (2) his assumptions concerning the adequacy of these words for *expressing* what it is that he means to say; one supposes, mistakenly, that what justifies (2) must be included in what justifies (1). A Frenchwoman not yet sure of her English, may utter the words "There are apples in the basket," intending thereby to express her belief that there are potatoes in the basket. If we show her that she has used the word "apples" incorrectly, and hence that she is mistaken in her assumption about the ways in which English speaking people use and understand the word "apples," we have not shown her anything relevant to her *belief* that there are apples in the basket.

Logicians now take care to distinguish between the *use* and *mention* of language (e.g., the English word "Socrates" is mentioned in the sentence "'Socrates' has eight letters" and is used but not mentioned, in "Socrates is a Greek.")[39] As we shall have occasion to note further in the next chapter, the distinction has not always been observed in writings on epistemology.

11

If we decide, then, that there is a class of beliefs or statements that are "self-justifying," and that this class is limited to certain beliefs or statements about our own psychological states and about the ways in which we are "appeared to," we may be tempted to return to the figure of the edifice: our knowledge of the world is a structure supported entirely by a foundation of such self-justifying statements or beliefs. We should recall, however, that the answers to our original Socratic questions had *two* parts. When asked "What is your justification for thinking that you know *a*?" one may reply "I am justified in thinking I know *a*, because (1) I know *b* and (2) if I know *b* then I know *a*." We considered our justification for the *first* part of this answer, saying "I am justified in thinking I know *b*, because (1) I know *c* and (2) if I know *c* then I know *b*." And then we considered our justification for the first part of the second answer, and continued in this fashion until we reach the point of self-justification. In thus moving toward "the given," we accumulated, step by step, a backlog of claims that we did not attempt to justify—those claims constituting the *second* part of each of our answers. Hence our original claim— "I know that *a* is true"—does not rest on "the given" alone; it also rests upon all of those other claims that we made en route. And it is not justified unless these other claims are justified.

A consideration of these other claims will lead us, I think, to at least three additional types of "stopping place," which we are concerned, respectively, with memory, perception, and what Kant called the a priori. I shall comment briefly on the first two and turn to the third in the following chapter.

It is difficult to think of any claim to empirical knowledge, other than the self-justifying statements we have just considered, that does not to some extent rest on an appeal to memory. But the appeal to memory—"I remember that A occurred"—is not self-justifying. One may ask "And what is your justification for thinking that you remember that A occurred?" and the question will have an answer—even if the answer is only the self-justifying "I think that I remember that A occurred." The statement "I remember that A occurred" does, of course, imply "A occurred"; but "I think that I remember that A occurred" does not imply "A occurred" and hence does not imply "I remember that A occurred." For we can remember occasions—at least we think we can remember them—when we learned, concerning some event we had thought we remembered, that the event had not occurred at all, and consequently that we had not really remembered it. When we thus find that one memory conflicts with another, or, more accurately, when we thus find that one thing that we think we remember conflicts with another thing that we think we remember, we may correct one or the other by making further inquiry; but the results of any such inquiry will always be justified in part by other memories, or by other things that we think that we remember. How then are we to choose between what seem to be conflicting memories? Under what conditions does "I think that I remember that A occurred" serve to justify "I remember that A occurred"?

The problem is one of formulating a rule of evidence—a rule specifying the conditions under which statements about what we think we remember can justify statements about what we do remember. A possible solution, in very general terms, is "When we think that we remember, then we are justified in believing that we do remember, provided that what we think we remember does not conflict with anything else that we think we remember; when what we think we remember does conflict with something else we think we remember, then, of the two conflicting memories (more accurately, ostensible memories) the one that is justified is the one that fits in better with the other things that we think we remember." Ledger Wood made the latter point by saying that the justified memory is the one that "coheres with the system of related memories"; C. I. Lewis used "congruence" instead of "coherence."[40] But we cannot say precisely what is meant by "fitting in," "coherence," or "congruence" until certain controversial questions of confirmation theory and the logic of probability have been answered. And it may be that the rule of evidence is too liberal; perhaps we should say, for example, that when two ostensible memories conflict neither one of them is justified. But these are questions that have not yet been satisfactorily answered.

If we substitute "perceive" for "remember" in the foregoing, we can formulate a similar set of problems about perception; these problems, too, must await solution.[41]

The problems involved in formulating such rules of evidence, and in determining the validity of these rules, do not differ in any significant way from those that arise in connection with the formulation, and validity, of the rules of logic. Nor do they differ from the problems posed by the moral and religious "cognitivists" (the "nonintuitionistic cognitivists") mentioned in the first section. The status of ostensible memories and perceptions, with respect to that experience which is their "source," is essentially like that which such "cognitivists" claim for judgments having an ethical or theological subject matter. Unfortunately, it is also like that which other "enthusiasts" claim for still other types of subject matter.

12

What, then, is the status of the doctrine of "the given"—of the "myth of the given"? In my opinion, the doctrine is correct in saying that there are some beliefs or statements that are "self-justifying" and that among such beliefs and statements are some that concern appearances or "ways of being appeared to"; but the "phenomenalistic version" of the doctrine is mistaken in implying that our knowledge may be thought of as an edifice that is supported by appearances alone.[42] The cognitive significance of "the empirically given" was correctly described—in a vocabulary rather different from that which I have been using—by John Dewey:

The alleged primacy of sensory meanings is mythical. They are primary only in logical status; they are primary as tests and confirmation of inferences concerning matters of fact, not as historic originals. For, while it is not usually needful to carry the check or test of theoretical calculations to the point of irreducible sensa, colors, sounds, etc., these sensa form a limit approached in careful analytic certifications, and upon critical occasions it is necessary to touch the limit. . . . Sensa are the class of irreducible meanings which are employed in verifying and correcting other meanings. We actually set out with much coarser and more inclusive meanings and not till we have met with failure from their use do we even set out to discover those ultimate and harder meanings which are sensory in character.[43]

The Socratic questions leading to the concept of "the given" also lead to the concept of "rules of evidence." Unfortunately some of the philosophers who stressed the importance of the former concept tended to overlook that of the latter.

Reason and The A Priori

The identity of each essence with itself and difference from every other essence suffices to distinguish and define them all in eternity, where they form the Realm of Essence. True and false assertions may be made about any one of them, such, for instance, as that it does not exist; or that it includes or excludes some other essence, or is included or excluded by it. [George Santayana, *The Realms of Being.*]

Pure reason is unable to produce any real knowledge, its only business is the arrangement of symbols which are used for the expression of knowledge. [Morris Schlick, "A New Philosophy of Experience."]

Our apprehension of such truths as the following is traditionally ascribed to "reason": being a square includes being rectangular, and excludes being circular; being a man includes being an animal, and excludes being an angel. Or, what may come to the same thing, it is *necessarily true* that if anything is a square then it is a rectangle and not a circle, and that if anything is a man then it is an animal and not an angel. Or it is true, not only in this world but in *all possible worlds,* that all squares are rectangles and no squares are circles, and that all men are animals and no men are angels. But being a square neither includes nor excludes being red, and being a man neither includes nor excludes being a Greek. Again: some men being Greek includes some Greeks being men and excludes no Greeks being men; it is necessarily true, or true in all possible worlds, that if some men are Greek then some Greeks are men; but some men being Greek neither includes nor excludes some men being Roman.

The period of American philosophy with which we are here concerned has been dominated by an attitude of skepticism toward such truths and faculties. The keynote of this attitude was struck by Moritz Schlick in his second public lecture at the College of the Pacific: "Empiricism now has the right and power to claim the whole field of knowledge. We know nothing except by experience, and experience is the only criterion of the truth or falsity of any real proposition."[44] Subsequent debate has indicated, I think, that Schlick's confidence was not justified.

To understand the debate and the issues it involved, we must consider the following topics: (1) the Kantian distinction between analytic and synthetic judgments, its reinterpretation by recent philosophers as a distinction between types of *statement*, and the relation of "analytic statements" to statements that are sometimes said to be "logically true"; (2) the Kantian distinction between a priori and a posteriori knowledge; (3) the attempt to construe the a priori knowledge, which is expressed in analytic statements, as a type of knowledge that is intimately connected with language; and (4) the question whether there is any a priori knowledge that is not expressible in statements that are either analytic or logically true.

1

An analytic judgment, according to Kant, is a judgment in which "the predicate adds nothing to the concept of the subject." If I judge that all squares are rectangles, then, in Kant's terminology, the concept of the subject of my judgment is the property of being square, and the concept of the predicate is the property of being rectangular. The concept of the predicate—and this is the reason for using the term "analytic"—helps us to "break up the concept of the subject into those constituent concepts that have all along been thought in it."[45] Kant would have said that the "constituent concepts" of being square are being equilateral and being rectangular; perhaps it would be clearer to say that being a square is a "conjunctive property" the components of which are being equilateral and being rectangular. In either case, the predicate of the judgment that all squares are rectangles may be said to "analyze out" what is already contained in the subject.

Synthetic judgments, on the other hand, are those in which the concept of the predicate is *not* thus "contained in" that of the subject. The judgment that all men are mortal is a synthetic judgment since the concept of being mortal is not included in that of being a man; hence, in the terminology of Leibniz, the judgment though true of this world is not true of "all possible worlds."

Anything that exemplifies the concept of the subject of an analytic judgment will, ipso facto, exemplify that of the predicate; anything that is a square is, ipso facto, a rectangle. To *deny* an analytic judgment—to judge that some squares are *not* rectangles—would be to contradict oneself, for it would be to judge that there are things that both do and do not have a certain property. Kant made this point by saying that "the common principle of all analytic judgments is the law of contradiction."[46]

All analytic judgments are true, but synthetic judgments may be either true or false. The synthetic judgment that all men are mortal is true; the synthetic judgment that all men are Greeks is false. If we deny the former judgment, holding that some men are not mortal, we go wrong but we do not contradict ourselves.

In recent philosophy, the terms "analytic" and "synthetic" are applied not to judgments but to statements or sentences. The linguistic concept of a *statement* is in some respects clearer than the psychological concept of a judgment; but the emphasis on statements, particularly in recent American philosophy, has led some philosophers to confuse certain fundamental questions of epistemology with certain quite different questions of the philosophy of language.

One of the best contemporary accounts of the distinction between analytic and synthetic statements is that given in C. I. Lewis's Carus Lectures, *An Analysis of Knowledge and Valuation* (Open Court, 1946). His account is substantially the following:

The word "square" has as its meaning the property of being square; it denotes, or applies to, anything that happens to have that property. The word "rectangle," similarly, has for its meaning the property of being rectangular, and it denotes, or applies, to anything that happens to have that property. The property of being rectangular, we have noted, is included in that of being square—i.e., it is a component of the conjunctive property of being both equilateral and rectangular; hence the meaning of "rectangular" is included in that of "square." We may say, then, that an affirmative subject-predicate statement, such as "All squares are rectangles," is *analytic* if the meaning of the predicate is included in that of the subject, and a negative subject-predicate statement, such as "No spinster is married," is analytic if the meaning of the negation of the predicate (in this case, the meaning of "nonmarried") is included in the meaning of the subject. A subject-predicate statement may be called *synthetic* if it is not analytic. "All men are mortal" is therefore synthetic, since the meaning of "mortal" is not included in that of "man"—even though, as it happens, the predicate applies to all those things that the subject applies to.[47]

The statement "Socrates is mortal or it is false that Socrates is mortal" is not analytic, as "analytic" has just been defined, for it is a compound statement and not a simple subject-predicate statement; but it is similar, in important respects, to those statements that are analytic. It is necessarily true, or true for all possible worlds, since Socrates being mortal excludes Socrates not being mortal. Kant would have said that it "has its principle in the law of contradiction" and we may express the same point by saying that it is a logical truth.

W. V. Quine proposed a useful definition of "logically true," as a phrase that may be predicated of statements or sentences. After we have formulated his definition, we will be in a position to understand some of the philosophical questions that these concepts involve.

Quine first enumerates a list of words to be called "logical words"; the list includes "or," "not," "if," "then," "and," "all," "every," "some." A sentence or statement is then said to be logically true if it is one in which only the logical words *occur essentially*. In "Socrates is mortal or it is false that Socrates is mortal," which is logically true, the expressions "or" and "it is false that" occur essentially, but the nonlogical words, "Socrates," "is," and "mortal," do not. What this means, put somewhat loosely, is that the truth of the statement is independent of the particular nonlogical words that happen to occur in it. Put somewhat more exactly: a logically true statement is one such that, if, for any nonlogical word in the sentence, we replace each of its occurrences by any other "grammatically admissible" word (making sure that all occurrences of the old word are replaced by occurrences of the same new word), then the new statement we derive will also be true. If the word "Socrates," in "Socrates is mortal or it is false that Socrates is mortal," is replaced by "these stones," if "is" is replaced by "are," and "mortal" by "blue," then the result—"These stones are blue or it is false that these stones are blue"—will be true. On the other hand, if we replace the logical words by other grammatically admissible words, the result may be false—as it would be if, in our example, we replaced "or" by "and." A logical truth on this interpretation, then, is "a statement that is true and remains true under all reinterpretations of its components other than logical particles.[48] (But if, in the logical truth "All elderly thieves are thieves," the nonlogical term "elderly" is replaced by such a term as "suspected," "possible," or "potential," the result will be a false statement. Certain qualifications must be added to "grammatic admissibility" to preclude this type of result. Moreover, as Quine recognized, such a definition of "logical truth" has this limitation: the question of *which* statements thus remain true under all reinterpretations of their nonlogical words remains problematic. The following are often said to be logical truths: "If it is true that either I am now in Providence or I am not now in Providence, then either it is true that I am now in Providence or it is not true that I am now in Providence," and "If it is true that either Zeno is in Athens or Zeno is in Sparta, and if it is also true that Zeno is walking either one mile an hour or Zeno is walking two miles an hour, then it is true that either Zeno is in Athens and walking one mile an hour, or Zeno is in Athens and walking two miles an hour, or Zeno is in Sparta and walking one mile an hour, or Zeno is in Sparta and walking two miles an hour." But if we change the tense of the first of these statements from present to future, then, according to some philosophers, we must reject the result on the ground that it conflicts with certain doctrines about freedom and human agency.[49] And if the second statement is revised, so as to refer to the position and velocity, not of Zeno, but of certain subatomic particles, then, according to some philosophers, we must reject the result on the ground that it conflicts with certain doctrines of contemporary quantum physics.[50] These issues involve epistemological questions similar to those discussed in the first section. For the present discussion, we may assume that we have a general characterization of logical truth, even though we have no definite way of fixing the boundary between logical and nonlogical truth.)

The analytic statements "All squares are rectangles" and "No spinsters are married" are not themselves logical truths on the above account. If in the former we replace the nonlogical word "squares" by "circles," the resulting statement will be false; and if in the latter we replace the nonlogical word "married" by "happy," the result will be false. But we may paraphrase any analytic statement—we may re-express what it expresses—by means of statements that *are* logically true. The term "squares" has among its synonyms (i.e., those terms having the same meaning that it has) a term—viz., "equilateral rectangles" —that includes the predicate term of "All squares are rectangles"; if we replace "square" by this synonym, then the result—"All equilateral rectangles are rectangles"—will be a logical truth. The term "spinster" has among its synonyms a term—viz., "adult lady who is nonmarried" —that includes the negation of the predicate of "No spinster is married"; replacement will thus yield the logical truth "No adult lady who is nonmarried is married." And similarly for other analytic statements; e.g., "All ornithologists are students of birds" and "All quadrupeds have feet." In each case by providing the proper synonyms and then substituting, we can turn the analytic statement into a logical truth. And we can recognize a logical truth, informally, by noting that it is a statement that is explicitly redundant —e.g., "All professional students of birds are students of birds," "No adult ladies who are nonmarried are married," and "All things that have four feet have feet." It will be convenient to describe both analytic statements and logical truths as redundancies—the former being sometimes implicit, and the latter always explicit.

In opposition to the view, mentioned at the beginning of this chapter, that these truths are concerned with relations among essences or properties, and relations among situations or possible states of affairs, and that they are apprehended by a kind of "rational insight," it has been maintained in recent years that they are expressions of our linguistic "rules" or "conventions" and strictly speaking, not truths at all. It has also been held that the distinction between analytic and synthetic is untenable. These views exhibit that "insurgence against reason," which, according to Morris Cohen, "has its roots deep in the dominant temper of our age." What Cohen said about the limitations of "psychologism," "historicism," and "empiricism," may also be said, if I am not mistaken, about these more recent doctrines.

2

"In the realm of logic and pure mathematics," Cohen wrote in *Reason and Nature* (Harcourt, 1931), "we have absolute and a priori truth." Even if "the more objective classical philosophies have overreached themselves in their abuse of the tests of self-evidence and self-contradiction, and in their sanctioning of false and meaningless propositions as a priori, it still remains true that in the Platonic ideas they have recognized the objectivity of the logical and mathematical forms of nature" (pp. 144-45). We can understand the concept of the a priori if we return to our Socratic questions about justification. What if such questions were raised in connection with that knowledge that is expressed in statements that are analytic or logically true? (The reader is referred again to the type of dilemma discussed in the first section. If there is doubt whether anyone *can* be said to know that all squares are rectangles, or that if some men are Greeks then some Greeks are men, it may well be that such doubt is incapable of being resolved. But we may still discuss the consequences of supposing that people *do* have such knowledge. And it will be well to note, so far as *this* question is concerned, that skepticism with respect to what is thought to be such knowledge is not to the point.)

"What justification do you have for believing you know that all squares are rectangles, or for believing you know that if some men are Greeks then some Greeks are men?"

If a man *does* know, as most of us think we do, that all squares are rectangles, or that if some men are Greeks then some Greeks are men, then there are only two ways he could answer our Socratic question. (1) He could say, simply: "I *see* that all squares are rectangles—that whatever is a square must be a rectangle—that being a rectangle is part of what it is to be a square. And I *see* that if some men are Greeks then some Greeks are men, that some men being Greeks and some Greeks being men are one and the same thing." Here we have a stopping place again for our Socratic questioning—but a stopping place that differs in a significant way from those considered in the previous section. (2) He might justify his claim to know these statements, not by saying that he sees that they are true, but rather by showing how to deduce them logically from *other* statements that are analytic or that are logically true. If we ask him what his justification is for believing he knows these other statements to be true, and if we continue our questioning, then sooner or later, he will stop with some such statements and say that he simply sees that they are true.

Let us now contrast the two statements "I see that Mr. Jones is in his garden" and "I see that all squares are rectangles." Both have subordinate statements as the objects of their principal verbs, and both are such that, if they are justified, then their subordinate statements are also justified. I may justify my claim to know that Mr. Jones is in his garden by saying "I see that he is" and I may justify my claim to know that all squares are rectangles by saying "I see that they are." And, as we have seen, if I am asked "What justification do you have for believing you *see* that Mr. Jones is in his garden?" then, if I do see that he is there, I can state my justification for believing that I see that he is there—and what I say will not merely reiterate the claim to see that he is there. But if I am asked "What justification do you have for claiming to see that all squares are rectangles?" and if my justification does not consist in the fact that I can deduce it logically from other analytic statements or from statements that are logically true, then I can *not* provide any further answer; in this case, unlike the case of Mr. Jones being in his garden, I can only reiterate that I *do* see it.

It is traditional to say, following Kant, that most, if not all, of the analytic statements and logical truths that express what we know are statements that express what we know a priori, and to say that what is known, but not known a priori, is known a posteriori. The point of using "a priori" and "a posteriori" may be suggested by this fact: we can know that all squares are rectangles *before* we have examined any particular square; but we cannot know that all men are mortal until *after* some particular men have been examined. One might speak of contemplating certain members of the realm of essence before examining any of their particular exemplifications in the realm of matter; this is the way that Santayana and Cohen expressed themselves. But we need not speak in this way, for one may also "contemplate" essence, or properties, in their particular exemplifications. As Aristotle said, "I may come to see that man is a rational animal—that the property of being rational and animal includes that of being rational—by considering some particular man, Callias; but what I thus learn will not be restricted to this particular fact, nor will it depend for its justification upon this particular fact."[51] And I may, by reflecting on some particular situation (say, on the fact that this apple is not, in the same part at the same time, both red and not red), come to know some more general fact that holds of all possible situations (say, that, for any possible object, being red excludes not being red). According to R. M. Eaton, this is the way we come to know some of the truths of logic.[52]

The statements we know a priori to be true differ in a number of respects from the "self-justifying" statements described in the previous chapter. For one thing, the "self-justifying" statements—e.g., "I believe that Socrates is mortal" and "That appears white"—are restricted to a psychological or subjective subject matter, but a priori statements are not so restricted. (The program of "psychologism," referred to in the first section, might be described as an attempt to reduce the a priori to the self-justifying, by transforming the statements of logic and mathematics into statements about the way in which people think.) For another thing, as Kant pointed out, the statements that we know a priori are statements that are *necessarily* true. All squares are rectangles—in this world and in all possible worlds. But "I cannot help believing that if a thing is a square it is a rectangle" is contingent and not necessary. (Consequently the program of "psychologism" was not successful.) Finally, if what I suggested in the previous chapter is accurate, a person's statement may be said to be "self-justifying" for her provided that her justification for thinking she knows it to be true is simply the fact that it *is* true; the point may be put alternatively by saying that such statements are "neither justified nor unjustified" but may constitute one's justification for other statements. Whether we may speak similarly of a priori statements remains problematic.[53]

What it is that we thus know a priori may seem meager and not worthy of being called "knowledge" at all. Schlick said, in his California lectures, that the statements of logic are "empty" and even Santayana, who wrote about "the realm of essence," said that there can be no *knowledge* of essences, that "there are no necessary truths," and that truth "never enters the field of mathematics at all."[54] But Schlick was saying only that the statements of logic *are* statements of logic and are not synthetic, and so, too, apparently was Santayana. (When Santayana wrote about the "realm of truth," he restricted the adjective "true" to what can be truly said only about the "realm of matter," about *this* possible world, and he did not apply the adjective — as he did the quotation at the beginning of this chapter — to what can be truly said about the "realm of essence." But he did truly say, of essences, and this is what matters, that "every essence involves its parts, considered as the elements which integrate it," and, "excludes everything not itself."[55] The interesting question is not whether analytic statements and the statements of logic are "empty truths," but whether they are truths at all.

3

Schlick had contended, and many still agree, that once we have exposed the relations between logic and language, we will be able to account for our "so-called 'rational knowledge.'" But just what relation between logic and language would account for such knowledge remained obscure.

Schlick said three quite different things in his California lecture: (1) that the so-called propositions of logic and mathematics are "nothing but certain rules which determine the use of language, i.e., of expression by combination of signs"; (2) that their "absolute truth" cannot be denied; and (3) that "they do not deal with any facts, but only with the symbols by means of which the facts are expressed."[56] Herbert Feigl and Albert Blumberg, reporting to America in 1931 on the speculations of the Vienna Circle (of which Schlick was one of the leading members), said substantially the same three things: (1) logic is "the system of conventions which determines the syntactical order required if we are to have a consistent language"; (2) the propositions of logic are "tautologically true"; and (3) "all formal sciences are engaged, then, in elaborating symbol-patterns and assert nothing about experience"[57] What, then, is the relation between logic and language that provides the key to our so-called rational knowledge? If we say, as in (1), that logical statements are *rules*, or *conventions*, then it may seem strange to go on to say, as in (2), that they are *true*; for we do not ordinarily think of rules, or of conventions, as being true, or as being false. Statements *about* rules, however, are either true or false; and what (3) suggests is, not that logical statements are themselves the rules or conventions of our language, but rather that they are statements *about* the rules of conventions of our language, statements telling us *what* these rules or conventions happen to be. Statements *about* the rules or conventions of language, however, need not be "tautologically true" (consider, e.g., "In French, adjectives of color are customarily placed after the noun they modify")—and the statements of logic with which we are concerned (e.g., "Either Socrates is mortal or it is false that Socrates is mortal") *are* tautologically true, and are *not*, in any clear sense, statements *about* the rules or conventions of our language.

What is usually maintained, in the face of such objections, is that the sentiments of logic are true *because* of the rules or conventions of our language. Thus Feigl and Blumberg said: "For example, '*p* or not-*p*' is tautologically true because of the very definitions of 'or' and 'not'" (p. 284). Others have said that analytic statements are true *because* of the way in which we use the words that make them up. What does this mean?

The doctrine of "truth by convention" will seem most plausible in the case of analytic statements. It may be recalled that the concept of the meaning of the words that make up a statement is essential to the definition of "analytic statement." The statement "All squares are rectangles," as it is understood in ordinary English, is analytic, inasmuch as the meaning of the predicate term is included in that of the subject term. But, as Plato had argued in the *Cratylus*, it is "by custom" and "convention," and not "by nature," that our words have the meanings they happen to have. Had the English language developed in a different way, as it quite conceivably could have, then those statements that happen now to be analytic might not be analytic and might even be false. If the word "square" were used to denote, not the geometrical objects that it does happen to denote, but, say, those things we now call "horses," then the English statement "All squares are rectangles" would be synthetic and false. Therefore, one may say that the English statement "All squares are rectangles" is analytic— and thus true—because we happen to use words the way we do. Similarly for the class of logical truths: if the word "some," for example, were used in the way in which, as it happens, we now use "all," then the statement "If some men are Greeks then some Greeks are men" would not be logically true.

May we infer from all of this that statements that are analytic or logically true are "true only by convention" and that the so-called rational contemplation of essence is merely knowledge or belief about our language? If such reasoning were valid, then we could infer, not only that analytic and logical statements are "true only be convention," but also that all of those *synthetic* statements that are true are "true only by convention." For, as Quine was to point out, "even so factual a sentence as 'Brutus killed Caesar' owes its truth, in part, to our using the component words the way we do."[58] Had "killed," for example, been given the use which the phrase "was survived by" came to have, then "Brutus killed Caesar" would be false—unless, of course, Brutus were called "Caesar" and Caesar "Brutus."

What if it is said that an analytic statement—e.g., "All squares are rectangles"—owes its truth *solely* to the fact that we use the component words the way we do, or, as the matter is sometimes put, that it is true "solely in virtue of the rules of our language"? We may suppose that the following is a "rule of English":

a) When the word "square" is used in English to designate something, the thing it designates should be square.

The rule seems more significant, of course, when it is formulated in a language other than English, e.g., as "Wenn das Wort 'square' auf Englisch angewendet wird, um etwas zu bedeuten, muss das, was es bedeutet, quadratisch sein." The following, then, would also be a "rule of English":

b) When the word "rectangular" is used in English to designate something, the thing it designates should be rectangular.

("'Rectangular' darf nur das bedeuten, was rechtwinkelig ist.") According to the thesis in question, the analytic statement "All squares are rectangles" owes its truth to the fact—and only to the fact—that the following is also a "rule of English":

c) When the word "square" is used in English to designate something, the thing it designates should be rectangular.

But (c) is a rule of quite a different sort from either (a) or (b). This may be seen as follows. If we were to teach English to an educated man, say to a native German, and taught him that (a) and (c) are rules of English, he would not be able to find out on his own that (b) is also a rule of English; or if we were to teach him that (b) and (c) are rules of English, he would not be able to find out on his own that (a) is a rule of English. But if we were to teach him that (a) and (b) are rules of English, he *would* then be able to find out on his own, to see by himself, that (c) is, or ought to be, an additional rule of English. How is it, then, that his knowledge of (a) and (b) enables him to know that (c) is also a rule? The only answer that seems reasonable to me is that, since he knows that all squares are rectangles, he knows that if (a) and (b) are rules, then (c) ought to be a rule as well. And, *ex hypothesi*, his knowledge that all squares are rectangles is now knowledge about the rules of English. I would say, therefore, that "All squares are rectangles" does not "owe its truth" solely to the fact that we use the component words the way we do; it owes it also to the fact that the conjunctive property of being both equilateral and rectangular has the property of being rectangular as one of its components.

Lewis wrote, in *An Analysis of Knowledge and Valuation*: "The *mode of expression* of any analytic truth is . . . dependent on linguistic conventions; as is also the manner in which any empirical fact is to be formulated and *conveyed*. But the meanings that are conveyed by symbols, on account of a stipulated or a customary usage of them, and the relation of meanings conveyed by an order of symbols, on account of syntactic stipulations or customary syntactic usage, are matters antecedent to and independent of any conventions affecting the linguistic manner in which they are to be conveyed" (p. 148).[59] What this passage makes clear to us is the need of keeping the following two questions distinct:

1) How does one find out whether the English statement "All squares are rectangles" is analytic?
2) How does one find out whether all squares are rectangles?

We can answer the first question only by making a linguistic investigation of English speaking people; but the answer to the second refers to what is a priori and depends only upon the "contemplation of essences," or however else we wish to describe that consideration of properties which is the source of our a priori knowledge. The linguistic study that is essential to the answer of (1) is not essential to the answer of (2); to realize this, we have only to consider that many people do not know English, and do not, therefore, know the answer to (1), but do know the answer to (2)—do know that all squares are rectangles. We need not answer (1), then to answer (2), but—and this is still another point—we *do* need to answer (2) to answer (1). For when we answer (1) we study the "linguistic behavior" of English speaking people and find out, as best we can, what properties constitute, for most such people, the meanings of the words "square" and "rectangle"; then, having found one property that we suppose to be the meaning of "square" and another that we suppose to be the meaning of "rectangle," we "look to see" whether the latter is included in the former—and this is something we can know a priori.[60]

To be sure, when I formulate question (2)—"How does one find out whether all squares are rectangles?"—I assume that the reader will understand what I have written; I assume, indeed, that I have used the words "squares" and "rectangles," as well as most of the other words that appear, in the way in which they are ordinarily used in English. But if the reader is tempted to infer from these facts that, when I write that all squares are rectangles, I am saying something *about* the English language, then he may be referred back to the possible confusion between "use" and "mention" noted at the end of the previous section.

In *Mind and the World-Order* (1929) and earlier, C. I. Lewis had defended a "pragmatic conception of the a priori," a view that was easily misread as being a kind of conventionalism. But this "pragmatic conception" was a view, not about the nature of a priori truth or our knowledge of it, but about our ways of classifying things. Whether, for example, it is better to use the word "fish" in such a way that it will apply to whales, or in such a way that it will not apply to anything that is a mammal—such questions as these are to be decided wholly on the basis of practical utility. "I *may* categorize experience as I will; but what categorical distinction will best serve my interests . . . ?" (p. 265). I *may* let properties A, B, and C be the properties that constitute the meaning of "fish," as I use the word, or I may choose properties B, C, and D instead; the choice is a matter of convenience. In the first use, but not the second, "All fish are A" will be analytic, and in the second, but not the first, "All fish are D" will be analytic. But (as Lewis recognized) the choice of these two classifications has no effect on the two a priori truths—that the properties A, B, and C include the property A, and that the properties B, C, and D include the property D—truths that do not at all depend on anyone's convenience. Thus Lewis said that "the pragmatic element in knowledge concerns the choice in application of conceptual modes of interpretation," but does not touch that "abstract a priori truth" which is "absolute and eternal (pp. 272-73).

I think it is fair to say that, for any clear interpretation that has been found for the phrase "true only by convention," the phrase cannot be said to refer to any merely *linguistic* characteristic that is peculiar to analytic statements and the truths of logic. There remains, however, the possibility that the statements *are* linguistic conventions —not that they are *true* "by convention" but that they are themselves conventions, rules, or stipulations and are thus not true (or false) at all. This possibility, as we saw, was suggested by Schlicks's California lecture and by Feigl and Blumberg's report; it was defended by Ernest Nagel, writing on "Logic without Ontology." Logical principles, he said, are "regulative principles," which are "*prescriptive* for the use of language"; the choice between alternative systems of such principles may be grounded "on the relatively greater adequacy of one of them as an instrument for achieving a certain systematization of knowledge."[61] But even if it be conceded that some logical statements are no more than rules or conventions, there is a difficulty of principle in saying that *all* such statements are rules or conventions. "Briefly the objection is that whatever rules one may have initially stipulated, and however arbitrary such stipulations may be, one will thereafter have to *find out* what these rules entail, and the statement that such and such is entailed by the rules could hardly be characterized as itself a rule."[62] What we find out, when we discover with respect to two statements in our language that our rules allow us to derive one from the other, includes a logical truth—something that we can know a priori.

I think that Schlick and his followers were mistaken, then, in saying that there are certain facts about language that will enable us to set aside our "so-called rational knowledge." Other attacks on the traditional conception of the a priori have proceeded from a skeptical position—a skepticism about our knowledge of properties and states of affairs. According to Lewis, as we have noted, if the word "square" is used to mean the property of being square and if the word "rectangular" is used to mean the property of being rectangular, then the statement "All squares are rectangular" is analytic; for, as he said, one can *see* by a kind of experiment in the imagination, that the property of being rectangular is included in that of being square (i.e., in that of being equilateral and rectangular). Morton White was skeptical about this kind of seeing or understanding: "One either sees or doesn't see the relationship and that is the end of the matter. It is very difficult to argue one's difficulties with such a position and I shall only say dogmatically that I do not find this early retreat to intuition satisfactory."[63] On the basis of a similar skepticism, Quine concluded that acceptance of the traditional distinction between analytic and synthetic is "an unempirical dogma of empiricists, a metaphysical article of faith."[64]

Here again I take the liberty of referring the reader to the discussion of skepticism in the first section.

4

There remains the question of the synthetic a priori. Is anything that is known a priori to be true expressible only in statements that are synthetic, i.e., in statements that are neither analytic nor logically true? Or, as we may say for short, do we have any synthetic a priori knowledge? According to the tradition of British empiricism, which has dominated much of the philosophical thought of the period with which we are concerned, all of our a priori knowledge is "empty" and "nonfactual"—that is to say, all of our a priori knowledge is expressible in statements that are analytic or logically true. But some American philosophers have argued, with some plausibility, that some of our a priori knowledge can be expressed only in statements that are synthetic.

The concept of the synthetic a priori, however, has been taken in two quite different ways, with the result that our question—"Do we have any synthetic a priori knowledge?"—has a certain ambiguity that is often overlooked. The technical term "a priori" is sometimes taken in a positive sense, as it has been here, and "a posteriori" is then defined as what is not a priori. If, for the moment, we take "rational knowledge" as a synonym for this positive sense of "a priori," then we may say that our a posteriori knowledge is any knowledge that is not rational knowledge. But sometimes "a posteriori" is taken as the positive term and the "a priori" is then defined as what is not a posteriori. When "a posteriori" is taken in this positive sense it then becomes a synonym for "empirical knowledge." (Our empirical knowledge may be thought of roughly, as comprising: first, what we know by means of the "external senses"; second, those facts about our own psychological states and about appearing that were discussed in the previous section; third, those facts of the first two types that we *remember*; and, last, whatever is inductively supported by any of the foregoing. The concepts of *empirical knowledge* and *rational knowledge* are thus exclusive but not necessarily exhaustive. If Burch's views about revelation, referred to in the first section, are correct, then there is a religious knowledge that is neither empirical nor rational.) Hence our question "Do we have any synthetic a priori knowledge?" may be taken in these two ways:

A) Is there any rational knowledge that is expressible only in synthetic statements?

B) Is there any knowledge that is not empirical and is expressible only in synthetic statements?

An affirmative answer to (A) would imply an affirmative answer to (B). An affirmative answer to (B), however, need not imply an affirmative answer to (A); for if there is knowledge that is neither empirical nor rational, and if that knowledge is the only nonempirical knowledge that must be expressed in synthetic statements, then (A) would be answered in the negative and (B) in the affirmative. In the present chapter, we are concerned with (A).

Our problem may be discussed by reference to the following six statements, each of which has been taken, by some American philosopher, to indicate an area of synthetic a priori knowledge:

1) Anything that is red is colored.
2) Nothing is both red and green.
3) If anything is orange, then it has a color that is intermediate between red and yellow.
4) Anything that is colored is extended.
5) Anything that is a cube has twelve edges.
6) Seven and five are twelve.

If we wish to show that there is no synthetic a priori knowledge, then we must show, with respect to each of these statements, either that it is analytic, or that it expresses what is known but not known a priori, or that it does not express what is known at all. The statements may thus be thought of as presenting us with six puzzles or riddles. The way in which we deal with these puzzles or riddles will obviously have important implications concerning the nature of our knowledge.

C. H. Langford has defended the thesis of the synthetic a priori with respect to statements (1), (2), (3), and (5); Hector Neri Castañeda, following Kant, has defended it with respect to (6); and various philosophers have defended it with respect to (4).[65]

Statement (1)—"Anything that is red is colored"—is very much like our earlier statement, "Anything that is square is rectangular." I think we may assume that, if the latter can be known a priori, then so, too can the former; in each case, knowledge of a single instance of the generalization is enough, if not more than enough, to enable us to see that the generalization itself is true. To show that "Anything that is square is rectangular" is analytic, we may "analyze the predicate out of the subject" in such a way that we turn the statement into an explicit redundancy; that is to say, we replace the subject term "square" with a synonymous expression, "equilateral and rectangular," containing the original predicate, and the result—"Anything that is equilateral and rectangular is rectangular"—is a statement that is logically true. Can we similarly "analyze the predicate out of the subject" in the case of statement (1)? Can we find some term, which along with "colored" can be used to make up a synonym for "red," and which will then enable us to turn "Anything that is red is colored" into an explicit redundancy? I believe that no one has been able to find a term that will do.

Suppose, however, that we had a list of all the colors, and suppose (for simplicity) that the list comprised just the colors red, yellow, green, and blue. Could we then say that "colored" is synonymous with "either red, yellow, green, or blue?" If we could, then by replacing the *predicate* instead of the subject we could turn "Anything that is red is colored" into the following logical truth: "Anything that is red is either red, yellow, green, or blue." But if our list of colors is not complete, then, of course, we cannot say that "colored" is synonymous with "either red, yellow, green, or blue," for the color that our list omits will be a color and neither red, yellow, green, nor blue. And even if our list of colors should happen to be complete, we may, at least, speculate on the possibility that it is not: "Were we all in the position of those people we now call 'color-blind,' we would have been mistaken about the completeness of any list we might have made. Might it not be that we are also mistaken about this present list? Perhaps there is some color that none of us is acquainted with, and that therefore is not on our list, but is such that if we were to become acquainted with it we would see that it is a further color to be added to our list." This speculation may be false, but, as Langford said (concerning a slightly different example), "it is logically and conceptually possible, which is all that is required for our purposes."[66] If it is logically and conceptually possible that a thing be colored and neither red, yellow, blue, nor green, then "colored" cannot mean "either red, yellow, blue, or green"; for there is *no* possibility that a thing could be either red, yellow, blue, or green, but neither red, yellow, blue nor green. And so runs the principal objection to this method of showing that statement (1) is analytic.

But if the objection is unfounded and if we can say that the list "red, yellow, blue, and green" (possibly with some additions), constitutes a complete list of colors, then we may also be able to say that statement (2)—"Nothing is both red and green"—is analytic. We might say, for example, that "green" means the same as "colored, but neither red, yellow, nor blue," and statement (2) could then be transformed into the logical truth "Nothing is both red and colored but neither red, yellow, nor blue." But if the objection we have just considered is valid, then we will have to deny that "green" means the same as "colored, but neither red, yellow, nor blue," and this method of transforming (2) into a logical truth will have to be rejected.

More technical devices have been proposed: we might try to our color vocabulary in such a way that, in our revised vocabulary, we can say everything we need to say about colors but cannot formulate the troublesome statement (2). If we can do this—and the technique that has been applied with considerable success elsewhere in philosophy and in logic—then perhaps we can say that our difficulties with (2) can be traced, not to the fact that (2) is synthetic a priori, but to the fact that our ordinary color vocabulary is defective. In applying this method, however, we must be on guard lest, when we use our new vocabulary, our difficulties reappear in connection with some other sentence. The following is a simple example of this method.

Think of two objects, A and B, which are red and green, respectively; define "is red" as "has the same color as A and does not have the same color as B," and define "is green" as "has the same color as B and does not have the same color as A"; then "Nothing is both red and green" may be replaced by "There is nothing that has the same color as A and does not have the same color as B and has the same color as B and does not have the same color as A," which latter statement is a logical truth. But, if I am not mistaken, we will have only transferred the problem of the synthetic a priori—transferred the problem from "Nothing is both red and green" to "If one object is red and another object is green, then the two objects do not have the same color." A method somewhat similar to this, though with added technical detail and refinement, was proposed by Hilary Putnam.[67] Arthur Pap subsequently suggested that the troublesome statements with which such an analysis leaves us—e.g., "Red and green are different colors"—*are* synthetic a priori, but that they are *also* statements that have "a linguistic origin" and therefore "may even be purely *verbal* and not 'about the world' at all! . . . What capital could a rationalist make of such synthetic a priori knowledge?"[68] We have noted, however, that serious difficulties are involved in saying, of statements that do not mention language, that they are "purely verbal" or that they have their "origin in language." I think it is more plausible to say of statement (2)—"Nothing is both red and green"—that it has its "origin" in the relation of *exclusion*, which obtains between the properties of being red and being green, and to which Santayana referred in the quotation at the beginning of this section.

Statement (3) on our list—"If anything is orange, then it has a color that is intermediate between red and yellow"—raises no new questions of principle. Of (3), Langford wrote: "We may suppose a person who has never seen anything that was either red or yellow, but has seen all his life things that were orange in color. Such a person will easily be able to understand the antecedent of this proposition; but he will not be able to understand its consequent, and that will not be due merely to a defect in vocabulary."[69] And this Langford took to be evidence for saying that (3) is synthetic a priori.

Perhaps we may deal with statement (4)—"Anything that is colored is extended"—in a simpler way. Instead of trying to prove that it is analytic, we might suggest, on the ground that it is not known at all, that it is now known a priori. For how are we to tell, of things that are not extended, whether or not they are colored?

What of statement (5), "Anything that is a cube has twelve edges"? Langford proposed the following argument to show that this statement, which seems clearly a priori, is not analytic. There are many people, he said, who know *what* a cube is, who can recognize dice and other such objects as being cubes, and who do *not* realize that being a cube requires having twelve edges. From this he deduced that "the notion of having twelve edges can be no part of the notion of being a cube" and hence that the statement "Anything that is a cube has twelve edges" is not analytic.[70] The conclusion follows, however, only if we assume that a man cannot recognize an object as exemplifying a certain complex of properties unless he also recognizes it as exemplifying each of the components of that complex. But it is at least problematic, I think, whether this assumption is true; the theories of the Gestalt psychologists suggest that it may be false.[71]

Our statement (6)—"Seven and five are twelve"—involves technical questions of logic and mathematics that fall outside the scope of the present survey. According to Kant and Castañeda, such mathematical statements are synthetic a priori; according to John Stuart Mill, they are synthetic but not a priori; and according to the "logistic thesis," defended in Russell and Whitehead's *Principia Mathematica* and elsewhere, such statements may be translated into the statements of logic and are therefore not synthetic. The status of (6) in contemporary controversy turns upon the question whether the "logistic thesis" is true. If the thesis is true, then the translations of (6) and the other statements of pure mathematics would turn out to be very long; Professor Quine told a Brazilian audience in 1942 that, if the binomial theorem were written out in the vocabulary of logic and in type the size of this, it would "extend from the North Pole to the South Pole.[72] But the objection to the "logistic thesis" is not, of course, to the length of the translations in question; the controversy concerns, first, whether these lengthy translations *would* be translations of such statements as (6), as the statements are ordinarily understood, and, second, whether all of the statements needed for the logistic translation or paraphrase of (6) are statements that are logically true. But these are not questions of epistemology.

Other statements sometimes thought or be synthetic a priori involve questions of ethics and of metaphysics; examples are "To the extent that an act is charitable it is good, whatever its consequences" and "If there are complexes, then there are simples."[73] The philosophical significance of the particular examples we have considered lies partly in this fact: if some of them must be acknowledged as exemplifying the synthetic a priori, then, in order to defend skepticism with respect to the statements of ethics and of metaphysics, it will not be sufficient merely to point out that some such statements, if they are known to be true, are synthetic a priori.

Appearances and Reality

1

"No man doubts," wrote A. O. Lovejoy in his Carus Lectures, *The Revolt Against Dualism* (Norton, 1930), "that when he brings to mind the look of a dog he owned when a boy, there is something of a canine sort immediately present to and therefore compresent with his consciousness, but that it is quite certainly not that dog in the flesh" (p. 305). The image—the something of a canine sort that is immediately before the mind—is not itself a physical object, Lovejoy said; it is a private, psychological object, conditioned by a series of physiological and psychological events, reaching back to the earlier dog that it now reveals.

If a man now looks at his desk, then, according to Lovejoy, another series of physiological and psychological events occurs, this time involving the activity of sense organs, but resulting as before in a private, psychological object—a sensation, this time something of a desk sort, a "visible desk" that in certain respects serves to duplicate the real, external, physical desk that it makes known to us. More generally, Lovejoy said, "the datum or character complex presented in the perception of a given moment" is never more than "the report, more or less tardy and more or less open to suspicion, from the original object which we are said to know by virtue of that perception" (p. 20).

Both of these examples—the earlier dog being now presented by a private and transitory mental dog and the external desk being presented by an inner visual desk—provide us with the essentials of two philosophical theories, which Lovejoy had referred to as "epistemological dualism" and "psychophysical dualism." According to "epistemological dualism," which is a thesis about our knowledge, we have direct or immediate knowledge only of certain private or subjective states of mind; some external objects, past or present, are duplicated in these states of mind and it is in virtue of this duplication that we know what we do about the rest of the world. Our knowledge of external things and of past events involves a "cleavage" between the *object* of our knowing and the subjective *vehicle* that makes that object known. And according to "psychophysical dualism," which is a thesis about reality, the world is constituted out of at least two fundamentally different kinds of stuff—the physical or material things that are studied by physics, and the psychical or mental things that make up our states of mind. When asserted in conjunction, as they were by Lovejoy, and in the seventeenth century by Descartes and Locke, these two forms of dualism imply that our knowledge of physical or material things is derived from our knowledge of the mental or psychical duplicates of physical or material things.

2

Future historians of British and American philosophy, Lovejoy suggested, might well describe the period from 1905 to 1930 as the period of the "Great Revolt Against Dualism"—an age in which philosophers sought to avoid epistemological and psychophysical dualism without falling into the subjectivism or skepticism that seemed to be the only alternatives. The appearance of *The New Realism* (Macmillan, 1912) had been an early American contribution to this revolt. The six New Realists—E. B. Holt, Walter T. Marvin, William Pepperell Montague, Ralph Barton Perry, Walter B. Pitkin, and E. G. Spaulding —had proclaimed, in opposition to the thesis of "epistemological dualism" (and in opposition to the thesis of nineteenth century "idealism"), that the objects of external perception and of memory are "directly presented to consciousness" and are "precisely what they appear to be." No inner visual desk is needed to present the one that is outside, and the dog of thirty years ago can present itself again today. For "nothing intervenes between the knower and the world external to him. Objects are not presented to consciousness by ideas; they are directly presented" (p. 2).

The New Realists had formulated their objection to dualism in the following way. If the two forms of dualism are true, then, they said:

The only external world is one that we can never experience, the only world that we can have any experience of is the internal world of ideas. When we attempt to justify the situation by appealing to inference as the guarantee of this unexperienceable externality, we are met by the difficulty that the world we infer can only be made up of the matter of experience, that it can only be made up of mental pictures in new combinations. An inferred object is always a perceptible object, one that could be in some sense experienced; and, as we have seen, the only things that according to this view can be experienced are our mental states. Moreover, the world in which all our interests are centered is the world of experienced objects. Even if, *per impossibile*, we could justify the belief in a world beyond that which we could experience, it would be but a barren achievement, for such a world would contain none of the things that we see and feel. Such a so-called real world would be more alien to us and more thoroughly queer than were the ghostland or dreamland which, as we remember, the primitive realist sought to use as a home for certain of the unrealities of life [p. 5].

This is an accurate statement, I think, of the absurdity which some of the versions of dualism involve. The New Realists rejected epistemological dualism outright (though Montague had misgivings), and at least two of them—Perry and Holt—seemed also to reject psycho-physical dualism. Subsequent philosophers, both in England and in America, were to construct metaphysical systems in the interests of this "Great Revolt Against Dualism."

Lovejoy's own activity, as Arthur Murphy said, was thus counter-revolutionary. He was one of the seven Critical Realists who contributed to a second cooperative study, *Essays in Critical Realism* (Macmillan, 1920). The adjective "critical" was used to distinguish the realism of the seven from the admittedly "naïve" realism of the six. All of the Critical Realists—Durant Drake, J. B. Pratt, A. K. Rogers, George Santayana, Roy Wood Sellars, C. A. Strong, and Lovejoy—accepted something very close to the thesis of epistemological dualism; and all but Drake, Sellars, and Strong accepted the thesis of psychophysical dualism.

By 1930, Lovejoy thought, the matter was finally settled. He concluded his book by saying, concerning the two types of dualism, that "there is no conclusion of empirical science about the physical world—assuming that there in any sense *is* a physical world—which is better established" (p. 319).

3

"Epistemological dualism," as Lovejoy understood it, involved the following three theses:

1) The only things that are ever *immediately given* to anyone are sensible appearances, memory images, and other such ideas.
2) Sensible appearances, memory images, and ideas are *subjective* in that they depend for their existence on the physiological and psychological state of the subject to whom they are immediately given.
3) Perceiving a physical thing to have a certain characteristic consists, in part, of (a) being given a sensible appearance that has that characteristic and (b) attributing that characteristic to the physical thing; analogously, remembering something to have had a certain characteristic consists, in part, of (a) being given a memory-image that has that characteristic and (b) attributing the characteristic to a prior state of the thing.

I have discussed, in the second section, the issues which the first of these three theses involves; we may now turn to the second and third.

I shall refer to the second thesis as the "subjective premise," since it asserts the "subjectivity" of appearances and images. Some of the metaphysical systems that were developed in the course of the "Great Revolt Against Dualism" depended on denying the subjective premise.

I shall call the third thesis the "messenger promise." Lovejoy had used the word "messenger" in this connection (p. 20); in perceiving, he suggested, we read the message contained in the appearance and thus (we suppose) learn something about the stimulus objects from which the message was sent. At times Lovejoy and some of the other Critical Realists seemed to take the messenger premise in a literal sense: In perceiving and in remembering, we attribute to the object of knowledge *just those characteristics* that we directly apprehend in the subjective vehicle of knowledge. At other times, however, the messenger premise seems not to have been taken in a literal sense.

4

Of the three theses that epistemological dualism involved, the least objectionable might seem to be the one that I call the "subjective premise"—the thesis that appearances and images depend for their existence on the physiological and psychological state of the subject to whom they are given, and are thus "subjective." But to the New Realists, who had been the leaders in the American revolt against dualism, and to the "objective relativists" and "perspective realists" who were to oppose "Mr. Lovejoy's Counter-Revolution," the hope for a realistic account of our knowledge of the world seemed to depend on denying, or at least qualifying, the subjective premise.

The New Realists had written: "The content of knowledge, that which lies in or before the mind when knowledge takes place is numerically identical with the thing known."[74] By the "content" of knowledge, they seemed to mean just those sensible appearances that Lovejoy was to describe as the "vehicles" of knowledge. But where Lovejoy, as an "epistemological dualist," distinguished the "vehicle" from the object it makes known, the New Realists said that the "content" and the object are one and the same. E. B. Holt had written that the sensible appearance of a physical object is "a part of the object."[75] Hence, according to the New Realism, the physiological and psychological processes involved in perception cannot be said to "create" or "generate" the sensible appearances that "lie before the mind" when perception takes place; these processes serve merely to "select" among appearances that already lie outside the mind and beyond the skin of the perceiver's body. "What is selected," Perry said, "is there to be selected, and is not instituted by the act of selection."[76] Where the dualist thought of perception as involving something like "a painter's canvas or photographic plate on which objects in themselves imperceptible are represented," the New Realists spoke of perception as "analogous to a light which shines out through the sense organs, illuminating the world outside the knower."[77]

In rejecting the subjective premise, the New Realists exposed themselves to the puzzling questions that are sometimes thought to constitute the subject matter of epistemology. What of the appearances of such objects as the straight stick that looks bent when partially immersed, the railroad tracks that appear to converge in the distance, the rectangular tabletop that looks diamond-shaped from the corner, the distant star that no longer exists but still appears in the heavens? Do the appearances of *these* objects exist along with the objects when no one is looking? Santayana wrote: "For the human system whiskey is truly more intoxicating than coffee, and the contrary opinion would be an error; but what a strange way of vindicating this real, though relative, distinction, to insist that whiskey is more intoxicating in itself, without reference to any animal; that it is pervaded, as it were, by an inherent intoxication, and stands dead drunk in its bottle!"[78] The plausibility of the subjective premise lies in the fact that the ways in which things appear depend in part on the state of the observer.

Arthur E. Murphy proposed "objective relativism" as a way of meeting such difficulties. "Objective relativism" was both a metaphysics and an epistemology, and had been influenced by Samuel Alexander, A. N. Whitehead, and John Dewey.[79] Murphy summarized the view, in 1939, in the following words:

The experienced world is *at once* in some of its major features dependent on and conditioned by the special relations in which sentient (and more particularly human) organisms stand to their environment *and also* a direct presentation of that environment itself, or the order of natural events, as it is under such conditions. Nature is not something essentially beyond the range of perceptual inspection, having its exclusive being in characters independent of all relation to human responses to it. Far more in the natural world than we can ever experience there certainly is and must be. But unless what we experience *also* belongs to and is, under the special but entirely natural conditions of organic interaction, a sample of the nature to which we claim to refer, then our relation to this ulterior nature becomes problematic, and the conditions of interaction which are in fact our means of getting in touch with it are treated as barriers to knowledge of what it is.[80]

It is an "objectively relative" characteristic of the distant star that, long after the star has ceased to exist it still appears in a certain way to those who look toward its former place in the heavens—"objective" because it is an objective fact about the star that the star *does* appear in this way, but "relative" because the star would *not* appear in this way unless some sentient being were there to be appeared to. When she *is* thus appeared to, the sentient being has a "sample" of what is in the heavens. The term "sample" is appropriate because, if we can accept the Whiteheadian cosmology that had influenced this view, we can say that the star is made up of such "concrete events" as its appearing in certin ways under certain conditions.

E. B. McGilvary defended a similar thesis. The star is made up of its "perspectives" (among other things); some of these perspectives are conditioned by perceiving organisms; and every perceptual experience may be regarded "as the real objective world appearing in the perspective of an experiencing organism."[81] McGilvary called his view "perspectivism," or "perspective realism," but he also accepted Murphy's term "objective relativism." Lovejoy had argued that nothing that is past can be conditioned by anything that is present; we cannot say that the characteristics of a star no longer exists may yet depend on some observer who looks into the heavens tonight. McGilvary replied: "There is such a character as that of 'being an ancestor of a president of the United States.' Had Mr. Hoover not been elected president in 1928 an indefinitely large number of men and women of bygone days would not have acquired this character."[82]

But the epistemology, as distinguished from the cosmology, of "objective relativism" does not seem to differ significantly from that of "epistemological dualism." Let us compare the ways in which Lovejoy and Murphy described the experience of the astronomer. According to Lovejoy, the astronomer has an experience that is conditioned by his own organic state and that contains a "message" about a star; according to Murphy, the astronomer has an experience that is conditioned by his own organic state and that contains, or constitutes, a "sample" of the star. In each case, we seem to have a "vehicle" that informs us about an object; in the one case the vehicle contains a "message," in the other a "sample"; both the "sample" and the "message" tell us something that is in the sky; and both the "sample" and the "message"—or that which contains the message— are dependent on the state of the perceiver. Thus Montague said that "these relativistic objects" bear "a suspicious resemblance" to the sensible appearances of Lovejoy's dualism.[83]

What the revolt against dualism needed was an attack on what I call the "messenger premise."

5

According to the messenger premise, perceiving a physical thing to have a certain characteristic consists in part of (a) being "given" a sensible appearance that has that characteristic and (b) attributing the characteristic to the physical thing; and analogously for remembering. Let us now consider the implications of (a).

The term "picture theory" that the New Realists had applied to dualism was not unacceptable to Lovejoy. If a man perceives a physical object or remembers one, Lovejoy said, the "transcendent reference" that his cognitive state involves consists in ascribing to the object of knowing a characteristic that the sense-datum "actually and certainly" possesses (p. 314); perceiving and remembering involve the "faith" that the object has, or had, this same characteristic. Some of the other Critical Realists had written in similar terms: the "immediate datum" that is "private" to the knower was said to have characteristics that the knower, acting in "animal faith," attributes to the object. C. A. Strong said that the perceiver "predicates the sense-datum of the external thing" and Roy Wood Sellars said that the vehicle of knowing has "a sort of revelatory identity with the object."[84] But these philosophical statements, when interpreted literally, seem clearly false.

The error had been noted by Durant Drake in his contribution to *Essays in Critical Realism*. Suppose, he said, that I perceive "a round wheel about three feet in diameter, moving away from me and now between this house and the next." The messenger premise would have us say that the characteristics, which I thus perceive a group of material things to have, are characteristics "actually and certainly" belonging to a sensible appearance. But it is clear, Drake said, that the complex sensible appearance I experience on this occasion "is not round (on any theory), since the wheel is endwise towards me; nor is it three feet in diameter, or moving away from me, or between this house and the next; nor does it have many, if any, of the qualities connoted by the word 'wheel.'"[85] Lovejoy had said that his memory-image had the characteristics that he attributed to his dog. But *which* characteristics? Perhaps he remembered the dog to be wearing a collar, and to be friendly and obedient; but surely he did not experience a sensible appearance possessing any of *these* characteristics.

Certain words do seem to apply both to appearances and to physical things—for example, "red," "bitter," "hard," "cold." And one might wish to say that the messenger premise does apply when it is restricted to the characteristics that these words connote. But these words, as Aristotle had said, are ambiguous, meaning one thing when applied to appearances and another thing when applied to phsyical things.[86] The distinction between these two uses was clearly drawn by C. J. Ducasse. When we say of a tree that it is green, then the term "green" refers to a property that is causal, or dispositional, in the same sense in which such terms as "abrasive" and "corrosive" refer to properties that are causal, or dispositional. If we are physicists, we may mean that the tree is such that, when it is struck by light, it reflects light vibrations of one frequency and absorbs the others; but those of us who are not physicists are more likely to mean that "the tree, whether or not it be at the moment looked at, is such that under the conditions of observation that are the standard ones for such an object," it would cause a sentient observer to have the sensation of green.[87] And when we say of the sensation, or appearance, that *it* is green, we do not intend the adjective in this causal or dispositional sense. To understand the nondispositional sense of such adjectives, we must look more closely at such terms as "appearance," "sense-datum," and "sensation."

As the quotation from Durant Drake suggests, to see something that appears to be a wheel is not to experience an *appearance* that *is* a wheel; this fact alone should make us wary of transforming "Something appears green to me" into "I experience a green appearance of something." The latter expression, moreover, seems to complicate matters beyond necessity; where the former involves the one category of *appearing* the latter involves the two categories of *experiencing* and *appearance*. Ducasse proposed, in effect, that we retain the verb "to experience" (or use "to sense" as a synonym) and that we reject the implication that there are *appearances* that are objects of experience. When we use such adjectives as "green" and "blue" in the locutions "appears blue, or green" and "presents an appearance, or sensation, which is blue, or green," the adjectives

are names not of objects of experience, nor of species of objects of experience, but of *species of experience itself.* What this means is perhaps made clearest by saying that to sense blue is then to sense *bluely* just as to dance the waltz is to dance "waltzily" (i.e., in the manner called "to waltz."). . . . Sensing, that is to say, is a mental process having to sensing blue the same logic relation which obtains, for example, between the process in a string called "vibrating" and a particular mode in which it vibrates—say, the middle-C mode. . . . Sensing blue, I hold, is thus a species or modulation of sensing.[88]

It would hardly be fair to say that, when Lovejoy contrasted the "visible desk" with the "'real' desk" that it makes known (p. 16), he took the statement "Something *appears* to me to be a desk" to imply that something presents me with an appearance that *is* a desk. But once we see that the messenger premise cannot be taken literally, we also see, if I am not mistaken, that we have no reason to suppose that the "real desk" has *any* kind of "internal duplicate."

It should be noted, in passing, that if the picture theory of *epistemological* dualism is false, then *one* of Lovejoy's arguments for *psychophysical* dualism is inconclusive. For Lovejoy had argued: (1) we see desks and stars and other objects by means of internal desks and stars that are not identical with the objects they enable us to perceive; but (2) no place among physical objects can be found for such internal desks and stars; therefore (3) the latter objects inhabit "the world of the mind" and not "the world of matter." But if premise (1) is false, *this* argument for psychophysical dualims is no longer available. Since there *are* no internal desks and stars, the materialist need not be asked to find a place for them.[89]

Variants of the picture theory defended by other Critical Realists had similar limitations. Roy Wood Sellars said, in *Essays in Critical Realism*, that sensible appearances serve as "substitutes" for external things: "these sensible characteristics which are open to inspection and so readily taken to be literal aspects, surfaces, and inherent qualities of physical things are *subjective substitutes* for the corresponding parts of the physical world" (p. 191). And he said elsewhere, of external physical things, that "we tend to mistake our sensations *for* these things"; "a patch of color, for instance, is *interpreted as* the surface of a thing"; and "analysis shows that the only literally intuited object is the sensory datum but that, in perceiving as such, it is given a context which makes the percipient *regard* it *as* an appearing thing."[90] Sellars did not say, as Lovejoy did, that there *are* two desks, one an appearance and the other an external thing; no appearance *is* a desk, according to Sellars, but people tend mistakenly to *believe* that certain appearances are desks. If what I have been saying is true, however, Sellars' account is also inadequate. People do not mistake appearances for desks; and when a man is mistaken in thinking that he perceives his desk, his mistake does not consist in believing, with respect to some appearance, that the appearance is his desk. The "transcendent reference" involved in perception—and in memory— does *not* consist in ascribing to a physical thing a characteristic or property that some sense appearance "actually and certainly" possesses, or even in ascribing to the thing a characteristic or property the sense appearance is mistakenly supposed to possess.

Aristotle taught that, in knowing, the soul "receives the form of the object" and that "actual knowledge is identical with its object."[91] Subsequent Aristotelians attempted to compromise between epistemological dualism and epistemological monism by saying that what is "in the mind" is "formally identical" with, but "materially different" from, the object that is known. "The thing *is* in the mind intentionally; the mind is or becomes the thing intentionally. Thus the thing actually known and the mind actually knowing it are identical."[92] This doctrine, which was developed by Thomas Aquinas and his commentators, is expounded in Thomistic manuals of epistemology; it was also set forth in 1948 as part of the "Platform" of a group of American philosophers called the "Association for Realistic Philosophy."[93] Where Lovejoy might be interpreted as saying that, when a man perceives a dog, an *appearance* takes on *some* of the characteristics of the dog, the Thomistic doctrine could be taken to say that, when the man perceives a dog, then the *man*, or his soul, takes on *all* the characteristics of the dog, though without becoming "identical with the matter" of the dog, and that when the man perceives a dog and a bird together, then the *man* becomes "formally identical" with the *dog*, and *also* with the *bird*. There have been many attempts to make this doctrine intelligible, but I cannot feel that they have been successful.

In *The Degrees of Knowledge* (Scribner, 1959; translated from the fourth French edition) Jacques Maritain reasoned in the following way: (1) "By an apparent scandal to the principle of identity, to know is to be in a certain way something other than what one is: it is to become a thing other than the self." But (2) the man who perceives a bird does not become identical with a bird in the precise sense in which the feathered object in the tree is identical with a bird. Hence (3) "there is a kind of union, transcending every union of a material sort, between the knower and the known." And therefore (4) "there is a vigorous correspondence between knowledge and immateriality. A being is a knowing being to the extent that it is immaterial" (p. 2).

Nicholas of Cusa, opening his argument in a similar way ("Intellegere est esse similitudinem omnium"), and assuming that the principle of identity is true, deduced that knowledge is impossible—a conclusion that Maritain avoids only by means of the qualifying premises (2) and (3). What his first three premises tell us, it seems to me, is merely that the relation between knower and known is quite unlike any of those relations that hold among the objects of physical science. I prefer Lovejoy's statement of the latter point:

To be known (except in the way in which immediate sensory content is sometimes, but, as I think, unfortunately said to be "known") things must—to use a happy phrase of Professor Dewey's—be "present-as-absent"; but since . . . a given bit of reality cannot be literally *both* present and absent, knowing must be a function of a unique and anomalous (but not a self-contradictory) sort. It must consist (partly) in the existence, at a given time and within an individuated field of consciousness, of particulars which do duty for other particulars, extraneous to that time and that field; and the former particulars must have associated with them in consciousness, the peculiar—but, as I submit, empirically the perfectly familiar—property which some of the Schoolmen termed "intentionality" and later dualistic epistemology has called "self-transcendent reference." The "intentional" or referential quality of a given bit of content present *now* in *my* cognitive experience is itself an item in the same present experience.[94]

The problem is, as Lovejoy suggests: in what way do certain particulars thus "do duty" for other particulars? Traditionally there have been two alternatives to the "identity," or "resemblance," theories of knowledge. These alternatives have also been defended by American philosophers.

6

Sextus Empiricus said, in his treatise *Against the Dogmatists*, that the function of appearances in perceiving is that of being *signs*—but signs only of *other* appearances. The appearances caused by smoke may signify those that are caused by fire; and they perform this sign function, not because they *resemble* the appearances that they signify, but because appearances of both kinds have been associated in the past. Indeed, according to Sextus, to say that appearances of smoke are a sign for some person of appearances of fire, is to say only that when that person experiences the smoke appearances she will be led to expect the fire appearances. Bishop Berkeley proposed, in his *Three Dialogues between Hylas and Philonous* (1713), that this relation between appearances gives us the clue to the nature of perception: the immediate apprehension "of ideas by one sense suggests to the mind others, perhaps belonging to another sense, which are wont to be connected with them." W. T. Stace, in *The Theory of Knowledge and Existence* (Oxford, 1932), and C. I. Lewis, in *An Analysis of Knowledge and Valuation* (Open Court, 1946), defended sophisticated versions of this theory.

Stace said that, when a man sees an apple, the man experiences certain visual appearances and "interprets" them by taking them to be signs of possible future appearances; "thus the reddish colour and the shape become signs to me that the visual experiences which I have of them will be followed in certain circumstances by another quite different experience, [for example] the sweet taste in the mouth" (p. 245). Lewis said, similarly, that the cognitive function of appearances is that of signifying *other* appearances. Stace described the "external world" as a "mental construction," and Lewis said that any meaningful statement about a physical thing is "translatable" into conditional statements about appearances (or, somewhat more accurately, into statements of the form "If I experience an S kind of appearance, then, if I undertake to do A, I will experience an E kind of appearance"). The relation of physical things to appearances, according to this "constructional" or "translation" thesis, is like that of "the average man" to particular men; statements ostensibly about the former may be translated, or paraphrased, into statements that mention the latter and do not mention the former. If it is true (1) that people do perceive external physical things and (2) that perception consists of appearances thus signifying *other* appearances, actual or possible, then some version of this translation, or construction, thesis must be true. But the thesis—which has come to be known as "phenomenalism"—involves serious difficulties.

The difficulties may be traced to the "perceptual relativity" that the Critical Realists had stressed—to the fact that the ways in which things appear depend, not only on the objective properties of the thing, but also on the conditions under which the thing is perceived and on the state of the person who perceives it. To translate or paraphrase a simple thing statement into a collection of appearance statements, or even to find a single appearance statement implied by the thing statement, we must find some appearance or appearances that can be uniquely correlated with the physical fact described by the thing statement. But we are not able to correlate any group of appearances with any particular physical fact unless we specify those appearances by reference to some *other* physical fact—by reference to some set of observation conditions and to the state of the particular person who is to sense the appearances. For it is the joint operation of the things we perceive and of the conditions under which we perceive them that determines the ways in which the things are going to appear to us. And this constitutes a difficulty in principle for the attempt to translate thing statements into appearance statements; whenever we seem to reach such a translation, we find that our translation still includes some set of thing statements that describe physical observation conditions and that have not been translated into statements about appearances. The problem is not unlike that of trying to define "uncle" in terms only of "descendant" and without use of the terms "male" or "female."[95] If the translation thesis is false, and if, as I have been assuming, we are justified in our beliefs about our ability to perceive the world, it will follow, I think, that we cannot describe perceiving, as Sextus had thought, in terms of sign relations that hold among appearances.

7

Long before the publication of *Essays in Critical Realism* (1920), John Dewey had argued that the "message premise" is false. Perceiving, he said, does *not* consist in inspecting sensible appearances, reading off their characteristics, and then attributing these characteristics to physical things. For example, in *The Schools of To-morrow* (Dutton, 1915), he quoted with approval a passage from Rousseau's *Émile* and then observed:

This passage . . . indicates how far ahead he was of the psychology of his own day in his conception of the relation of the senses to knowledge. The current idea (and one that prevails too much even in our time) was that the senses were a sort of gateway and avenue though which impressions traveled and then built up knowledge pictures of the world. Rousseau said that they are a part of the apparatus of action by which we adjust ourselves to our environment, and then instead of being passive receptacles they are directly connected with motor activities—with the use of hands and legs. In this respect he was more advanced than some of his successors who emphasized the importance of sense contact with objects, for the latter thought of the senses simply as purveyors of information about objects instead of instruments of the necessary adjustments of human beings to the world around them [pp. 11-12].

Dewey's criticisms of "sensationalistic empiricism" and of other "spectacular theories" of knowing are clear and penetrating; it is more difficult, however, to understand his positive account of perception or to put it into a precise terminology. A comparatively clear statement is the following, from the second edition of *Experience and Nature* (Norton, 1929):

That a perception is cognitive means, accordingly that it is used; it is treated as a sign of conditions that implicate other as yet unperceived consequences in addition to the perception itself. That a perception is *truly* cognitive means that its active use or treatment is followed by other consequences which follow independently of its being perceived. To discover that a perception or an idea is cognitively invalid is to find that the consequences which follow from acting upon it entangle and confuse the other consequences which follow from the causes of the perception, instead of integrating or coordinating harmoniously with them [pp. 323-24].

What Dewey meant, I think, may be illustrated as follows: if a driver now perceives that the road is clear before her, then the road that she perceives is for her a source of sensible stimulation; a "transaction" occurs with the result that the person acts, or becomes prepared to act, on the belief that the road *is* clear before her. If the road were *not* clear, or if there *were* no road, these ways of acting would lead to a state of "disruption," "imbalance," or "disequilibration" and the person would find herself in an "indeterminate situation"—a situation that would then precipitate further inquiry. But since (on our assumption) the road *is* clear before her, such "disruption," "imbalance," or "disequilibration" will not result.[96]

Were it possible on any occasion to act *only* on what one perceives, then it might also be possible to correlate the "cognitive validity" of the perception with the consequences of acting. But in everything we do, we act on an indefinite number of propositions, many of them true, and, at times at least, some of them false. Our driver, in acting on the proposition that the road is clear before her, is also acting on the proposition that the road will take her where she wants to go, that the car will continue to be in working order, that she will continue to be able to drive it, and so on and on. If any one of these propositions is false, then the whole set of propositions—the true ones as well as the false ones—may lead to "disequilibration." The propositions we know, or believe, to be true, as Quine has said in a somewhat different connection, face the tribunal of reality "not individually but as a corporate body."[97] Our driver, seeing that the road is clear, acts on this "truly cognitive" perception; she sets out and then finds herself in a "doubtful situation" because the road, though clear enough, is not the road she thought it was. The perception was "truly cognitive," yet the consequences that followed from acting on it "entangled and confused the other consequences which followed from the causes of the perception." To be sure, if she had not been mistaken about where the road would take her, she would not now be in a "doubtful situation." But this fact does not absolve the true belief; for it was *also* this "truly cognitive" perception of the road that led her to act in the way that she did.

Suppose, on the other hand, that her perception of the road has not been "truly cognitive." Because she thought, mistakenly, that the road was *not* clear, she took another road instead. The other road turned out to be shorter and better, with the consequence that the driver did not land in any state of "disequilibration," "imbalance," "disruption," or "shock."

Action on a "truly cognitive" perception, then, is no guarantee that "disequilibration" will *not* result, and action on an *un*veridical perception is no guarantee that it will. For this reason, it seems to me, we cannot describe the "cognitive validity" of any perception, or of any belief, in terms merely of the consequences of deliberating and acting.

The "specific response" theory of Holt and Perry—two of the New Realists—was an attempt to construe *believing*, as well as perception, in terms of bodily adjustment and behavior. This theory, which is considerably simpler than Dewey's "transactional" account, also seems to be quite obviously inadequate. In recent years, however, Reichenbach and Carnap have defended it.

3

When psychologists talk about the behavior of animals, they may describe certain kinds of responses by reference to the stimuli with which such responses are usually associated. An animal's "food responses," for example, may be described in terms of what the animal does only when it is in the presence of food. A man's "fire responses," similarly, might be those things he does when and only when he is in the presence of a fire. Thus Perry wrote: "If, for example, I suppose or 'entertain the idea' that the barn is on fire, I in some measure set my fire-response in readiness. . . . An expectation, then, is an implicit response unreservedly set for a specific occasion; as when, believing that my train leaves the station at three o'clock, I correlate my readiness to depart, or my train-taking activities, with a place and time in my field of action."[98] If this way of talking is satisfactory, we might be able to define, by reference to a man's "X-responses," what it is for the man to believe that there is an X nearby; to say that a man believes that there is a horse nearby, for example, might be to say that he "puts his horse responses in readiness." By incorporating this account of believing into our description of perceiving, we might then hope to describe perceiving in terms merely of sensible stimulation, behavior, and adjustment.

But what would a man's "horse responses" be? Would they be those ways in which he acts, or is prepared to act, *only* when he is in the presence of horses? If we described his "horse responses" in *this* way, then we would not be able to say that believing a horse to be in the vicinity consists in "putting one's horse responses in readiness." For suppose we were to say (1) that a man's "horse responses" are those responses he puts in readiness *only* when he is in the presence of horses, and (2) that when a man believes that there is a horse nearby, then—and only then—the man puts his "horse responses" in readiness. In such a case our definitions would have the unacceptable consequence that no one can ever *mistakenly* believe that there is a horse in the vicinity. Should we say, then, that a man's "horse responses" are responses that are *similar* to those he makes when he is in the presence of horses? Unfortunately, any two responses are similar in *some* respect or other; hence this account would have the consequence that *all* of the responses a man may make are "horse responses and thus we could never say, of a man in action, that he does *not* believe there are horses nearby. A man's "horse responses," of course, are those responses that are similar in *relevant* respects to those he makes in the presence of horses. But what are the respects that are relevant?

The concept of *sign* does not help at this point. We could say, to be sure, that when a man perceives something to be a horse, then, as a result of sensible stimulation, something serves for him as a *sign* of the presence of a horse—or something *signifies* a horse. But when we attempt to say what it is for something to signify a horse, we find ourselves saying either that the something calls up the man's "horse responses," or that it leads to a "transaction" that would be "fulfilled" only by the presence of a horse, or, more simply, that it causes him to *believe* that he is in the presence of a horse.

In recent years philosophers investigating language have tried to construct more subtle versions of the specific response theory, in which "horse response" and the like have been replaced by more technical concepts. But each of these attempts, I believe, suffers from one or another of three defects. If one attempts to define "the belief that there is a horse" in terms of the concept of "horse response" (or its more recent equivalents), one will find: either (1) a man's "horse responses" become responses that *only* a horse could call up, in which case we cannot say that a man may believe falsely that he is in the presence of horses; or (2) they become responses he may make when he does *not* believe he is in the presence of horses, in which case we cannot define the belief in terms of the responses; or (3) the theory makes use, in the last resort, of some synonym for "believes," "takes," or "perceives," and thus leaves us at the point at which we began.[99]

9

What, then, can we say positively about perception and the problem of "objective reference"?

When we perceive, with respect to some physical thing, that the thing has a certain property, then, because the thing does have that property and because it is a source of sensible stimulation, it appears to us in a certain characteristic way. If we are justified in our belief that what we call perception is a reliable source of knowledge, then we may say with Lewis:

The given appearance may not be discernibly different from that of some other kind of object, under conditions other than those which affect this observation —so that the appearance could "deceive" us under conditions which, for all we know, may presently obtain—but because the condition which would lead to this "deception" is one which is exceptional, there is a high correlation between just this given character of the appearance and the objective property it leads us to ascribe to the thing observed.[100]

But it would be a mistake, I have suggested, to suppose that the appearance itself *has* the property—or at least that it has *all* the properties—that it leads us to ascribe to the thing. We are so constituted that, because the thing appears to us in just the way it does appear, we have a kind of spontaneous belief about the thing.[101] We may be led to expect subsequent appearances of some definite sort, and doubtless, as a result of our perceptions, we set ourselves to act in various appropriate ways; but neither of these facts, if what I have been saying is correct, may be said to constitute the belief that the perception involves.

The problem of objective reference persists in the concept of belief. What is it for a psychological state—in the present instance, a belief —to be *about* some object other than itself? Franz Brentano held that "intentional reference" is a distinctive mark of the psychological and that it cannot be described in physical terms. "Intentionality" is

characteristic not only of believing and perceiving, but also of remembering, thinking, loving, hating, and other such states or dispositions; each of these states or dispositions, Brenanto suggested, may
be said to "have an object" in a sense in which no nonpsychological
thing may be said to have an object. This concept of "reference," or
"intentionality," has now become a subject of intensive philosophical investigation; I think it is likely that there will be important de-
velopments in the next few years.[102]

Let us now return to the concept of *justified* belief—and consider
its relation to truth.

10

"The true sceptic," Santayana said, "merely analyses belief, dis-
covering the risk and the logical uncertainty inherent in it. He finds
that alleged knowledge is always faith; he would not be a sceptic if
he pretended to have proved that any belief, much less all belief, was
wrong."[103] Let us suppose that we are no longer confused about bent
sticks, distant stars, and converging railroad tracks, that we are sensitive to the risks that "appearance" and other philosophical terms involve, and that we are clear about the general epistemological predicament I have tried to describe in the first section of this essay. What
may we say now for the claim that our knowledge, in particular that
knowledge we attribute to perception, involves an element of "animal faith"—for Lovejoy's assertion in *The Revolt Against Dualism*
(p. 318) that "we know by faith?"

In its application to perception, the assertion is based, I think, on
the following considerations. (1) As we noted in the second section,
there are beliefs, or statements, about some of our own psychological
states and about some of the ways we are "appeared to," that can be
said to be "self-justifying" in a sense in which no other belief, or
statement, can be said to be "self-justifying"; thus the statements expressing what we attribute to perception cannot, in this sense, be
"self-justifying." (2) "Our senses do at times deceive us"; that is to
say, there are occasions when we *think* we perceive that some state
of affairs obtains and when, as a matter of fact, that state of affairs
does *not* obtain. And (3) if we were to make use *only* of premises
that are "self-justifying," in the present sense of this term, then we
could not construct a good argument, deductive or inductive, for the
thesis that any of the beliefs we normally attribute to perception are
true.

The first two of these three points are incontovertible, I believe. The third is more problematic, for we do not as yet have a generally accepted and clear account of what a good *inductive* argument might be. It is clear that we cannot construct a good *deductive* argument from directly justified premises to a conclusion saying that any of the beliefs we attribute to perception are true. And we cannot construct an *enumerative* inductive argument—an argument where the directly justified premises are of the form "Some As are Bs," and the conclusion is of the form "All As are Bs," or "Most As are Bs," or even "Some other As are Bs." For the As and Bs in the conclusion must refer to certain properties of the kind we normally attribute to the things we think we perceive; but the As and Bs in the premises can refer to our own psychological states and to certain ways of being appeared to. What remains problematic is the question whether we can construct a good argument by means of what is sometimes called *hypothetical induction*—an argument in which the conclusion (saying that some of the beliefs that we normally attribute to perception are true) is advanced as being the most likely explanation of the facts asserted in the self-justifying premises. Any controversy concerning this point is likely to turn on the questions "What constitutes a good argument by hypothetical induction?" and "What are the criteria for determining what constitutes the 'most likely explanation' for any set of data?" During the past twenty years an extraordinary amount of important work has been done in this area, especially by American philosophers, but most of it is still controversial. (In a series of articles in 1933 and 1934, Donald Williams defended "realism as an inductive hypothesis," but the premises he made use of were not restricted to those that I have called "self-justifying."[104] Much of what he wrote was a criticism of various forms of skepticism and subjectivism.)

The relevant epistemological question is this: If we suppose that the three considerations I have listed are true—if we suppose that our "self-justifying" beliefs are what I have said they are, that "our senses do sometimes deceive us," and that our "self-justified" beliefs do not warrant any inferences about the reliability of the senses—then, what implications does our supposition have concerning the knowledge that we attribute to perception? We should first note, as a point of logic, that the three considerations by themselves do not imply that we are *not* justified in putting our faith in the "external senses." If the skeptic wished to *prove* to us logically that such faith is unreasonable, then he would need to find an additional premise that, when added to our three, would yield his conclusion—a premise describing the conditions under which the faith is justified. If we cannot accept his conclusion, then we may deny his additional premise while retaining our original three, and his proof we are misguided will fail. Yet *we* cannot prove, on his grounds, that *he* is wrong; if we attempt to prove from some set of directly justified premises that the senses *are* generally reliable, then, as I have suggested, *our* proof will fail, too.[105] If the reader feels that I have done an injustice to our position, or to that of the skeptic, he is referred to the first section.

Why *should* one suppose that to justify what we attribute to perception we should construct an argument using only "directly justified" statements as premises? The supposition proceeds, I think, from the tendency, discussed at the end of the second section, to emphasize "the given" at the expense of the related concept of "rules of evidence." Since we find that our senses do sometimes deceive us, we cannot say that *every* belief we attribute to perception is true. But "if one who trusts his senses is sometimes deceived, he is more wretchedly deceived who never trusts them."[106] According to the assumptions we made at the beginning, we are justified in thinking, with respect to a large class of our beliefs, including those that we attribute to perception, that they are instances of knowing; or, what comes to the same thing, we are justified in thinking that we have adequate evidence for those beliefs. But since our senses do sometimes deceive us, it follows that some of the beliefs for which we have adequate evidence are in fact false—or, in other words, that some of the things we are justified in thinking, that we know are *not* in fact things that we know. If this, as I believe, is what is intended by the statement "Our knowledge involves an element of animal faith," then I think the statement is correct.

It is necessary, finally, to say something about the relations between evidence and truth.

11

In light of all the foregoing, we may make some general observations about criteria of evidence. A person may be said to have adequate *evidence* for a given statement—or the statement may be said to be *evident* to her—provided it meets one of these three conditions: (1) it is "directly justified"; (2) it is "a priori"; or (3) it expresses what the person thinks she remembers and is not logically incompatible with any statement expressing what she thinks she remembers.

I believe we should also specify a certain subclass of perceptual judgments and say that a statement may be evident provided (4) it expresses what the person thinks she perceives (where the perceptual
judgment is of the kind specified). Possibly we should add, further,
that a statement is evident provided (5) it is logically implied by anything that is evident in the first four senses; this addition would have
the result that a person may have adequate evidence for certain statements (e.g., some of the theorems of logic and mathematics) that, in
fact, are not among those statements that she believes to be true. If,
moreover, we are justified in saying that some of the conclusions of
modern science (e.g., "There are nine planets") have the status of
being evident, we should add that a statement is evident provided (6)
it is highly probable in relation to all of those statements that are evident in the first five senses. (Generally speaking, an inductive conclusion that is probable—even highly probable—in relation to what is
evident cannot itself be added *to* the evidence and then used to com-
pute the probability, in relation to what is evident, of other statements.[107] The statement "There are nine planets" is one most scientists would wish to count as evident, but its justification lies in the
fact that it is highly probable in relation *to* the evident. What degree
of probability—of probability less than one and in relation to other
statements that are evident—is necessary in order that a statement
may itself be counted evident, is an unanswered question of the
theory of induction.) And perhaps there are still other criteria of evidence—associated with some of the other "sources" of knowing
mentioned in the first section.

A fundamental dilemma for the theory of knowledge is the following. If (3), (4), and (6) are omitted from our list of criteria of evidence
—that is to say, if the only statements that are to be counted as evident are those that are "self-justifying" or "a priori" or are logical
consequences of what is "self-justifying" or "a priori," then our
knowledge is restricted to a much smaller class of statements than
anyone, other than the skeptic, believes that it is. But if we include
(3), (4), and (6) in our list, then we must say that, from the fact that
a statement is evident it does not follow that the statement is true.

What follows is based on the assumption that the second of these
courses is the lesser evil.

12

One can say of the belief that Socrates is mortal, or of any statement
that says that Socrates is mortal, and hence of the English statement

"Socrates is mortal," that it is *true* if and only if Socrates *is* mortal. But one cannot say, of the belief or of the statement, that it is evident if and only if Socrates is mortal; for the belief or statement that Socrates is mortal may be evident even though Socrates is not mortal, or may not be evident even though he is mortal. More generally, the *conditions of truth* and the *criteria of evidence* for most beliefs and statements do not coincide. To state the conditions of truth for any belief or statement, we have only to assert the belief or statement; to state the criteria of evidence, if any, for any belief or statement (other than one that is "self-justifying"), we ordinarily must assert many other beliefs or statements.

We should be prepared, then, for an ambiguity in the philosophical expression *"criteria of truth."* Sometimes the expression is used to mean *conditions of truth*, but at other times it is used to mean what I have called *criteria of evidence*.

Conflicting "theories of truth" arise partly because some philosophers consider the concept of *truth* in terms of the problem of "objective reference" and others consider it in terms of the concept of *evidence*. Thus philosophers who seem to have conflicting theories of truth may agree with the traditional dictum that truth consists in the "adequacy" of the intellect and reality: Veritas est aedequatio rei et intellectus. Some consider this "adequacy" in terms merely of objective reference, as I believe they should and are thus able to accept Aristotle's simple statement: "To say of what is that it is not, or of what is not that it is, is false, while to say of what is that it is, or of what is not that it is not is true."[108] (The term "believe," or "judge," may also be used where this passage uses "say.") Other philosophers, mistakenly I think, seem to consider "adequacy" in terms of evidence. Thus Dewey said that he accepted a "correspondence theory of truth" and that he took the term "correspondence" to have an "operational" meaning: "the meaning, namely, of *answering*, as a key answers to conditions imposed by a lock, or as two correspondents 'answer' each other; or, in general, as a reply is an adequate answer to a question or a criticism — as, in short, a *solution* answers the requirements of a problem"[109] If we consider correspondence, or adequacy, in this second way, we will be led to the false conclusion that where no "solution" is available, i.e., where adequate evidence is not available, there is no truth. It was in this way, I think, that Otto Neurath was led to make the following paradoxical statement: "We should be doubtful even in admitting a definition of 'true' which implies that the saying, 'There is an elephant here,' may be called true if and only if there is an elephant here. Even this sounds like an 'absolute' expression . . . which we do not know how to fit into a framework based on observation statements."[110]

An adequate theory of evidence, I have suggested, will not imply that the belief or statement that Socrates is mortal is a belief or statement that is *evident* if and only if Socrates is mortal. But an adequate theory of objective reference must be one that implies that any belief or statement, which is a belief or statement *that* Socrates is mortal, is a belief or statement that is *true* if and only if Socrates is mortal. (Thus the stoics, according to Sextus Empiricus, defined the truth of statements in terms of what the words making up the statements *refer* to: 'This man is sitting' or 'This man is walking,' they declare it is true when the thing predicated such as 'sitting' or 'walking' belongs to the object indicated.")[111]

Thus if we were to accept a "copy theory" of reference (e.g., "a state of mind refers to a thing if and only if it takes on the properties of that thing") then we might also accept a "copy theory" of truth (e.g., "a state of mind is *true* if and only if it does thus refer to a thing—if and only if it does succeed in copying what exists"). William James's so-called pragmatic theory of truth was, as he realized, essentially a theory of reference, a theory about the nature of belief. He said, in effect, that if a man *believes* that there are tigers in India, then the man is in a bodily state that is such that, if the man were to go to India, then the bodily state (1) would turn out to be disrupted, or frustrated, if and only if there were *no* tigers in India, and (2) would be fulfilled or satisfied, if and only if there *were* tigers in India; hence, on this theory, the man's belief is *true* if and only if the bodily state would be fulfilled or satisfied; and James thus concluded, somewhat misleadingly, that truth consists in "satisfaction."[112] The limitations of this theory of reference, and hence of the account of truth, are substantially those of the theory of reference attributed to Dewey, above.

In the nineteenth century, "idealistic" philosophers attempted to formulate a "coherence theory" of truth. Believing that everything is mental and hence that nothing nonmental for the intellect to be adequate to, they thought of truth as a kind of systematic consistency of beliefs, or "ideas." Many philosophers rejected the theory on the grounds (1) that since a system of false propositions may be internally consistent, consistency alone is not a condition of truth, (2) that the theory did not give a clear account of the respect in which "coherence" differs from mere consistency, and (3) that the possible interpretations of "coherence" seemed to presuppose the kind of "adequacy" or "correspondence" that the theory was designed to avoid.

In the present century, "logical positivists" defended for a time a "restrained coherence theory of truth." Believing that statements can be "compared" only with other statements, and hence that "statements are never compared with a 'reality,' with 'facts,'" they concluded that the "cleavage between statements and reality" that the "correspondence theory" seemed to presuppose is "nothing but the result of a redoubling metaphysics, and all the problems connected with it are mere pseudo-problems."[113] They admitted that mere consistency is not enough, and said that what distinguishes a system of true statements from a consistent fairy tale is that the former, unlike the latter, agrees with the "protocol statements of science," i.e., with the observation statements of science. The "protocol statements" were characterized as "true" only in the sense of being those observation statements that, as it happens, are "actually adopted by mankind, by the scientists of our culture circle."[114] It was noted that any observation statement is subject to being revoked at some later time, and that "the adoption of any observation statement has, after all, the character of a *convention*."[115] The latter quotation suggests the "postulational" theory of evidence, or justification, which I mentioned in the second section, number 7, p. 55. I believe it would now be conceded that this "restrained coherence theory of truth" resulted from failure to distinguish criteria of evidence from conditions of truth.

The "coherence theory of truth" was also developed by Brand Blanshard, in *The Nature of Thought* (Macmillan, 1940), as part of a general theory of reality, or a metaphysics.[117] Blanshard's theory of truth depends partly on a theory of reference, partly on a theory of evidence. Following Josiah Royce's *The World and the Individual* (Macmillan, 1899), Blanshard says that "the relation between idea and object must be conceived teleologically, as the relation of that which is partially realized to the same thing more fully realized" (vol. 1, p. 473). Hence "the idea can then be *both* the same as its object *and* different; the same because it *is* the object *in posse*; different because that object, which is its end, is as yet incompletely realized" (vol. 1, p. 494). The theory (which may recall the Thomistic attempt, mentioned above, to find a mean between literal identity and difference) implies, concerning what I take to be my idea of Julius Caesar, either (1) that the idea is *not* an idea of Julius Caesar, or (2) that it is capable of becoming Julius Caesar himself, or (3) that Julius Caesar is capable of becoming my idea of him, or (4) that both Julius Caesar and my idea have purposes that are such that, if these purposes were realized, then my idea and Julius Caesar would both become the same thing. It is clear that Blanshard took the fourth of these courses; the metaphysical system that such a view must involve does not lie within the scope of the present work.

But Blanshard's theory of truth depends also on his theory of evidence. His procedure is as follows: he poses the question "What are the tests of truth?" and examines various possibilities—authority, mystic insight, correspondence, self-evidence, and coherence—rejecting all but the last; he then concludes (1) that "coherence is our sole criterion of truth" (vol. 2, p. 259) and, given this conclusion, attempts to demonstrate (2) that truth *consists* in coherence. "Assume coherence as the test, and you will be driven by the incoherence of your alternatives to the conclusion that it is also the nature of truth" (vol. 2, p. 269).

If what I have said about the nature of evidence and of justification is accurate, and if I have interpreted Blanshard correctly, then there would seem to be two errors in his account. He seems to suppose that coherence is a sufficient condition of evidence; I discussed this supposition in the second section. He also seems to suppose that, if we have found necessary and sufficient conditions for saying that a proposition is evident, we have also found, *ipso facto*, necessary and sufficient conditions for saying that the proposition is true. This second supposition does indeed give us the mark of those psychological propositions that I have called "self-justifying"; but if there are any other propositions that are evident, then, according to what has been said, the supposition is false. "I think I remember" (with the qualifications noted earlier) may imply "I have adequate evidence for that which I think I remember," but it does not imply "I remember." And a good inductive argument may guarantee that we have adequate evidence for its conclusion, but it does not guarantee that the conclusion is true.

The thesis that evidence does not imply truth is doubtless discomfiting and we may be tempted to think, therefore, that by redefining our terms we can somehow avoid it. Franz Brentano held that a belief may be called true provided it is a belief that would be held by one who "judged with evidence."[118] C. J. Ducasse said, similarly, that truth "means capacity to compel belief in a rational person who has the relevant evidence."[119] Charles Saunders Peirce said that a true opinion is one that accords "with the ideal limit towards which endless investigation would tend to bring scientific belief"—a view that Dewey also accepted (though without accepting the "conditional idealism" that Peirce took his theory to imply.)[120] But any theory that defines "evidence," or "truth," in such a way that "evidence" may be said to imply "truth," may be interpreted either as *restricting* the concept of evidence to confine it to propositions that are true, or as *relaxing* the concept of truth in order that it might apply to any proposition that is evident. In the former case, we succeed only in making evidence as *remote* as truth; we will not know whether a good inductive argument yields evidence unless we know that its conclusion is true. In the latter case, we succeed only in making truth as *relative* as evidence; the belief that there are nine planets could be true in this relaxed sense of "true," even if there were not nine planets.

Notes

Notes

Chapter 1. A Version of Foundationalism

1. John Maynard Keynes, *A Treatise on Probability* (London: Macmillan and Company, 1952), p. 322.

2. Bertrand Russell, *Human Knowledge: Its Scope and Limits* (New York: Simon and Schuster, 1948), pp. 381-82.

3. Compare C. I. Lewis, *The Ground and Nature of the Right* (New York: Columbia University Press, 1955), chap. 2; and James Van Cleve, "Foundationalism, Epistemic Principles, and the Cartesian Circle," *The Philosophical Review*, 88 (1979), 55-91, esp. 84-91.

4. Other principles are set forth in the second edition of my book, *Theory of Knowledge* (Englewood Cliffs, NJ, Prentice-Hall, Inc., 1976), pp. 138-39. The principles are there restricted to de dicto form; but their analogues for direct attribution are obvious.

5. I am indebted to Robert Shope for his penetrating criticisms of earlier attempts to define the concept of self-presentation.

6. We may say that a property P *entails* a property Q, provided only that P is necessarily such that, whoever attributes it to anything, attributes Q to something.

7. This distinction was proposed by Guido Küng in "Understanding and Rational Justification," in *Dialectica*, III (1979), 217-232; see p. 227.

8. The relations among *implication, entailment,* and *involvement* are discussed in detail in "The Paradox of Analysis" in Part Two of this book.

9. *Principles of Philosophy*, Part 1, Principle 9, in E. S. Haldane and G. R. T. Ross, eds., *Philosophical Works of Descartes* (Cambridge: The University Press, 1931), p. 222.

10. Compare William P. Alston, "Two Types of Foundationalism," *Journal of Philosophy*, 73 (1976), 165-85, esp. 170; and Ernest Sosa, "The Foundations of Foundationalism," *Nous*, 15 (1981).

11. Otto Neurath, "Protokollsatze," *Erkenntnis*, Band III (1932-1933), 204-14; the quotation is on page 206.

12. Compare Ernest Sosa, "The Raft and the Pyramid," *Midwest Studies in Philosophy*, 5 (1980). Sosa makes clear that the two figures do not exclude each other.

13. Compare *Sextus Empiricus*, vol. 2, Loeb Classical Library (London: William Heineman, Ltd., 1933), p. 95; "Against the Logicians," I, 176-77. Compare the following definition

proposed by John Pollock: "'P is prima facie justified for S' means: 'It is necessarily true that if S believes (or were to believe) that P, and S has no reason for thinking that it is false that P, then S is (or would be) justified in believing that P.'" John Pollock, *Knowledge and Justification* (Princeton: Princeton University Press, 1972), p. 30.

14. See the chapter called "Three Uses of Appear Words," in my book *Perceiving: A Philosophical Study* (Ithaca: Cornell University Press, 1957), pp. 43-53; the distinction is further defended in "Comments and Replies," *Philosophia*, (1978), 599-602.

15. See Franz Brentano, *Untersuchungen zur Sinnespsychologie*, 2nd ed. (Hamburg: Felix Meiner Verlag, 1979), pp. 157-63; compare H. P. Grice, "Some Remarks about the Senses," in R. J. Butler, ed., *Analytic Philosophy*, First Series (Oxford: Basic Blackwell, 1963), pp. 133-53.

16. Compare Fred Dretske, *Seeing and Knowing* (Chicago: Universty of Chicago Press, 1969), p. 23.

17. See A. Meinong, *Über die Erfahrunsgrundlagen unseres Wissens* (1906), in A. Meinong, *Gesamtausgabe*, Band 5 (Graz: Akademische Druck- und Verlagsanstalt, 1973); see esp. pp. 398-404.

18. H. H. Price, *Perception* (New York: Robert M. McBride & Company, 1935), p. 185.

19. Compare Bertrand Russell: "beliefs caused by perception are to be accepted unless there are positive grounds for rejecting them." *An Inquiry into Meaning and Truth* (New York: W. W. Norton & Company, 1940), p. 166.

20. I have discussed negative perception in detail in chapter 8 of *The First Person*.

21. *Theory of Knowledge*, 2d ed., p. 63.

22. This point is recognized by Frederick L. Will in *Induction and Justification* (Ithaca: Cornell University Press, 1974), part 2; compare Michael Williams in *Groundless Belief* (Oxford: Basil Blackwell, 1977), p. 115.

23. See Alvin Goldman, "Discrimination and Perceptual Knowledge," in G. S. Pappas and M. Swain, eds. *Essays on Knowledge and Justification* (Ithaca: Cornell University Press, 1978), pp. 120-45. Goldman attempts to develop the "reliability" theory for perceptual knowledge; hence what he says is not strictly applicable to our three examples above. And I think he would concede, moreover, that he has set forth a program rather than a finished theory, for he makes use of the undefined expression "S's propensity to form an F-belief as a result of percept P has an *appropriate* genesis" (p. 142, my italics). Compare Fred Dretske, *Seeing and Knowing* (London: Routledge & Kegan Paul, 1969), chap. 2, and "Conclusive Reasons," in *Australasian Journal of Philosophy*, 48 (1971), 1-22. Compare James van Cleve's criticism of "naturalistic" theories of epistemic justification, "Foundationalism," section 10.

24. One could, of course, make use of a principle such as our P3 and then compensate for its overpermissiveness by making certain further epistemic *stipulations*. Compare Keith Lehrer, *Knowing* (Oxford: The Clarendon Press, 1974), chap. 6. I believe that Lehrer does not intend his theory to be adequate to the type of example I have cited; but if this is so, then the theory should not be thought of as an alternative to the present theory.

25. Compare Keith Lehrer, *Knowledge*, chap. 8, and Nicholas Rescher, *The Coherence Theory of Truth* (Oxford: The Clarendon Press, 1973), chap. 13. The theories proposed by these authors are not readily applicable to our three cases.

26. Keith Lehrer, *Knowledge*.

27. Compare James Cornman, "Foundational versus Nonfoundational Theories of Empirical Justification," in Pappas and Swain, *Essays*, pp. 229-52.

28. The quotation is from Jaegwon Kim's article, "Explanation in Science," in Paul Edwards, ed., *Encyclopedia of Philosophy* (New York: The Macmillan Company, 1967), vol. 3, pp. 159-63; the quotation is from page p. 161. Kim also cites additional "epistemic conditions" that must be fulfilled if a theory or hypothesis is to serve as an explanation;

one of these is "the requirement of total evidence" (p. 161). Compare Lehrer, *Knowledge*, chap. 5.

29. Thus Cornman, in the article referred to above, makes use of the undefined expression "x explains y," but he does not introduce "x explains y for S."

30. For a definitive study of the relations between the epistemic and ethical senses of "justify," or "warrant," see Roderick Firth, "Are Epistemic Concepts Reducible to Ethical Concepts?" in A. Goldman and J. Kim, eds., *Values and Morals* (Dordrecht: D. Reidel Publishing Company, 1978), 215-29.

Chapter 2. Confirmation and Concurrence

1. This type of definition has been proposed by Carnap: "To say that the hypothesis *b* has the probability *p* (say 3/5) with respect to the evidence *e*, means that for anyone to whom this evidence but no other relevant evidence is available, it would be reasonable to believe in *b* to the degree *p*, or, more exactly, it would be unreasonable for him to bet on *b* at odds higher than p: (1-p) (in the example, 3:2)." Quoted from "Statistical and Inductive Probability," in Edward Madden, ed., *The Structure of Scientific Thought* (Boston: Houghton Mifflin and Company, 1960), pp. 269-79; the quotation is on p. 270.

2. Compare the similar procedure proposed by Earl Conee, "Propositional Justification," *Philosophical Studies*, 38 (1980), 65-8.

3. We could say that a proposition e is a priori false provided only that the negation of e is necessarily such that (i) it is true and (ii) whoever understands it accepts it.

4. I am indebted to Philip Quinn for simplifying this example. Another example of failure of transitivity is provided by these three propositions: (e) Exactly 95 of the 100 balls in the urn are black; (h) at least 95 of the 100 balls in the urn are black; and (i) all of the 100 balls in the urn are black.

5. This property, though not self-presenting, may be entailed by something that is self-presenting—for example, the property of being such as to believe there are stones and not to believe that some birds are red.

6. Richard Foley, "Chisholm on Coherence," *Philosophical Studies*, 38 (1980), 53-63; the example is quoted from page 57. This paper is expanded on in "More on Chilsholm and Coherence," presented to the Eastern Division of the American Philosophical Association on December 30, 1980.

7. The distinction between epistemic principles and inductive principles is discussed in "*Verstehen*: The Epistemological Problem," in Part II of this book.

Chapter 3. Knowledge as Justified True Belief

1. E. L. Gettier, "Is Knowledge Justified True Belief?" *Analysis*, 23 (1963), 121-23.

2. The relevant sense of "makes evident" is explicated in the previous essay.

3. It should be noted that our formulation of e contains a blank and is therefore incomplete. The conjunction of propositions that are explicit in our formulation of e is *not* sufficient to make f evident for the subject of Gettier's example.

4. Keith Lehrer, "Knowledge, Truth and Evidence," *Analysis*, 25 (1965), 168-75.

5. Earl Conee has pointed out to me that my earlier attempts to deal with the Gettier problem do not satisfy the third condition. See his "The Analysis of Knowledge in the Second Edition of *Theory of Knowledge*," *Canadian Journal of Philosophy*, 10 (1980), 295-300.

6. Possibly this is true of the example of the pyromaniac proposed by Brian Skyrms in "The Explication of 'S knows that P,'" *Journal of Philosophy*, 64 (1967), pp. 373-89. Skyrms considers these two propositions, e and h: (e) "Sure-Fire matches have always and

often lit for me when struck except when wet, and this match is a Sure-Fire and is dry"; (h) "This match will light now as I strike it." He assumes—mistakenly, it seems to me—that e makes h evident. I believe the most we can of e in this connection is that it makes h such as to be beyond reasonable doubt.

Chapter 4. Knowing that One Knows

1. H. A Prichard, *Knowledge and Perception* (Oxford: The Clarendon Press, 1950), p. 86.

2. See the first essay in Part II.

3. Compare William P. Alston, "Two Types of Foundationalism," *Journal of Philosophy*, 73 (1976), 165-85; Ernest Sosa, "The Foundations of Foundationalism," in *Nous*, 4 (1981).

4. This objection is adapted from one set forth by Richard Feldman, "Fallibilism and Knowing that One Knows," *The Philosophical Review*, XC (1981), 266-82.

5. Compare Wilfrid Sellars, "More on Givenness and Explanatory Coherence," in G. Pappas, ed., *Justification and Knowledge* (Dordrecht: D. Reidel, 1979), 169-82. Compare Ernest Sosa, "The Raft and the Pyramid: Coherence versus Foundations in the Theory of Knowledge," *Midwest Studies in Philosophy*, 5 (1980). Sosa would view nonderivative epistemological principles as normative principles that are such that it is an intellectual virtue to regulate one's beliefs in accordance with them.

Chapter 5. The Problem of the Criterion

1. Published in London in 1917 by Longmans, Green and Co.

2. The eighth edition of this work was published in 1923 in Louvain by the Institut Supérieur de Philosophie, and in Paris by Félix Alcan. The first edition was published in 1884. It has been translated into Spanish, Polish, Portuguese and perhaps still other languages, but unfortunately not yet into English.

3. The quotation is a paraphrase. What Montaigne wrote was: "Pour juger des apparences que nous recevons des subjects, il nous faudroit un instrument judicatoire; pour verifier cet instrument, il nous y faut de la demonstration; pour verifier la demonstration, un instrument; nous voylà au rouet. Puisque les sens ne peuvent arrester notre dispute, éstans pleins eux-mesmes d'incertitude, il faut que se soit la raison; aucune raison s'establira sans une autre raison: nous voylà à reculons jusques à l'infiny." The passage appears in Book 2, Chapter 12 ("An Apologie of Raymond Sebond"); it may be found on page 544 of the Modern Library edition of *The Essays of Montaigne*.

4. *Critériologie, Op. cit.*, eighth edition, p. 234.

5. See the reply to the VIIth set of Objections and Coffey, vol. 1, p. 127.

6. Thomas Reid, *Inquiry into the Human Mind*, chap. 1, sec. 8.

7. Unfortunately Cardinal Mercier takes Reid to be what I have called a "methodist." He assumes, incorrectly I think, that Reid defends certain principles (principles that Reid calls principles of "common sense") on the ground that these principles happen to be the deliverance of a faculty called "common sense." See Mercier, pp. 179-81.

8. *On Improvement of the Understanding*, in *Chief Works of Benedict de Spinoza*, vol. 2, trans. R. H. M. Elwes, rev. ed. (London: George Bell and Sons, 1898), p. 13.

9. The logic of these concepts, though with a somewhat different vocabulary, is set forth in Roderick M. Chisholm and Robert Keim, "A System of Epistemic Logic," *Ratio*, 15 (1973).

10. *The Disputed Questions on Truth*, Question One, Article 9; trans. Robert W. Mulligan (Chicago: Henry Regnery Company, 1952).

11. Coffey, vol. 1, p. 146. I have been unable to find this quotation in Hobbes.

12. *New Essays concerning Human Understanding*, book 4, chap. 7, n. 1.

13. *Exposition of the Posterior Analytics of Aristotle*, Lectio 4, No. 10; trans Pierre Conway (Quebec: M. Doyon, 1956).

14. I have attempted to do this to some extent in *Theory of Knowledge* (Englewood Cliffs, NJ: Prentice-Hall, Inc., 1966). Revisions and corrections may be found in my essay "On the Nature of Empirical Evidence" in Roderick M. Chisholm and Robert J. Swartz, eds., *Empirical Knowledge* (Englewood Cliffs, NJ: Prentice-Hall, Inc., 1973).

Chapter 6. The Foundation of Empirical Statements

1. This objection applies also to Leonard Nelson's statement: "If one asks whether one possesses objectively valid cognitions at all, one thereby presupposes that the objectivity of cognition is questionable at first" (*Socratic Method and Critical Philosophy* [New Haven, 1949], p. 190). One of the unfortunate consequences of the work of Descartes, Russell, and Husserl is the widely accepted supposition that questions about the justification for counting evident statements *as* evident must be *challenges*, or expressive of *doubts*. The objections to this supposition were clearly put by Meinong (cf. vol. 2 of his *Gesammelte Abhandlungen* [Leipzig, 1913], p. 191).

2. We may also ask, of course, for a justification of the rule of evidence; the problems that such questions involve are beyond the scope of the present paper. Note that the reply described above does not say that the rule of evidence is evident.

3. See Leonard Nelson's *Über das sogenannte Erkenntnisproblem* (Göttingen, 1930), reprinted from *Abhandlungen der Fries'schen Schule*, vol. 2 (Göttingen, 1908); esp. pp. 479-85, 502-3, 521-24, 528. Compare also his "The Impossibility of the 'Theory of Knowledge'" in *Socratic Method*, esp. pp. 190-92.

4. Compre L. Wittgenstein, *Philosophical Investigations* (Oxford, 1953, p. 89e: "It can't be said of me at all (except perhaps as a joke) that I *know* I am in pain. What is it supposed to mean — except perhaps that I *am* in pain?"

5. "We do not ask for one torch to help us to see and another to help us to recognize what we see" (Gilbert Ryle, *The Concept of Mind* [London, 1949], p. 162.)

6. Some of Ajdukiewicz's *Sinnregeln*, but, I believe, not all of them, could be regarded as telling us what statements are "basic" in our present sense; see K. Ajdukiewicz, "Sprache und Sinn," *Erkenntnis*, 4 (1934), 100 ff. A similar remark may be made of the simple "acceptance rules that Carnap formulates in "Truth and Confirmation"; see esp. pp. 124-25, in the version of that article in H. Feigl and W. S. Sellars, ed., *Readings in Philosophical Analysis* (New York, 1949).

Chapter 7. *Verstehen*: The Epistemological Question

1. I have attempted to show this in *Theory of Knowledge*, 2nd ed. (Englewood-Cliffs, NJ: Prentice-Hall, Inc., 1977), chap 4.

2. See A. Meinong, *Über die Erfahrungsgrundlagen unseres Wissers* (1906), in A. Meinong, *Gesamtausgabe*, Band 5 (Graz: Akademische Druck- und Verlagsanstalt, 1973); see esp. pp. 398-404.

3. H. H. Price, *Perception* (New York: Robert M. McBride & Company, 1935), p. 185.

4. See A. Meinong, "Zur erkenntnistheoretischen Würdigung des Gedächtnisses" (1886), in A. Meinong, *Gesamtausgabe*, Band 2, (1971), pp. 185-213.

5. C. I. Lewis, *An Analysis of Knowledge and Valuation* (La Salle, II:3 The Open Court Publishing Company, 1946) +, p. 334.

6. One of his clearest statements is in "*Die Entstehung der Hermeneutik*" (see especially

the *zusätze aud den Handschfiften"*) of 1900, in Wilhelm Dilthey, *Gesammelte Schriften*, Band 5 (Leibzig and Berlin: B. G. Teubner, 1924), pp. 317-38. He discusses the problem of other minds ("*Der Glaube an die Realität anderer Petersonen"*) in *Beiträge zur Losung der Frage vom Ursprung unseres Glaubens an die Realität der Aussenwelt und Seinem Recht"* (1890) in the same volume, pp. 110-13. This latter discussion, in which he stresses the importance of the argument from analogy, is, for our purposes, particularly unrewarding.

7. Alfred Schuetz, "Scheler's Theory of Intersubjectivity and the General Thesis of the Alter Ego," *Philosophy and Phenomenological Research*, (1942), 323-47; the quotation is from page 334. Schuetz is here expounding the theory as set forth in Scheler's *Wesen und Formen der Sympathie* (1923).

8. *Op. cit.*, p. 449. Reid cites this as one of ten "first principles of continent truths."

9. *Essays on the Intellectual Powers of Man*, in *The Works of Thomas Reid*, essay 6, chap. 5, pp. 449-50. Of the types of "sign" distinguished in the first two sentences of this passage, the Stoics called the first "commemorative" and the second "indicative"; Sextus Empiricus, as a skeptic, held that there are no "indicative signs." See Sextus Empiricus, *Against the Logicians*, Book 2, chap. 3, in *Sextus Empiricus*, The Loeb Classical Library (Cambridge: Harvard University Press, 1930), vol. 2, pp. 313-97.

10. *Philosophical Investigations* (Oxford: Basil Blackwell, 1953), p. 98e.

11. *Works of Thomas Reid*, p. 449.

12. Guido Küng, in his contribution to the symposium which this essay originally appeared, has set forth an accurate and sympathetic account of the present point of view. I believe that his distinction between what he calls "the self-presenting" and the "self-presented" is one of the first importance. It can also be used to illuminate the distinction between (i) merely being in a certain mental state and (ii) noticing that one is in that state. See G Küng, "Understanding and Rational Justification," *Dialectica*, 33 (19790, 217-32.

Chapter 8. What Is A Transcendental Argument?

1. "I entitle *transcendental* all knowledge which is occupied not so much with objects as with the mode of our knowledge of objects in so far as this mode of knowledge is to be possible *a priori.*" *Critique of Pure Reason*, B25.

Chapter 9. The Paradox of Analysis

1. We note that entailment as here defined differs from that relation that holds between two properties P and Q, when and only when P both implies and involves Q. The property of *being red and heavy and if colored then round* implies and involves the property *being round*, but it does not *entail* the property *being round*.

2. These concepts are discussed in detail in Roderick M. Chisholm, "Objects and Persons: Revision and Replies," *Grazer Philosophische Studien*, 7/8 (1979), 317-88; see especially, 350-51. Compare Roderick M. Chisholm, "Events, Propositions and States of Affairs," in Paul Weingartner and Edgar Morscher, eds., *Ontologie und Logik* (Berlin: Duncker & Humblot, 1979), pp. 27-47.

3. Why not put the third condition more simply by omitting the last occurrence of "properly" and saying this: "If Q is analyzed by P, then P does not properly invoke anything that involves Q"? This simpler condition would not enable us to say that "being a man" is analyzed by "being a rational animal." For being a rational animal does properly involve being a man (it involves being a man, and being a man does not involve it), and being a man involves being a man.

Chapter 10. Theory of Knowledge in America

1. George Burch, "The Place of Revelation in Philosophical Thought," *Review of Metaphysics*, 15 (1962), 396-408; the quotation is from p. 407.

2. *Ibid.*, p. 406. I think that John Hick's *Faith and Knowledge* (Cornell, 1957) may be interpreted as a defense of the second type of religious cognitivism. For a different point of view of the same problem, compare Morton White, "Reflections on Anti-Intellectualism" *Daedalus*, 91 (1962), 437-68.

3. Maurice Mandelbaum, "Societal Facts," *British Journal of Sociology*, 6, 307; reprinted in Edward Madden, ed., *The Structure of Scientific Thought* (Houghton, 1960). In an interesting monograph, *On the Epistemology of the Inexact Sciences* (Rand Corp., 1958), Olaf Helmer and Nicholas Rescher have defended making use of "experts' personal probability valuations" in a way that suggests that their view is close to the one I have submitted to Mandelbaum.

4. An excellent statement of the limitations of this view may be found in Rudolf Carnap, *The Logical Foundations of Probability* (U. of Chicago, 1950), pp. 37-51.

5. Alonzo Church, "Abstract Entities in Semantic Analysis," *Proceedings of the American Academy of Arts and Sciences*, 80 (1951), 100-12; the quotation is from p. 104.

6. Paul Edwards, "Bertrand Russell's Doubts about Induction," in A. G. N. Flew, ed., *Essays on Logic and Language*, first series (Blackwell, 1951). Cf. F. L. Will, "Will the Future Be Like the Past?" *Mind*, 56 (1957), 332-47; Norman Malcolm, "Certainty and Empirical Statements," *Mind*, 51 (1942), 18-46; O. K. Bouwsma, "Descartes' Skepticism of the Senses," *Mind*, 54 (1945), 313-22; Max Black, "Linguistic Method in Philosophy," *Philosophy and Phenomenological Research*, 8 (1948), 635-49; John Hospers, *An Introduction to Philosophical Analysis* (Prentice-Hall, 1953), chap. 3.

7. Norman Malcolm, "Moore and Ordinary Language," in P. A. Schilpp, ed., *The Philosophy of G. E. Moore* (Northwestern, 1942). Malcolm subsequently conceded that this view was mistaken; cf. Malcolm's symposium with the present author, Philosophy and Ordinary Language," *Philosophical Review*, 60 (1951)., 317-40.

8. "In the case of all expressions the meanings of which must be *shown* and cannot be explained . . . , it follows, from the fact that they are ordinary expressions in the language, that there have been *many* situations of the kind which they describe; otherwise so many people could not have learned the correct use of those expressions" (Norman Malcolm, "Moore and Ordinary Language," p. 361).

9. In recent American philosophy, for example, by Max Black, *Language and Philosophy* (Cornell, 1949), chap 1, and *Problems of Analysis* (Cornell, 1954), chap. 2

10. Peirce's article is reprinted in vol. 5 of his *Collected Papers* (Harvard, 1934); the quotations are from p. 258. Cf. Williams James's *Pragmatism* (Longmans, 1907), chap. 2.

11. *Wissenschaftliche Weltauffasung: Der Wiener Kreis* (1929); see esp. pp. 15-20. The classic statement of the development of this doctrine is Carl G. Hempel's "Problems and Changes in the Empiricist Criterion of Meaning," *Revue internationale de philosophie*, quatrième année, no. 11 (1950), pp. 41-63; reprinted in Leonard Linsley, ed., *Semantics and the Philosophy of Language* (U. of Ill., 1952), and in A. J. Ayer, ed., *Logical Positivism* (Free Press of Glencoe, 1959).

12. Cf. R. M. Blake, "Can Speculative Philosophy Be Defended?" *Philosophical Review* (1943), 127-34; W. T. Stace, "Positivism," *Mind*, 53 (1944), 215-37.

13. C. G. Hempel, "Problems and Changes in the Empiricist Criterion of Meaning, p. 42.

14. Assuming that his argument was sound, Malcolm proposed a theory concerning the "uses" of those sentences that ostensibly attribute mental activities to sleeping persons. This theory falls outside the scope of this essay.

15. "If language is to be a means of communication, there must be agreement not only in definitions but also (queer as this may sound) in judgments." (Ludwig Wittgenstein, *Philosophical Investigations* [Blackwell, 1953], p. 88e).

16. The third quoted example is taken from John Canfield, "Judgments in Sleep," *Philosophical Review*, 70 (1961), 224-30.

17. Philosophers in other traditions also noted these confusions. See, for example, John Wild, "The Concept of the Given in Contemporary Philosophy," *Philosophy and Phenomenological Research*, 1 (1940), 70-82.

18. The expression "myth of the given" was used by Wilfrid Sellars in "Empiricism and the Philosophy of Mind," in Herbert Feigl and Michael Scriven, eds., *Foundations of Science and the Concepts of Psychology and Psychoanalysis*, Minnesota Studies in the Philosophy of Science, vol. 1 (U. of Minn., 1956), pp. 253-329.

19. Dewey also said that, instead of trying to provide "Foundations for Knowledge," the philosopher should apply "what is known to intelligent conduct of the affairs of human life" to "the problems of men." John Dewey, *Problems of Men* (Philosophical, 1946), pp. 6-7.

20. C. I. Lewis, *Mind and the World-Order* (Scribner, 1929), p. 29.

21. *Ibid.*, p. 19. Cf. Hans Reichenbach, *Experience and Prediction* (U. of Chicago, 1938), p. 6; C. J. Ducasse, "Some Observations Concerning the Nature of Probability, *Journal of Philosophy*, 38 (1941), esp. 400-401.

22. Hans Reichenbach, "Are Phenomenal Reports Absolutely Certain?" *Philosophical Review*, (1952), 147-59; the quotation is from p. 150.

23. Brand Blanshard, *The Nature of Thought*, vol. 2 (Macmillan, 1940), p. 276.

24. C. G. Hempel, "On the Logical Postivists' Theory of Truth," *Analysis*, 2 (1935), 49-59; the quotation is from p. 57.

25. Rudolf Carnap, "Truth and Confirmation," in Herbert Feigl and W. S. Sellars, eds., *Readings in Philosophical Analysis* (Appleton, 1949), p. 125. The portions of the article quoted above first appeared in "Wahrheit und Bewährung," *Actes du congrès internationale de philosophie scientifique*, 4 (Paris; 1936), 18-23.

26. Cf. Nelson Goodman, *The Structure of Appearance* (Harvard, 1951), p. 104. If Goodman's book, incidentally, is not discussed in his collection of essays, the fault is with our conventional classification of philosophical disciplines. The book, which is concerned with an area falling between logic and metaphysics, is one of the most important philosophical works written by an American during the period being surveyed.

27. C. G. Hempel, "Some Theses on Empirical Certainty," *Review of Metaphysics*, (1952), 621-29; the quotation is from p. 621.

28. *Ibid.*, p. 628. Hempel's remarks were made in an "Exploration" in which he set forth several theses about "empirical certainty" and then replied to objections by Paul Weiss, Roderick Firth, Wilfrid Sellars, and myself.

29. C. J. Ducasse, "Propositions, Truth, and the Ultimate Criterion of Truth," *Philosophy and Phenomenological Research*, 4 (1939), 317-40; the quotation is from p. 339.

30. Cf. Norman Malcolm, "Knowledge of Other Minds," *Journal of Philosophy*, 55 (1958), 969-78. Reprinted in Malcolm, *Knowledge and Certainty: Essays and Lectures* (Prentice-Hall, 1963).

31. The principle behind this way of looking at the matter is defended in detail by Max Black in *Language and Philosophy*, p. 116 ff.

32. One of the best criticisms of the "appearance" (or "sense-datum") terminology was O. K. Bouwsma's Moore's Theory of Sense-Data," in *The Philosophy of G. E. Moore*, pp. 201-21. In *Perceiving: A Philosophical Study* (Cornell, 1957), I tried to call attention to certain facts about appearing which, I believe, Bouwsma may have overlooked.

33. Augustine, *Contra academicos*, xi, 26; translated by Sister Mary Patricia Garvey as

Saint Augustine Against the Academicians (Marquette, 1942); the quotations are from pp. 68-69.

34. *Experience and Prediction*, p. 176.

35. It may follow, however, that "the vaunted incorrigibility of the sense-datum language can be achieved only at the cost of its perfect utility as a means of communication" (Max Black, *Problems of Analysis* p. 66), and doubtless, as Black added, it would be "misleading to say the least" to speak of a "language that cannot be communicated" — cf. Wilfrid Sellars, "Empiricism and the Philosophy of Mind" — but these points do affect the epistemological question at issue.

36. This doctrine was modified in Lewis's later *An Analysis of Knowledge and Valuation* (Open Court, 1946) in a way that enabled him to preserve the theory of the given.

37. *The Nature of Thought*, vol. 2, pp. 269-70. Blanshard added, however, that "for all the ordinary purposes of life" we *can* justify some beliefs by showing that they cohere "with the system of present knowledge"; and therefore, he said, his theory should not be described as being "simply sceptical" (vol. 2, p. 271). Cf. W. H. Werkmeister, *The Basis and Structure of Knowledge* (Harper, 1946), part II.

38. Quoted by A. E. Murphy in "Dewey's Epistemology and Metaphysics," in P. A. Schlipp, ed., *The Philosophy of John Dewey* (Northwestern, 1939), p. 203. Dewey's theory of inquiry, however, was not intended to be an epistemology and he did not directly address himself to the questions with which we are here concerned.

39. Cf. W. V. Quine, *Mathematical Logic* (Norton, 1940; rev. ed., Harvard, 1951), sec. 4.

40. Ledger Wood, *The Analysis of Knowledge* (Princeton, 1941), p. 81; C. I. Lewis, *An Analysis of Knowledge and Valuation*, p. 334.

41. Important steps toward solving them were taken by Nelson Goodman in "Sense and Certainty," *Philosophical Review*, 61 (1952), 160-67, and by Israel Scheffler in "On Justification and Commitment," *Journal of Philosophy*, 51 (1954), 180-90. The former paper is reprinted in Roland Houde and J. P. Mullally, eds., *Philosophy of Knowledge*, (Lippincott, 1960), pp. 97-103.

42. Alternatives to the general metaphor of the edifice are proposed by W. V. Quine in the introduction to *Methods of Logic* (Holt, 1950; rev. ed., 1959), in *From a Logical Point of View* (Harvard, 1953), and in *Word and Object* (Wiley, 1960).

43. John Dewey, *Experience and Nature*, 2nd ed. (Norton, 1929), p. 327.

44. Moritz Schlick, "A New Philosophy of Experience, in P. A. Schlipp, ed., *Lectures . . . ,* (Publications in Philosophy, The College of the Pacific, 1932); reprinted in Schlick's *Gesammelte Aufsätze* (Vienna, 1938).

45. *Critique of Pure Reason*, A 7.

46. *Prolegomena to Any Future Metaphysics*, sec. 2.

47. For refinement of detail, see Lewis, *An Analysis*, book 1, and Rudolf Carnap, *Meaning and Necessity* (U. of Chicago, 1947), chap. 1.

48. W. V. Quine, *From a Logical Point of View*. Quine first set forth this view in "Truth by Convention," in Otis Lee, ed., *Philosophical Essays for Alfred North Whitehead* (Longmans, 1936).

49. Cf. Paul Weiss, *Nature and Man* (Holt, 1947), pp. 13, 203; Charles Hartshorne, *Man's Vision of God and the Logic of Theism* (Willett, 1941); Richard Taylor, "The Problem of Future Contingencies," *Philosophical Review*, 66 (1957), 1-28, and "Fatalism," *Philosophical Review*, 71 (1962), 56-66; Donald C. Williams, "The Sea Fight Tomorrow," in Paul Henle, Horace M. Kallen, and Susanne K. Langer, eds., *Structure, Method, and Meaning: Essays in Honor of Henry M. Sheffer* (Liberal Arts, 1951).

50. Cf. Garrett Birkhoff and John von Neumann, "The Logic of Quantum Mechanics," *Annals of Mathematics*, 37 (1936); Hilary Putnam, "Three Valued Logic," *Philosophical Studies*, 8 (1957).

51. *Posterior Analytics*, 100a-100b.

52. R. M. Eaton, *General Logic* (Scribner, 1931), pp. 495-501. Cf. W. P. Montague, *The Ways of Knowing* (Macmillan, 1925), chap. 11; Charles A. Baylis, "Universals, Communicable Knowledge and Metaphysics," *Journal of Philosophy*, 48 (1951), 636-44; Donald Williams, "The Nature and Variety of the *A Priori,*" *Analysis*, 5 (1938), 85-94.

53. "What we require is a picture of the employment of mathematical propositions and of sentences beginning 'I believe that . . . ,' where a mathematical proposition is the object of belief," (Luwig Wittgenstein, *Remarks on the Foundations of Mathematics* [Blackwell, 1956], p. 33e.)

54. George Santayana, *The Realms of Being* (Scribner, 1942), pp. 407, 421.

55. *Ibid.*, pp. 401, 82, 88.

56. *Gesammelte Aufsätze*, pp. 146-47.

57. Albert E. Blumberg and Herbert Feigl, "Logical Positivism," *Journal of Philosophy*, 28 (1931), 281-96. It was in this article that the name "logical positivism" was introduced.

58. W. V. Quine, "Carnap e la verità logica," *Revista di filosofia*, 48 (1957), 4.

59. Cf. Gustav Bergmann, *The Metaphysics of Logical Positivism* (Longmans, 1954), p. 45 ff.

60. On the problem of finding a definition or a criterion of *sameness of meaning* that does *not* refer to relations between properties, see: Nelson Goodman, "On Likeness of Meaning," in Leonard Linsky, ed., *Semantics and the Philosophy of Language*, pp. 67-74; Morton White, "The Analytic and the Synthetic: An Untenable Dualism," in the same book, pp. 272-86; W. V. Quine, *Word and Object*, chap. 2, and Paul Ziff, *Semantic Analysis* (Cornell, 1960).

61. Ernest Nagel, "Logic without Ontology," in Y. H. Krikorian, ed., *Naturalism and the Human Spirit* (Columbia, 1944); reprinted in Herbert Feigl and W. S. Sellars, eds., *Readings in Philosophical Analysis*.

62. Arthur Pap, *Semantics and Necessary Truth* (Yale, 1958), p. 184. Compare Quine's "Carnap e la verità logica," p. 11. The latter paper is an excellent statement of the entire problem. Quine's critique of conventionalism goes back to his "Truth by Convention" (1936), and "Is Logic a Matter of Words?" (1937), read at the Princeton meeting of the American Philosophical Association and abstracted in the *Journal of Philosophy*, 34 (1937), 674.

63. Morton White, "The Analytic and the Synthetic: An Untenable Dualism" p. 280. White also noted that attempts to define "analytic statement" *without* reference to meaning and to relations between properties were inadequate; he took these facts to indicate that the traditional distinction between analytic and synthetic is "untenable." For a criticism of this reasoning, see Richard Taylor, "Disputes about Synonymy," *Philosophical Review*, 63 (1954), 517-29.

64. *From a Logical Point of View*, p. 37. He also said, what is obviously true, that if the traditional distinction between a priori and a posteriori were replaced by a "behavioristic" contrast "between more or less firmly accepted statements," then the distinction might well turn out to be merely a matter of degree.

65. C. H. Langford, "Moore's Notion of Analysis," in Schilpp, ed., *The Philosophy of G. E. Moore*, and "A Proof That Synthetic A Priori Propositions Exist," *Journal of Philosophy*, (1949), 20-24; Hector Neri Castañeda, "'7 + 15 = 12' as a Synthetic Proposition," *Philosophy and Phenomenological Research*, 21 (1960), 141-58. For a useful general discussion, see Oliver A. Johnson, "Denial of the Synthetic *A Priori*," *Philosophy*, 35 (1960), 1-10.

66. "A Proof That Synthetic A Priori Propositions Exist," p. 24.

67. Hilary Putnam, "Reds, Green, and Logical Analysis," *Philosophical Review*, 45 (1956), 206-17.

68. Arthur Pap, "Once More: Colors and Synthetic A Priori," *Philosophical Review*, 66

(1957), 94-99. Pap's discussion of these questions in his *Semantics and Necessary Truth* is more in the spirit of what I have tried to say here than in that of the passage just quoted. His bok is a useful account of the issues that the concept of the a priori has involved in recent philosophy.

69. "A Proof That Synthetic A Priori Propositions Exist," p. 24.

70. *Ibid.*, p. 21.

71. Langford introduced this example in connection with what he called the "paradox of analysis"; viz., if the philosophical analysis of a concept is such that "the verbal expression representing the analysandum has the same meaning as the verbal expression representing the analysans, the analysis states a bare identity and is trivial; but if the two verbal expressions do not have the same meaning, the analysis is incorrect" ("The Notion of Analysis in Moore's Philosophy," p. 323). For further discussion of this "paradox," see: Moore's reply to Langford, *The Philosophy of G. E. Moore*, pp. 660-67; Morton G. White, "A Note on the 'Paradox of Analysis,'" *Mind*, 54 (1945); Max Black, "The 'Paradox of Analysis' Again: A Reply," *ibid.*, pp. 272-73; Morton G. White, "Analysis and Identity: A Rejoinder," *ibid.*, pp. 357-61; Max Black, "How Can Analysis Be Informative?" *Philosophy and Phenomenological Research*, 6 (1946), 628-31; a review of White's and Black's papers by Alonzo Church, *Journal of Symbolic Logic*, 11 (132-33; and Arthur Pap, *Semantics and Necessary Truth*, pp. 275-82.

72. W. V. Quine, "Os estados unidos e o ressurgimento da lógical," in *Vida intelectual nos estados unidos*, vol. 2 (União Cultural Brasil-Estados Unidos, São Paulo, 1946); the quotation is from p. 277. Quine's Truth by Convention" is a clear discussion of some of the issues that the "logistic thesis" involves.

73. On statements of the latter sort, see Henry Veatch, "Matrix, Matter, and Method in Metaphysics," *Review of Metaphysics*, 14 (1961), 581-600.

74. *The New Realism*, p. 34.

75. *Ibid.*, p. 357. Holt's essay was entitled "The Place of Illusory Experience in a Realistic World."

76. R. B. Perry, "A Note on Neutralism," in *Structure, Method, and Meaning: Essays in Honor of Henry M. Sheffer*, p. 223. Cf. James K. Feibleman, *The Revival of Realism* (U. of N. C., 1946), *passim*.

77. *The New Realism*, pp. 2, 4.

78. *The Winds of Doctrine* (Scribner, 1913), p. 146.

79. Cf. A. E. Murphy, "Objective Relativism in Dewey and Whitehead," *Philosophical Review*, 36 (1927), 212-44; "Mr. Lovejoy's Counter-Revolution," *Journal of Philosophy*, 28 (1931), 29-42, 57-71; "A Program for Philosophy, in Horace M. Kallen and Sidney Hook, eds., *American Philosophy Today and Tomorrow* (Furman, 1935). Reprinted in Murphy, W. H. Hay, and M. G. Singer, *Reason and the Common Good: Selected Essays of Arthur E. Murphy* (Prentice-Hall, 1963).

80. "Dewey's Epistemology and Metaphysics," in Schilpp, ed., *The Philosophy of John Dewey*, pp. 219-20.

81. E. B. McGilvary, *Toward a Perspective Realism*, ed. A. G. Ramsperger (Open Court, 1956), p. 6. This book, published posthumously, was prepared from the typescript of McGilvary's Carus Lectures, delivered in 1939, and from articles previously published.

82. "The Revolt Against Dualism," *Philosophical Review*, 40 (1931), 246-65.

83. W. P. Montague, "The Story of American Realism," *Philosophy*, 12 (1937), 1-22.

84. C. A. Strong, *Essays on the Natural Origin of the Mind* (Macmillan, 1930), p. 93; Roy Wood Sellars, "Knowledge and Its Categories," in Durant Drake, et al, *Essays in Critical Realism: A Cooperative Study of the Problem of Knowledge* (New York: Macmillan, 1920), p. 200.

85. Durant Drake, "The Approach to Critical Realism," in *Essays in Critical Realism*, p. 29.

86. *De anima*, III, ii, 426a; cf. *Metaphysics*, IV, v, 1010b.

87. C. J. Ducasse, "On the Attributes of Material Things," *Journal of Philosophy*, 31 (1934), pp. 57-72. Cf. "Introspection, Mental Acts, and Sensa," *Mind*, 45 (1936), 181-92.

88. C. J. Ducasse, *Nature, Mind, and Death* (Open Court, 1951), p. 259. The misleading character of "appearance" terminology has been discussed in detail by Martin Lean, in *Sense-Perception and Matter* (Humanities, 1953); see also the references in the second section, above.

89. But he must, of course, fit the fact of *appearing* into his scheme of things; the metaphysical problems that this very difficult project involves fall beyond the scope of this essay. Cf. Herbert Feigl, "The 'Mental' and the 'Physical,'" in Herbert Feigl, Michael Scriven, and Grover Maxwell, eds., *Concepts, Theories, and the Mind-Body Problem*, Minnesota Studies in the Philosophy of Science, vol. 2 (U. of Minn., 1958), pp. 370-497; John T. Stevenson, "Sensations and Brain Processes" *Philosophical Review*, 69 (1960), 505-10.

90. Roy Wood Sellars, "A Statement of Critical Realism," *Revue internationale de philosophie*, première année (1947), pp. 476, 478, 479.

91. *De anima*, II, 4, 5.

92. Gerald B. Phelan, "Verum sequitur esse rerum," in Roland Houde and J. P. Mullally, *Philosophy of Knowledge*, p. 209.

93. See the appendix to John Wild, ed., *The Return to Reason* (Regnery, 1953). Cf. John Wild, *Introduction to Realistic Philosophy* (Harper, 1948); Henry Veatch, *Intentional Logic* (Yale, 1952); Oliver Martin, *The Order and Integration of Knowledge* (U. of Mich., 1957); Francis H. Parker, "Realism, 'New' and 'Critical,' Reappraised," *Proceedings of the Association for Realistic Philosophy*, 1 (1952), 2-15.

94. A. O. Lovejoy, "A Temporalistic Realism," in G. P. Adams and W. P. Montague, eds., *Contemporary American Philosophy*, vol. 2 (Macmillan, 1930), pp. 85-105; the quotation is from p. 97.

95. Lewis discusses further aspects of the problem in "Professor Chisholm and Empiricism," *Journal of Philosophy*, 45 (1948), 517-24. The translation thesis is defended by Roderick Firth in "Radical Empiricism and Perceptual Relativity," *Philosophical Review*, 59 (1950), 1964-83, 319-31.

96. See Dewey's *Logic: The Theory of Inquiry* (Holt, 1938), p. 105 and *passim*, and his *Knowing and the Known* (Beacon, 1949), written in collaboration with Arthur F. Bentley. Dewey's theory of inquiry is similar in many respects to the theory that Charles Sanders Peirce first set forth in 1877; see volumes 2 and 5 of Peirce's *Collected Papers*. I regret that I am unable to determine the significance of Dewey's writings for epistemology; many believe, however, that they are of first importance. The following works were influenced by Dewey: Lewis E. Hahn, *A Contextualistic Theory of Perception*, University of California Publications in Philosophy, 22 (1942), 1-205; Justus Buchler, *Nature and Judgment* (Columbia, 1955); George Boas, *The Inquiring Mind* (Open Court, 1959).

97. W. V. Quine, *Methods of Logic*, p. xii.

98. R. B. Perry, *General Theory of Value* (Longmans, 1926), pp. 313-316; cf. E. B. Holt, *The Concept of Consciousness* (Macmillan, 1914), chap. 9, and "Eight Steps in Neuro-Muscular Integration," in *Problems of Nervous Physiology and of Behavior*, Symposium, Dedicated to Professor I. Beritashvili, The Academy of Science of USSR, Georgian Branch (Tiflis; 1936), pp. 25-36.

99. See, for example, Charles Morris, *Signs, Language, and Behavior* (Prentice-Hall, 1946); Hans Reichenbach, *Elements of Symbolic Logic* (Macmillan, 1947), esp. pp. 274-84; Rudolf Carnap, "Meaning and Synonymy in Natural Languages," *Philosophical Studies*, 4 (1955), 33-47, and "On Some Concepts of Pragmatics," *Philosophical Studies*, 6 (1957), 89-91; Wilfrid Sellars, "Mind, Meaning, and Behavior," *Philosophical Studies*, 3 (1952), 83-94. I have discussed some of these attempts in more detail in "Sentences about Believing,"

Proceedings of the Aristotelian Society, 56 (1955-56), 125-48; reprinted with alterations in Minnesota Studies in the Philosophy of Science, vol. 2 (U. of Minn., 1956), with an appendix consisting of correspondence with W. S. Sellars.

100. C. I. Lewis, "Professor Chisholm and Epiricism," pp. 519-20.

101. On the kind of "spontaneous belief" involved, compare Brand Blanshard's description of perceiving in *The Nature of Thought*, book 1, chap. 4-6, and my own account in *Perceiving: A Philosophical Study* (Cornell, 1957).

102. Recent suggestive articles are: Alonzo Church, "Logic and Analysis," *Proceedings of the Twelfth International Congress of Philosophy*, pp. 77-81; Arthur Pap, "Belief and Propositions," *Philosophy of Science*, 24 (1957), 123-36; Nicholas Rescher, "The Problem of a Logical Theory of Belief Statements," *Philosophy of Science*, 27 (1960), 88-95; Nelson Goodman, "About," *Mind*, 70 (1961), 1-24.

103. "Apologia pro mente sua," in P. A. Schlipp, ed., *The Philosophy of George Santayana* (Northwestern, 1940), p. 516. Fichte's term "posit" has come to replace Santayana's "animal faith" in recent writings (see the discussion of Reichenbach in the second section of this chapter). Quine writes, in the spirit of Santayana' "To call a posit a posit is not to patronize it . . . " (*Word and Object*, p. 22). In "Realism and the New Way of Words," Wilfrid Sellars speaks of "positing" languages and their subject matter; see *Readings in Philosophical Analysis*, pp. 424-56.

104. Donald Williams, "The *A Priori* Argument for Subjectivism," *The Monist*, 43 (1953), 173-202; "The Inductive Argument for Subjectivism, *The Monist*, 44 (1934), 80-107; and "The Argument for Realism," *The Monist*, 45 (1934), 186-209. Cf. Everett Nelson, "The Inductive Argument for an External World," *Philosophy of Science*, 3 (1936), 237-49; and "The External World," *Philosophy of Science*, 9 (1942), 261-67; George Chatalian, "Induction and the Problem of the External World," *Journal of Philosophy*, 39 (1952), 601-7.

105. The position of our hypothetical skeptic is taken by W. T. Stace, in "The Refutation of Realism," in *Readings in Philosophical Analysis*, pp. 364-72; first published in *Mind* (1934).

106. Augustine, *The City of God*, book 19, chap. 18.

107. See Rudolf Carnap, *The Logical Foundations of Probability*, pp. 382-86.

108. Aristotle, *Metaphysics*, III, 7, 27.

109. John Dewey, *Problems of Men*, p. 343.

110. Otto Neurath, *Foundations of the Social Sciences, International Encyclopedia of Unified Science*, vol. 2, no. 1 (U. of Chicago, 1944), p. 12. Cf. C. G. Hempel, "Le Problème de la vérité," *Theoria*, 2 (1937), 206-44, esp. 243-44; Hans Reichenbach, *Experience and Prediction*, p. 188 ff.

111. Sextus Empiricus, *Against the Dogmatists*, II, 100; Loeb Classical Library ed., vol. 2, p. 289. In Tarski's and Carnap's studies of the semantics of formalized languages, "truth" is defined in terms of the concept of *fulfillment*, or *satisfaction*—a concept that is exemplified in the relation between Socrates and the expression "X is mortal." Both authors emphasize, in effect, that to the truth conditions for any statement we have only to assert the statement. See Alfred Tarski, "The Concept of Truth in Formalized Languages," in *Logic, Semantics, Metamathematics* (Oxford, 1956); the paper referred to was published in Polish in 1933 and in German in 1935; "The Semantic Conception of Truth," *Philosophy and Phenomenological Research*, 4 (1944), 341-76 (reprinted in *Readings in Philosophical Analysis*); and Rudolf Carnap, *Introduction to Semantics* (Harvard, 1942).

112. James's clearer statements are in *Pragmatism*, lecture and in *The Meaning of Truth* (Longmans, 1909), chap. 2 ("The Tigers in India"); the latter was written under the influence of Dickinson Miller.

113. Carl G. Hempel, "On the Logical Positivists' Theory of Truth," *Analysis*, 2 (1935), 49-59; the quotations are from pp. 49, 50, 51.

114. *Ibid.*, p. 57.

115. Carl G. Hempel, "Some Remarks on 'Facts' and Propositions," *Analysis*, 2 (1935), 93-96; the quotation is from p. 96.

116. Cf. Rudolf Carnap on "the neglect of the distinction between truth and knowledge of truth (verification, confirmation)" in "Truth and Confirmation," *Readings in Philosophical Analysis*, pp. 119-27; and Tarski on truth and "provability" in "The Semantic Conception of Truth," p. 354.

117. W. H. Werkmeister, in *The Basis and Structure of Knowledge*, presented a similar theory, but combined it with a view enabling him to "identify 'truth' with 'warranted belief' and, therefore, with 'knowledge'" (p. 152). Cf. E. S. Brightman, *An Introduction to Philosopphy,* rev. ed. (Holt, 1951), pp. 80 ff.

118. Franz Brentano, *Wahrheit und Evidenz* (Leipzig, 1930), p. 139.

119. C. J. Ducasse, "Facts, Truth, and Knowledge," *Philosophy and Phenomenological Research*, 5 (1945), 330.

120. Charles Saunders Peirce, *Collected Papers*, vol. 5, 5-565, 5-494, 5-358n; John Dewey, *Logic: The Theory of Inquiry*, p. 345. Peirce also defined truth as follows: "For truth is neither more nor less than that character of a proposition which consists in this, that belief in the proposition would, with sufficient experience and reflection, lead us to such conduct as wouls tend to satisfy the desires we should then have" (5-375n).

Index

Index

Roderick Chisholm is Andrew W. Mellon Professor
of the Humanities in the department of philosophy at
Brown University. Among his books are *Perceiving:
A Philosophical Study, Theory of Knowledge, Person
and Object,* and *The First Person.* He has served as
president of the American Philosophical Association,
Eastern Division, and of the Metaphysical Society of
America, and is currently president of the Interna-
tional Phenomenological Society and editor of
Philosophy and Phenomenological Research.